D0217446

BANTON, Michael. Racial theories. Cambridge, 1987. 181p bibl index 86-32734.
44.50 ISBN 0-521-33456-X; 12.95 pa ISBN 0-521-33675-9. HT 1521. CIP
Banton here continues the valuable work he published as *The Idea of Race* (1978). Like its predecessor, *Racial Theories* examines the historical debates over race and race relations hermeneutically, that is, by placing the various positions firmly in sociohistorical context. The author's meticulous historical scholarship brings, for example, new appreciation to the influence Sir Walter Scott's *Ivanhoe* had on early formulations of the concept of race. Banton clearly demonstrates how difficult it was to explain human physical and cultural diversity, given the constraints of a general acceptance of biblical scriptures and an almost total lack of knowledge of genetics. Banton's general approach is to trace the historical twists and turns of the meanings attached to the idea of race—first as lineage, then as type, subspecies, and population, and, more currently, as status and class—since its emergence in 16th-century Anglo-European thought. The authority Banton brings to his subject is beyond dispute; he is admirably fair when examining the ideas of all protagonists, and he writes clearly, concisely, and engagingly. At once an insightful study in intellectual history and an exemplary analysis of sociological theory building. Upper-division undergraduates and above.—*W.P. Nye, Hollins College*

RACIAL THEORIES

Racial Theories presents a study of the main theories of race and ethnic relations, and traces the historical development of the concept of 'race'.

It begins with the eighteenth-century concept of race as lineage, and the nineteenth-century doctrines that have been called scientific racism. These doctrines, with their biological and theological foundations, were destroyed by the theory of natural selection; but the Darwinian revolution was complex; it took time before its lessons were learned and the foundations laid for a sociological approach to racial relations.

The book describes orthodox sociological theories in a chapter on race as status, and then looks at the major challenge to these theories. It maintains that these orthodox theories will not be superseded by attempts to interpret racial relations in terms of the relations between classes.

Anyone who wonders why racial theories were so widely accepted at the beginning of the present century has to understand their roots in nineteenth-century science. Anyone who wants to unravel the confusions of contemporary debate about racial conflict and racial harmony must follow the course of twentieth-century social science. *Racial Theories* tells them what they need to know.

RACIAL THEORIES

MICHAEL BANTON

Professor of Sociology, University of Bristol

674451

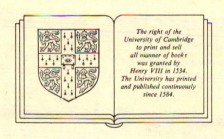

*The right of the
University of Cambridge
to print and sell
all manner of books
was granted by
Henry VIII in 1534.
The University has printed
and published continuously
since 1584.*

CAMBRIDGE UNIVERSITY PRESS

Cambridge
London   New York   New Rochelle
Melbourne   Sydney

Published by the Press Syndicate of the University of Cambridge
The Pitt Building, Trumpington Street, Cambridge, CB2 1RP
32 East 57th Street, New York, NY 10022, USA
10 Stamford Road, Oakleigh, Melbourne 3166, Australia

© Cambridge University Press 1987

First published 1987

Printed in Great Britain at the University Press, Cambridge

British Library cataloguing in publication data

Banton, Michael
Racial theories.
1. Race relations
I. Title
305.8′001   HT1521

Library of Congress cataloguing in publication data

Banton, Michael P.
Racial theories.
Bibliography.
Includes index.
1. Race. 2. Race relations. I. Title.
HT1521.B345 1987   305.8   86–32734

ISBN 0 521 33456 X hard covers
ISBN 0 521 33675 9 paperback

WD

Contents

Preface

A lot has been written about race and racial relations in the past one hundred and fifty years. To today's generation, much of it seems mistaken or pernicious, often because it is based upon tacit assumptions of a theoretical character. Consider the remarks of Gilbert Murray (1900: 156) the classical scholar, humanitarian and devoted supporter of the League of Nations:

> There is in the world a hierarchy of races . . . those nations which eat more, claim more, and get higher wages, will direct and rule the others, and the lower work of the world will tend in the long-run to be done by the lower breeds of men. This much we of the ruling colour will no doubt accept as obvious.

In these remarks nations, as political units, are equated with races, as biological units. The position of white people at the top of the hierarchy is attributed to their racial character and the future division of labour throughout the world is represented as an expression of this hierarchy. So the statements reflect a theory that is simultaneously biological and sociological. The theory, which was very widely accepted among Europeans of all political persuasions in Gilbert Murray's generation, was first attacked for its claims about white superiority. Indeed, when one of the earliest critics, the Frenchman Jean Finot (1906), entitled his book *Le préjugé des races* he understood racial prejudice to be not a psychological disposition but a belief in racial superiority. The theory of white superiority was unquestionably both of political importance, and wrong. Whites were superior to blacks and yellows in political and economic power but their superiority was not an expression of the kind of hierarchy Gilbert Murray had in mind. He was in error, not just in his conception of hierarchy but even more seriously in his acceptance of a theory of classification which misrepresented the nature of the units.

Mistaken theories are scarcely unusual. In a hundred years time people

vii

will marvel that the present generation could accept theories that have subsequently been exposed as inadequate or false. So in both the human and the natural sciences there is a central question: how does a research worker formulate better theories? In seeking an answer it is well to remember the testimony of Louis Pasteur, the discoverer of vaccines, who said that discoveries come only to the prepared mind. Those research workers who do not have a 'prepared mind' are likely to repeat old mistakes and to miss the significance of elements in their work that could point to new explanations. Research workers who know how previous discoveries have been made in their own field and have learned the lessons taught by past mistakes should be more imaginative and be more likely to make discoveries in their turn.

My own research has, I believe, been significantly assisted at several points by study of the philosophy of science and by its application to problems of intellectual history. In 1950, when I started research on black–white relations in England, the distinction between prejudice and discrimination was scarcely appreciated by anyone in Britain, even among academic social scientists (who, of course, were very few in number at that time). To get to the position where in *White and Coloured* (1959) I was able to write separate chapters on 'explaining prejudice' and 'explaining discrimination', and to analyze the relations between the two modes of explanation, required much hard intellectual work. Nothing helped me more than an acquaintance with the arguments then being advanced in favour of methodological individualism as opposed to methodological collectivism, and with the attempt to define an individualist method for sociology that avoided any tendency to reduce sociological problems to psychological ones. I argued for the view that the same event may pose different questions to the economist, the psychologist and the sociologist (though, of course, it may not be equally interesting to all three). All events can be looked at from many different angles, different aspects requiring different explanations. The sociologist might be interested in customary patterns of behaviour; these have a logic of their own quite apart from the expectations of individuals. Custom could have objective characteristics and the sociologist could build up a body of knowledge about it which was separate from the knowledge of psychologists.

Eight years later my book *Race Relations* was published. In it I surveyed the academic literature which was conventionally defined as constituting this field, classifying it in terms of what I called Six Orders of Race Relations. The publisher enquired whether I thought of up-dating the book after a while and preparing a second edition; I replied that I did not wish to do this because I was dissatisfied with the way in which I had organized the material. It was too eclectic, different theoretical approaches being used for different regions. I wanted a single synoptic approach or theory that could be applied to all regions. But where was I to find one? After a while I concluded that in order to move forwards I must first step backwards and learn more about how it had come to be thought that there was a distinctive field of study identified by the name 'race relations'. The results of these enquiries were published in 1977 as a book entitled *The Idea of Race*. In writing it I learned a great deal that helped my search. As an undergraduate I had been taught that there was a body of doctrine in the nineteenth century called 'scientific racism'. Up to the end of the 1960s I had assumed that the central concept in this doctrine was that of race. Therefore, it came as a surprise to me when (helped by an essay of Ernest Mayr's) I discovered on rereading the principal authors that the central concept was not race but type. This enabled me to isolate the main features of the theory of racial typology and place it in its historical context. Racial typology was a better name for the body of doctrine than scientific racism; in turn this meant that I could dispense with using the word 'racism' and disentangle myself from the confusions that spread after the late 1960s when this word came to be used in diverse new ways.

A second discovery which may seem quite trivial but which started me on a new train of thought, concerned the use of the word 'assimilation'. I noticed that in the *American Journal of Sociology* in 1901 the word was used in a wide sense, in line with that of some European writers who had been discussing social evolution. Any process by which peoples became more similar was designated assimilation. I realized that subsequently when commentators in the United States expressed anxiety that the new wave of immigrants were of poor racial stock and would not easily be assimilated, they were using the word in a more restricted sense in which it was being equated with Americanization. Something similar happened in Britain towards the end of the 1950s when assimilation came to be equated with Anglicization. The word was used to designate a process by which one collectivity (the majority society) was expected to absorb another (the immigrant minority) without itself undergoing any significant change. It identified one way in which people might become more similar and it was used in a manner which distracted attention from other modes of assimilation. Moreover, it was directed to change at the collective level and neglected the explanation of change at the individual level. For example, in many situations immigrant men learn the language of the receiving society more quickly than immigrant women. Language learning, which is one of the most fundamental features of assimilation, is a response to incentives. When people, men or women, want employment and need linguistic competence for this purpose, they set about acquiring it even though at the same time they may be trying to preserve their traditional ideas about relations in the home between husbands and wives, parents and children. Processes of ethnic change have to be studied separately for different spheres of life, and the various different directions and speeds of change have to be separately accounted for. Appreciation of these quite elementary distinctions helped me understand how the study of assimilation had been distorted by unconscious pressures originating in the social and political environment. It led me to believe that some of the sociological problems could be resolved by a theory which saw individual behaviour as a response to incentives and related that behaviour to features of the social structure, particularly those which demarcated one group from another. So in 1976 I wrote down these arguments as a set of propositions which I called the Rational Choice Theory of Racial and Ethnic Relations.

My decision to step back in time and attempt a critical review of the intellectual tradition in which I stood had paid off. It had shown me lines of argument implicit at earlier periods which had never been followed up, and lessons that had not been learned. Having formulated a theory of my own, I wondered if I should revise my manuscript of *The Idea of Race* to show how it had helped me to my new position? I decided against this course, partly because that manuscript was already with a publisher, and partly because I thought I should first write out a full exposition of my theory and why I thought it should be preferred to the other theories then available. This task took me six further years and resulted in a book which some readers considered too long, though I am conscious of respects in which it still was not long enough to do justice to the argument.

Instead of revising *The Idea of Race* I have written a new book with a much clearer structure than its predecessor; some of the earlier material has been used again but much that is in *The Idea of Race* is neither superseded nor replaced by this volume. The main task of this book, as of the earlier one, is to put forward an interpretation of the growth of knowledge about what people have called race or racial relations. (I prefer to write racial relations to make clear that the first word is an adjective and that the subject matter overlaps with ethnic relations, but 'race relations' has been the form more commonly used by other writers and so I employ it sometimes.) While I hope that the book will be of interest to some historians, it is written primarily for sociologists, seeking to persuade them of the relevance of intellectual history to theory-building in this field. This objective has been one of my criteria in deciding what to include and what could be omitted.

A particular difficulty in preparing such a study is that the word race has been used in so varied and imprecise a way that the modern reader is often left uncertain quite what earlier writers intended when they employed it. My claim is that many of the confusions about the growth of knowledge concerning racial relations can be reduced if this growth is seen as falling into three phases. This first is tied to the appearance of the word race in European languages from about the beginning of the sixteenth century. It deals with the increase in knowledge about the varied forms of life, the many proposals about how to classify and interpret that diversity, and the ways in which new knowledge fashioned the use of the word race. As the first phase is focused upon knowledge about race, so is the second upon knowledge about racial relations. It is the period in which relations between people who were not of the same race (or type) were thought to differ from relations between people who were of the same race. It was held that the difference was rooted in biological make-up, and that therefore inter-racial relations required different explanations from intra-racial relations, giving rise to the idea of racial relations as a special sphere of knowledge. This period started at the beginning of the nineteenth century and it took over a hundred years before the expression 'race relations' came into use. The third phase is one in which the errors of the second were identified, new explanations advanced, and attempts made to reformulate the field of study using sociological concepts in place of biological ones. Since this phase is still continuing and its outcome is uncertain, there must be dispute about the best name for it. The simplest solution is to see it as concerned with knowledge about ethnic relations, taking a lead from a book published in 1935 by Sir Julian Huxley and A. C. Haddon which criticized mistaken racial doctrines and proposed the use of 'ethnic group' in place of 'race' when discussing the social aspect, because the adjective 'ethnic' more clearly indicated a concern with social differences. These three phases overlap. Mistakes made during the first two persist to the present day and increase the confusion of biological and social issues, but mistakes are almost certainly being made in the third phase too, and their character will become more evident in a future period.

The three-phase view of racial thought can be elaborated by separation of some of the different senses in which the word race has been used. From the sixteenth to the nineteenth centuries, in English, the principal use was that of race as lineage, to refer to a group of persons, animals, or plants, connected by common descent or origin. In this phase the main dispute was whether all humans descended from Adam and Eve. The beginning of the second phase was signalled by the use of race in the sense of type, in which the word designated one of a limited number of permanent forms.

This perspective was destroyed by the discovery of the principles of natural selection which made possible an understanding of the evolutionary nature of species and subspecies. The second phase, therefore, contained a contest in which race as type was overcome by a Darwinian conception of race as subspecies, and then that conception was enriched by discoveries about the genetics of inheritance and the ways in which these were related to selective agencies in particular environments. The first sociological theory of racial relations was one which drew inspiration from ecological reasoning within biology. Physical features of the kind called racial were taken as indicators that the individuals in question were usefully assigned to particular populations distinguished by their gene frequencies. Both the biological and the sociological theory of the second period led to an understanding of human diversity which can be summarized in the notion of race as population. The third phase began with studies furnishing much better descriptions of black–white relations in the United States and which in their interpretations relied upon the idea of race as an indicator of minority status. Methods for analyzing race as status have been improved within the past twenty years by linkages between sociological and economic theory, but during the same period this approach has been forced on the defensive by challenges from writers elaborating the kinds of theory pioneered by Karl Marx. Their prescriptions can be designated, inadequately perhaps, by writing of race as class. So the third phase also contains a major contest; in this case I believe that the older theory will not be overcome, though it will surely be much improved by the criticisms to which it has been subjected.

One of the merits of presenting the history of racial thought in such a way is that it interprets this history as having a structure. Each of the various writers can be seen as having a place in this structure. Some of them are representative of a particular phase or viewpoint; others are transitional from one to the next; yet others are simply confused or are opportunists who put together incompatible elements to construct an unconvincing synthesis. Dividing up the subject and distinguishing different uses of the word race can also help the commentator avoid falling into the error of presentism. This is the tendency to interpret other historical periods in terms of the concepts, values, and understanding of the present time. Many writers about racial thought have failed to notice that when their predecessors wrote about groups distinguished in racial terms they did not see matters in the way that people would today. As a result, these earlier writings have not been located in their proper historical context. One reason why people have often fallen into this trap is that much of the debate has addressed the question 'what is race?' assuming that there was something best identified by this particular name. The 'something' was the difference in skin colour, facial features and kind of hair that is best called phenotypical variation by anyone seeking a neutral scientifically defensible name which can be translated without difficulty into many other languages. 'Race' cannot be translated so easily because in English and some other tongues it is a folk concept, a word in popular use with a significance deriving from popular understanding and varying from one historical period to another.

Folk concepts change with the growth of knowledge. Thus people in twentieth-century Europe do not explain misfortune and mental illness in terms of the concepts of witchcraft and madness used by their ancestors. Folk concepts are also modified in line with popular experience: ideas about other peoples change in step with the frequency and character of the encounters from which that experience is derived. So in the course of time folk concepts acquire additional meanings which increase their service-ability in everyday communication while introducing ambiguities. By con-trast, the building of scientific theories depends upon the reduction of ambiguities, so that the meaning of propositions becomes more certain. Theories are built with analytical concepts defined as precisely as possible in ways appropriate to the task in hand. Where folk concepts are ordinary language names of things, analytical concepts are terms necessary to expla-nations. In the social sciences the tendency has been to start from folk con-cepts and to elaborate definitions which will permit the same words to be used also as analytical concepts. For example, Augustin Thierry's study published in 1825, a *History of the Conquest of England by the Normans*, seems to have inspired others to try to transform the words race and class from folk into analytical concepts. W. F. Edwards, the founder of the *Société Ethnographique* in Paris, was stimulated to develop ideas about the significance of race in history by a reading of this book and some similar ones, while Karl Marx hailed Thierry as 'the father of the "class struggle" in French historical writing'.

There is today a folk concept of class used to identify what sociologists prefer to call differences of status. Many, but not all, sociologists would maintain that class can also be used as an analytical concept. The distinc-tion between these two kinds of concept furnishes a perspective from which to study the career of the word race as a concept. In English it has been used as a folk concept for four centuries, changing as the kinds of con-tacts between English and non-English have changed. Its meaning has also diversified and shifted because, with the growth of knowledge, theorists believed it possible to use the word analytically to explain the common characteristics of individuals thought to constitute first a type, then a subspecies, a population, a status category and finally a class category. What the theorists wrote has affected its use as a folk concept, so there has been a two-way traffic between the two spheres of discourse. In some other respects the folk-analytical distinction parallels that drawn between the world of appearances, and the world of determining relations in which the appearances are manufactured. There is often dispute about what are the determining relations, different theorists advancing contrasting views and advocating the use of different analytical concepts.

In what I have described as the second phase the word type was introduced as an analytical concept. The more systematic typological theorists, like Nott and Gliddon, recognized that the races of the contemporary world were historical creations assembling people of mixed origin. Yet appearances were deceptive. Men could migrate and mate with strange women but they could not overcome the anthropological laws of permanence of type, the infertility of hybrids and the restrictions upon acclimatization which determined the ultimate outcome. Others did not draw a clear distinction between race and type. For example, Robert Knox maintained that race was the key to the interpretation of history but his argument depended upon a definition of race that made it a synonym for type as used by Nott and Gliddon. This is the capital error and the central issue with which the history of racial thought must be concerned. It must explain how the error came about, why it has been so difficult to overcome, and why the elaboration of better explanations had to depend upon the establishment of new modes of analysis.

Imprecision in the nineteenth-century use of the word race was assisted by the upsurge in European nationalism and the readiness to see that sentiment as an expression of race, so that race was often equated with nation as well as type. After Darwin, races were seen by biologists as historical units that might sometime evolve into species. When genetics became established as a science, its practitioners could examine the underlying relations which determined the process of speciation. Instead of trying to identify a subspecies by drawing a line round a collection of individual specimens, geneticists selected a sample in order to study the frequency of particular genes within that population, and to examine the processes of change in gene frequencies. The theory of natural selection comprehended the determinants of biological patterns. Something additional was required to explain the social relations between people assigned to groups and categories on the basis of their physical characteristics. Ways had to be found of superseding the erroneous mid nineteenth-century explanations of the relation between race and social affairs. This search has provoked an animated controversy about the relative merits of status and class as analytical concepts capable of explaining the patterns of behaviour which constitute racial relations.

Anyone who seeks to explain how it is that some contributions led to a growth of knowledge and helped to move racial thought on from one phase to another, must draw upon some philosophy of science. Up to the middle of the present century the dominant view was the inductivist one formulated by Francis Bacon. It represented research as a procedure whereby people collected specimens, classified and named them, and then noted the generalizations that emerged. According to Bacon, the chief obstacle to the growth of knowledge was excessive self-confidence among research workers unable to recognize how they were blinded by their prejudices and superstitions. To avoid error they should purge their minds of preconceptions. According to his successors, the scientific procedure was to express the generalizations as explanatory hypotheses and try to verify them. The challenge to this prescription came from Karl Popper, who maintained that the mind could not be purged of preconceptions. Hypotheses occur to investigators as, working within particular intellectual traditions, they attempt to account for new as well as old observations. Discoveries come from the refutation of conjectures. Mistakes are made continuously: the task is to learn from them. In the study of racial thought, the Baconian philosophy revealed itself in the representation of race as 'a modern superstition' and in the claim that doctrines of racial superiority expressed the racial prejudices of their authors. Those who followed Popper's view of the matter stressed the relative inability of scientific institutions in the nineteenth century to regulate claims to scientific authority, especially when the political climate in Europe and North America encouraged the growth and distribution of the doctrines.

Popper's interest was in the discoveries which ushered in major scientific advances, the revolutions which were featured in the title of Thomas S. Kuhn's 1962 book, *The Structure of Scientific Revolutions*. Yet Kuhn's work attracted more attention for what it had to say about the paradigms, or patterns of 'normal science' in between the revolutionary upsets. It accompanied the revival of interest in the sociology of knowledge which encouraged historians to examine what Kuhn called the 'external social, economic and intellectual conditions' when analyzing changes in science. Kuhn wrote (1968, vol. 14: 76) of the 'internal approach' to the history of science as being concerned with the substance of science as knowledge. It concentrated upon the problems with which scientists grappled and their attempts to resolve them. He contrasted it with the 'external approach' which is concerned with the activity of scientists as a social group within the larger culture and looks at the ways in which their problem selection and their search for explanations are influenced by the social and political conditions of their time. Both are legitimate ways of writing history. The tension between them is not in the answers they offer but in their choice of questions. This is most marked in the case of Marxists. Since they subscribe to a theory about the course of historical change they think they can, in general terms, predict the course of future events. They then maintain that scholars have a moral obligation to study the sorts of problems which will help politically progressive people to select the sort of strategy that will be to the advantage of the majority. Non-Marxists are more likely to say that the individual scholar should be free to study the kinds of problem he or she finds interesting, and that often intellectual advances have come from the study of unfashionable problems. There are links here with contrasting philosophies of society. Someone who believes that the material conditions are vital to the understanding of any society is likely to think it important to concentrate upon questions of external conditions in the history of science. Someone who considers that the ideas people hold decide the use they make of their material resources, is more likely to interest himself or herself in the sort of questions that characterize the internal approach to the history of science.

To understand which questions scientists and scholars seek to answer, it is helpful to see each individual research worker as standing within an intellectual tradition. He (assuming it is a he) has received a training which has directed his attention to particular problems and to what is interesting about them. He has come to regard particular previous investigations as exemplars of the best way to conduct research and, on the other side, has come to believe that other procedures are unproductive and to be avoided or attacked. In this way research traditions are built up which incorporate ideas about good and bad practice. They are driven forward by internal controversy and new knowledge so that they change over time. They also vary from one country to another and sometimes from one university to another. Popper and Kuhn took their examples from physical science where the intellectual revolutions have been fairly clear cut and there is least opportunity for research in different countries to pursue idiosyncratic interpretations (the Lysenko affair in Soviet genetics is an illuminating example of these constraints). Biological science, so Ernst Mayr (1982: 36–45) argues, differs from physical science. General laws are less important and have to allow for exceptions that are not refutations. The study of evolution necessitates the use of concepts of a special kind. Social science differs even more, since the people who are being studied are constantly changing their behaviour in the light of what they have learned about the principles governing the operation of their societies. Social science traditions differ greatly from one country to another, partly for this reason, partly because of political constraints, and partly because the research workers concentrate upon what are perceived as the important problems of their own societies. The study of ethnicity and ethnic relations in the Soviet Union today is very different from that in the United States, while that in the United Kingdom has yet another character.

Most readers will not be interested in historical studies of racial thought for their own sake. They will want to know if such studies can throw light upon present-day problems of an intellectual or practical nature. I have tried to bear their concerns in mind by keeping to a minimum the descriptions of the work of particular authors (while providing references for those who wish to follow up such matters) and by concentrating instead upon the connecting tissue of enquiry which relates these authors to one another. I have neglected authors who in their time attracted much attention, like Houston Stewart Chamberlain, Madison Grant and Lothrop Stoddard, if they did not grapple with the intellectual problems. In any case, their arguments have been thoroughly examined in other works. Nor have I thought it feasible, in a work of this character, adequately to discuss the social and political background to all the various theories. That would be another and larger task. Underlying the selection of authors and topics for discussion in the period up to World War Two has been my assumption that no one can understand the debates about racial differences among humans who cannot relate them to the contemporary attempts to explain corresponding differences in the wider world of nature. The modern reader with the advantages of hindsight can see more clearly the shape of the problems with which these earlier writers contended. Too often he condemns his predecessors for being unable to see things that no one in an earlier generation could clearly perceive. Too often he explains the predecessors' mistakes as the outcome of moral deficiencies. No one knows how future generations will assess the moral deficiencies of our own time. Every commentator upon racial relations in the present judges them in the light of what he believes them to have been like in the past. Everyone who writes about present-day racial thought does likewise. If their beliefs about the past are wrong, their assessments of the present will be unreliable. Therefore they should check their assumptions. Historical studies can bring a measure of humility to the vigorous dialogue that is understandably characteristic of discussions about racial relations and racial equality.

For the period after World War Two, when the third phase was well established, the need to consider contemporary explanations of biological differences is less pressing. The volume of social science research started to increase dramatically in the 1950s and this makes the task of selection more difficult. For this period I have allowed my views of the Marxist challenge, and of the most satisfactory response to that challenge, to determine the selection of arguments for discussion, though this obliges me to neglect work in sociology and in other subjects that other readers will consider equally or more important. I have also tried to present the material selected in ways that will persuade readers that historical studies can open perspectives that should stimulate the formulation of better theories.

Acknowledgements

One of the pleasures of writing a book about racial theories is that the subject matter invites an author to cross so many academic boundaries. One of the pleasures of working in a university is that an author has colleagues with so many kinds of specialist knowledge who can guide his studies. I have benefited from the guidance of colleagues in departments of accounting and animal husbandry at one end of the alphabet across to theology and zoology at the other. Seeking advice from specialists has its perils as well, for they often insist that to clarify a problem it is necessary to go into the kind of detail that will frighten off most non-specialist readers. So I have tried to keep these tendencies in check.

I wish to thank all those colleagues and students who, sometimes without knowing it, have advised me or helped me develop my arguments. I owe a particular debt to John Hurrell Crook, until recently Reader in Ethology in the University of Bristol, who over the years has tutored me on many questions of a biological character and who commented in detail on this book when it was in draft.

May, 1986   MICHAEL BANTON

1

RACE AS LINEAGE

The word race entered the English language in 1508 in the poem *The Dance of the Sevin Deidly Sins* by the Scotsman, William Dunbar. Among those who followed the sin of Envy he listed:

> And flatteris in to menis facis;
> And bakbyttaris of sindry racis,
> To ley that had delyte.

It was introduced into an intellectual world in which the Bible was accepted as the authority on human affairs. All humans were descended from Adam and Eve. To understand what had happened to the various sections of humanity subsequently it was necessary to trace their histories back genealogically through the links in the ancestral chain. People were differentiated because they had migrated to different regions and because God had guided the course of events. He had punished some, as by putting the mark upon Cain and by permitting the curse upon Ham and his descendants. Different groups had doubtless been dispersed after the Flood and after the fall of the Tower of Babel. Yet the Bible was obscure in places and its answers seemed to be hidden, so it had to be studied with intelligence and faith. How was it possible to reconcile stories of people in distant lands with a Bible that made no mention of these lands? One possible solution was to maintain that Adam was the ancestor of the Jews alone, and that other peoples' nature and history could be traced back to other ancestors. Such an explanation, later called that of polygenesis, was first advanced by Paracelsus in 1520. It was taken up again in 1655 by the luckless Isaac de Peyrère, who wrote, 'I would that St Augustine and Lactantius were now alive, who scoffed at the Antipodes. Truly they would pity themselves if they should hear and see those things which are discovered in the east and west in this clear-sighted age . . . ' Yet his book was burned and its author forced to recant. Isaac de Peyrère was a man of Jewish descent who professed to be a Christian; his claim of separate origins seems to have been intended as testimony to the greater glory of the Jews (Poliakov, 1974: 132–4).

Classification

Though 'race' came into increasing use in the sense of lineage during the sixteenth and seventeenth centuries (as in the 1570 reference in Foxe's *Book of Martyrs* to 'the race and stocke of Abraham') its future significance was being decided in another realm of discourse, that of natural history. People looked to the Bible for explanations not of human origins only, but of all living things. One of the first to offer a systematic natural history was John Ray (1627–1705), a founder of the Royal Society, who in 1690 wrote *The Wisdom of God Manifested in the Works of the Creation*. John C. Greene (1959: 17) describes this as a reaffirmation of the Christian doctrine of the creation infused with the hopefulness generated by the scientific revolution of his time. Ray maintained that 'the number of true species in nature is fixed and limited and, as we may reasonably believe, constant and unchangeable from the first creation to the present day'. In the beginning God had created a limited number of animals and plants. The study of nature could bring humans to an understanding of the wisdom, power and benevolence by which the Creator ministered to their intellectual and spiritual as well as physical needs. Still, it was not always easy to discern God's design or to sort out the diversity of living forms. Ray's guiding principle was that what God had created was the species, and that 'a species is never born from the seed of another species', that is, it consisted of individual specimens linked by descent. His criteria for distinguishing the essential features of plant species from 'accidents' of variation in size, colour and number of leaves, were subjective and open to dispute. Just as Ray would not accept that a black cow and a white cow, or two similar fruits with a different taste, were necessarily separate species, so he would make no such distinction between a Negro and a European. But while he could experiment by sowing the seed of a plant and seeing whether it gave rise to a similar variety, when it came to the bigger animals he had to class together specimens whose common descent he could not verify.

This leads straight to the central problem of racial thought, one that runs through from the seventeenth century (if not earlier) to the present time, and is far from settled yet: What is the nature of species? There is nothing wrong in classifying humans according to their appearance. The problems revolve around the nature of the classes from which a classification is constructed and the significance of the differences between them. In this they reflect one of the oldest and most fundamental disputes in philosophy. In the Middle Ages a major battle was fought between the nominalists and the realists. According to Popper (1957: 27) the former held that universal terms like 'energy', 'velocity', 'carbon', 'whiteness', etc., differed from singular terms or proper names, like 'Alexander the Great', 'Halley's Comet' and 'World War One', in that the former were labels for sets or classes of individual things. The nominalists regarded the universal term 'white' as identifying a set composed of things as different as snowflakes, tablecloths and swans. The realists contended that whiteness was an intrinsic property: snowflakes shared this property along with tablecloths and swans. They believed that universal terms denoted universal objects (called 'forms' or 'ideas' by Plato) just as singular terms denoted individual things. The doctrine traditionally called realism has also been called idealism (which might seem to be its opposite) and so Popper concluded that it would be less confusing to speak of an opposition between nominalism and essentialism. Nominalists regard words as instruments of description which permit scholars to generalize about the behaviour or relations of individuals which are classed separately or together. Essentialists believe that research must seek the essence of things in order to explain them. Nominalists regarded the classification of individuals to constitute a species as a matter of convenience. Different classifications could be used for different purposes. In biology, Robinet, Buffon and Lamarck all at various times gave their assent to the view that 'there are only individuals, and no kingdoms or classes or genera or species'. Essentialists started from the Biblical story and believed that the task of classification was to grasp the essential character of the original form which explained the diversity of outward appearances.

The number and variety of forms was daunting. Were all dogs, for example, to be accounted one species? They inter-breed, but the differences between the spaniel, the terrier and the bulldog were striking. One scheme which assisted simplification was the notion of a Great Chain of Being, a *scala naturae*, to which Linnaeus referred when in 1754 he wrote:

> If we consider the generation of animals, we find that each produces an offspring after its own kind . . . so that all living things, plants, animals, and even mankind themselves, form one chain of universal being from the beginning to the end of the world. Of all the species originally formed by the Deity, not one is destroyed. (quoted, Bendyshe, 1865: 435)

The ambiguities in this conception can be seen in the passage quoted, for while it refers to a vertical or temporal chain in which individuals are linked to their ancestors and descendants of different generations, it also implies that plants, animals and humans are linked to one another in a horizontal or classificatory chain such that the individuals of each species shaded into those of the next, or intergraded, as if sharp differentiation was impossible. *Natura non facit saltum* (nature makes no leaps) was the slogan expressing the view that there were no discontinuities or breaks in natural variation. Linnaeus' dogmatic assertion that no species was ever destroyed was an attempt to eliminate a serious problem. John Ray had earlier been troubled by the discovery of the fossils of apparently extinct shell fish. He decided that such shell fish might still be lodged so deep in the seas or on rocks so remote that they had not been noticed. For why would God have created them if they were not necessary to his design? The natural historian felt obliged to assume that God's creation was perfect; to do otherwise would be to suggest that God was a poor craftsman. When in 1706, 1739, and later, the skeletal remains of mammoths were discovered in New York state, in Ohio, and in other parts of North America, it was inferred that there must somewhere be living mammoths because, in the words of Thomas Jefferson (in 1785), 'Such is the economy of nature, that no instance can be produced, of her having permitted any one race of her animals to become extinct . . . ' (Greene, 1959: 96–120).

Linnaeus (1707–78) is famous for his classificatory system, sometimes called binomial because he identified creatures by the names for the genus and the species. To these is also added another division, once called the variety but now known as the subspecies. Thus seagulls belong to the genus *Larus* and the Herring Gull is *Larus argentatus* or *Larus argentatus argentatus*. The species name is repeated to show that it is not divided at the subspecific level, unlike the Lesser Black Backed Gull which is *Larus fuscus britannicus* to differentiate it from *Larus fuscus antelius*. In the tenth edition of his *Systema Naturae* (1758) Linnaeus divided the species *Homo sapiens* into six diurnal varieties: *ferus* (four footed, mute, hairy); *americanus* (red, choleric, erect); *europaeus* (white, ruddy, muscular); *asiaticus* (yellow, melancholic, inflexible); *afer* (black, phlegmatic, indulgent); *monstrosus* (further subdivided to include deviant forms from several regions). The diurnal varieties were compared with a single nocturnal one, the troglodytes or cave-dwellers, exemplified by *Homo sylvestris* (man of the woods, or Orang Utan). Right up to the early years of the nineteenth century there were doubts about where the link was to be drawn between men and apes, and which side of that line Pygmies, Hottentots and Orang Utans belonged. Many travellers' tales asserted that the last-named was 'equally ardent for women as for its own females'. Believing that apes were men in a primitive stage of development, the whimsical Scottish judge and author Lord Monboddo maintained that

Orang Utan-human matings might be fertile; his views were satirized by Thomas Love Peacock in his 1817 novel *Melincourt* which tells how the central figure, Sir Oran Haut Ton, comes to be elected a Member of Parliament.

Linnaeus was too honest to deal with other problems as dogmatically as he dealt with that of extinct species. He encountered a striking mutation of flower structure in the plant *Linaria*, which he believed to be a new species. He also studied some hybrids which seemed to be new species. This led him after a while to the conclusion that perhaps only genera had been created in the beginning and that species were the product of hybridization among them (Mayr, 1982: 259).

The Linnaean classificatory enterprise depended upon the assumption that the various sets of individuals to be classified were stable, for how could they be classified if they were changing? Some new principle had to be incorporated into the scheme to deal with change. Linnaeus' great French contemporary Buffon (1707–88) moved further in this direction and there was, of course, a Biblical warrant for a change in the story of the expulsion of Adam and Eve from the Garden of Eden. If they had been sent to live in inferior environments might it not be expected that they would degenerate? In the first volume of his *Histoire Naturelle* (1749) Buffon rejected the concept of species, contending that only individuals existed. The idea of a species could be rendered intelligible only 'by considering Nature in the succession of time, and in the constant reduction and renovation of beings'. Yet Buffon abandoned this view in his second volume, asserting that two animals belong to the same species 'if by means of copulation they perpetuate themselves and preserve the likeness of the species'. The horse and the donkey were separate species because the product of their mating was sterile (the offspring of a male donkey and a mare is called a mule; that of a stallion and a female donkey is called a hinny). In the first volume Buffon also elaborated an environmental view of human variation, suggesting that after being diffused over the whole surface of the earth mankind 'underwent divers changes, from the influence of climate, from the difference of food, and of the mode of living, from epidemical distempers, as also from the inter-mixture, varied *ad infinitum*, of individuals more or less resembling each other . . .'

How environments might occasion organic change was far from clear. The philosopher Immanuel Kant (1724–1804) supposed that the ancestral human stock had been endowed with latent powers which could be evoked or suppressed in new circumstances. A somewhat similar interpretation was developed by Johann Friedrich Blumenbach (1752–1830), the German anatomist who has been called the father of anthropology. It was he who first advanced the fivefold classification: Caucasian, Mongolian, Ethiopian, American, Malayan, and maintained that the different kinds of humans differed only in degree. Blumenbach was puzzled by the way that acquired characters (in particular peculiarities of appearance made by accident or by intention, such as the binding of children's heads or feet) were not handed down to the next generation when other 'marks of race', organic disorders and deficiencies of speech were so transmitted. He concluded that there must be some hidden agencies which operated to change the bodies of animals. This change he called degeneration, but seems to have meant by it not deterioration so much as the kinds of modification that arise as one generation succeeds another (though cf. Sloan, 1973). He wrote of degeneration as an explanation of variation within a species and as opposed to separate creation. In his view the genital liquid interacted with other material to produce a formative force which resulted in the normal reproduction of the animal or plant unless it was deflected in some way; in which case it produced monsters, hybrids, or greater variation. Climate had great influence in 'diverting the formative force from its accustomed path'. Domestic animals showed greater variation than wild ones, because they had been subjected to more varied conditions, especially of food. All hogs, for example, descended from the wild boar. Yet endless differences could be seen between the kinds of domestic hogs to be found in various European countries. The original wild condition of man was not known, but in spreading over the earth he had exposed himself to so many different stimuli that he had developed even more variation than the hog.

If forms were changing, this complicated the problem of classification. It also had implications for the use of the word race. Kant distinguished between *Naturbeschreibung* (nature-description) and *Naturgeschichte* (natural history). The former was static, a classification at a moment in time which was based upon similarities between specimens ordered into genera, species and varieties. The latter dealt with relations between varieties, species and genera over time. What was species in *Naturbeschreibung* must in *Naturgeschichte* often be called only race since it was impossible to distinguish species from genus in the historical dimension (see especially Greene, 1957: 363 note 13). Johann Gottfried von Herder also in 1784 protested about the use of the word race to denote classes when it was properly used to designate a difference of origin; since all humans were of the same origin no racial difference existed in their species.

External conditions

The discovery of the hidden agencies of evolution is a story that belongs with the internal history of biology. Before sketching its outlines it will be appropriate to comment upon the external conditions of racial thought from the sixteenth to the eighteenth centuries. The first of these conditions must be the power of organized religion to prevent speculation coming to any conclusions which could not be fitted into the monogenetic view of humanity as the descendants of Adam and Eve. This conception was threatened by the new ideas arising from discoveries overseas. Contemplating reports about the life of peoples in the newly discovered regions of America, Europeans were bound to ask, 'Why are they not like us?'. Trying to identify what was distinctive about these other peoples, Europeans were forced into a new self-consciousness. They had to ask what was distinctive about themselves, and why their own way of life was to be preferred. Thus the French essayist Montaigne (1533–92) described what he had learned about the customs of the peoples near the bay of Rio de Janeiro and suggested that there was no more barbarism in their eating men alive than in some of the things he and his readers had lately seen in France. Three men of this foreign nation, he wrote, visited Rouen in the time of Charles IX, who talked with them a great while. Montaigne also did his best to question them on many points and reported: 'I find that there is nothing in that nation that is either barbarous or savage, unless men call that barbarism which is not common to them.' In 1721 Montesquieu's *Persian Letters* started a new fashion when it held up to a European nation a picture of itself as it might appear in the eyes of people from another culture.

The early explorers in the Pacific had only fleeting contacts with the islanders, who often received them in friendship. Their accounts were favourable, but the European writing inspired by them went further and built the myth of the Noble Savage. This was of importance politically, for to believe that the savage is noble is to believe that man is naturally good. If evil does not have its origin in human nature, it must spring from the faulty organization of society. As Rousseau urged: 'God makes all things good; man meddles with them and makes them evil.' To believe that man is naturally good is to believe that under another regime he could lead a better life, and such an outlook must therefore be a powerful spur to the radical reorganization of society. This kind of romanticism was an important influence in the changes of opinion leading up to the French Revolution in 1789. After the Revolution the myth disappeared and, as missionary activity in the Pacific increased, it was replaced, first by 'the evangelistic picture of an ignoble and degraded brute' and then by a conception of the savage as 'representative of the childhood of man, interesting because he possessed the unrealized accomplishments of the child' (Smith, 1960: 22–3, 108, 251).

Montesquieu's great work *The Spirit of Laws* (1748) was important for its elaboration of environmental explanations of cultural and physical variation. 'Cold air constringes the extremities of the external fibres of the body', he wrote; 'this increases their elasticity, and favours the return of the blood from the extreme parts to the heart.' He himself had frozen half of a sheep's tongue and examined it under a microscope to study these changes. Such processes meant that people were more vigorous in cold climates; national character was shaped by environmental influences while forms of government had to suit the character of the country's inhabitants. 'The people of India', he wrote, 'are mild, tender and compassionate. Hence their legislators repose great confidence in them.' Montesquieu also referred to 'countries where excess of heat enervates the body, and renders men so slothful and dispirited that nothing but the fear of chastisement can oblige them to perform any laborious duty: slavery is there more reconcilable to reason'. While acknowledging that in such environments slavery could be founded on natural reason, he still insisted that it had to be rejected since 'all men are born equal' and he deployed his heaviest sarcasm against those who thought they were justified in going off and enslaving Negroes. The message was that each people was adapted to its own environment and therefore should stay where they were. The same lesson was taught by Voltaire's story of Candide whose misadventures while travelling abroad led him to decide that he should stay at home and cultivate his own garden. It was widely believed that Europeans who migrated to North America were liable to degenerate because they were not suited to that climate (Echevaria, 1957). Indeed, the mortality from the new diseases that travellers encountered was often frightening.

In the eighteenth century Europeans wondered why their nations had recently made such great technological progress and were able to spread their influence. Why could not other peoples do likewise? What were the causes of progress? The environmentalist view went with a stress upon what were called the moral causes of progress, as by Adam Ferguson, a sociological fore-runner who maintained that progress depended upon having a social organization suited to the people's environment (cf. the contrast between physical cause and moral cause explanations in Curtin, 1964: 227–58).

Though there was a substantial literature in the seventeenth and eighteenth centuries about Africans and other non-Europeans, the word 'race' was rarely used either to describe peoples or in accounts of differences between them. Anthony J. Barker has combed through this literature. In 1748 David Hume, in a footnote to his essay *Of National Characters*, stated that since, among the races of the world, only the Negro race had never developed any major civilization, he suspected that Negroes might be 'naturally inferior to the Whites'. Noting that this remark had attracted attention because of Hume's eminence as a philosopher, Barker (1978: 77) replied that the very rarity of such comments was symptomatic of a pervasive apathy about problems of racial and cultural difference among the more innovative thinkers of the period. He overlooked the discussion of cultural variation in connection with the moral causes of progress, but this is not the main issue. Barker contended that there was a contemporary theory of African inferiority even if it was not to be found in the works of the intellectuals. It could be reconstructed piecemeal from the writings of more obscure authors. This reconstruction revealed a theory of the cultural inferiority of West Africa; of the African as shaped by a culture that was to be condemned, but with a human potential to be salvaged. They were black because the African environment had made them so; they were neither natural slaves nor were they especially well equipped to work in the tropics (Barker, 1978: 100, 62). Little use was made of the image of the black man in the romantic writing about the noble savage because people knew so much more about Africans than about Pacific Islanders and had formed an unfavourable estimate of African society as incapable of developing the region's potential wealth (cf. Curtin, 1964: 95). Therefore, when the agitation against the slave trade began (this can be dated from the formation in 1787 of the Committee for the Abolition of the Slave Trade) it started a debate that was conducted within a framework of existing knowledge. For the abolitionists the central issues were the morality and necessity of the trade. Only a handful of pro-slavery writers asserted that blacks were inferior; most of them pointedly rejected such views except in so far as they contended that only Negroes could work in extreme heat. The traders themselves formed a third party. They rationalized the problems they had experienced in their dealings with West Africans in mutually contradictory charges of native incompetence and sharp practice. The detailed information which many of them provided came from a context of mistrust and ethnocentric contempt and not from assumptions about racial inferiority.

Those who disputed about the slave trade agreed on some fundamental points, foremost among them being that the Negro was no more amenable to the regimentation of slavery than any other man. In 1730 Ralph Sandiford had complained that one of the great injustices of the slave trade lay in taking Africans to 'unnatural climates which is hard for them to bear whose Constitutions are tendered by the Heat of their Native Country; for God that made the World, and all Man of one Blood, that dwelt upon the Face of the Earth, has appointed them Bounds of their Habitations . . . ' In so saying he was repeating the text of the Acts of the Apostles 17: 26. Some had argued that whites could work in the West Indies as well as anyone else, but the British Government refused to transport white convicts to the islands and the belief that only blacks were suited to tropical drudgery gained ground. The idea of divinely ordained racial zones could be interpreted either way. The contending parties were united in the belief that because of their bad environment and their cultural backwardness, it could be to the Africans' advantage to be removed from their existing society provided that it could not be reorganized along European lines (and the vicissitudes of the attempted resettlement of blacks in Sierra Leone from 1787 onwards did not encourage any optimism on that score). What they disputed was whether the slave trade was a proper means for enabling Africans in some other setting to realise their full human potential.

The contrary view has often been sustained by a superficial reading of a passage in Eric Williams' *Capitalism and Slavery* in which he wrote:

> Slavery in the Caribbean has been too narrowly identified with the Negro. A racial twist has thereby been given to what is basically an economic phenomenon. Slavery was not born of racism: rather, racism was the consequence of slavery. Unfree labor in the New World was brown, white, black and yellow; Catholic, Protestant and Pagan. (1944: 7)

The thrust of this argument was in the first sentence. There was no reason for Williams to deny that there were white prejudices against blacks before New World slavery. There is now no reason for anyone else to deny that such prejudices were increased by slavery. The argument is about the interaction between racial attitudes and structures of exploitation. It is important because twentieth-century writers recognize in their own societies doctrines or practices they call racism and they ask when these originated. The first difficulty is that of defining sufficiently clearly just what it is whose origin is to be discovered; the second that of separating it from the various other beliefs and forms of behaviour with which it is associated. It has also to be remembered that an ideology is likely to be a synthesis of ideas, some of which will have been familiar for a long period. It may be a long time in the making before it is formulated in a way that commands widespread assent. One view sees racism as an ideology generated to defend the interests of whites who made great profits from sugar production in the West Indies; this ideology was then developed to serve the interests of the capitalist classes. The main alternative view relates the prejudices of whites towards blacks to status distinctions drawn within white society and sees it as starting to increase greatly after the middle of the nineteenth century.

A straightforward statement of the first position is to be found in a history of black people in Britain entitled *Staying Power* (Fryer, 1984), which dates English racism as originating among Barbados planters in the eighteenth century. They told one another that Negroes were beasts without souls who should not be baptized lest this encourage rebellion. Their attitudes were then brought home and adopted by whites in England who deplored marriages between black men and white women as polluting English blood. Since only a few people (perhaps four or five) wrote to this effect it is necessary to assess their representativeness and influence. The author most frequently quoted is Edward Long, son of a Jamaican planter who served there as a judge and who in 1774 published a *History of Jamaica* which shows that he hated colonial governors almost as much as he hated blacks. Long's views are said to demonstrate the existence and appeal of racism in England in the 1770s, but Barker (1978: 162) reports that other pro-slavery writers repudiated Long's views about race and that Long 'produced criticisms of the slave system so fundamental that his work, for all its racialism, came to be used far more by abolitionists than by pro-slavery writers'. William Wilberforce, the leader of the abolitionists, when speaking in Parliament, frequently quoted Long. It was his criticisms of slavery that were influential and not his views about race. So if Long's arguments are to be interpreted as an ideology advancing material interests these could not have been the interests of the slave-owners.

In the section of his *History* dealing with Negroes, Long begins with an unacknowledged extract from the most unfavourable contemporary description of Africa and then goes on to organize observations about the various kinds of apes and men in accordance with the postulate of a Great Chain of Being. Those who believed in such a chain regarded it as a static hierarchy, the links of which were the various species whose distinctiveness was proven by their inability to produce fertile offspring. Long knew well that in the West Indies blacks and whites did produce fertile offspring, and so did interested members of the British public who could observe the results of inter-racial mating in their own country, who heard reports of black–white liaisons in West Africa and the West Indies, and who could occasionally observe individuals who in their appearance were intermediate between blacks and whites. So Long maintained that while blacks and whites could inter-breed the results of such unions were of diminishing fertility: if two mulattoes had children they would not survive to maturity. This was scarcely a contribution to the development of a theory of racial inequality. There were such contributions but they came not from writers identified as spokesmen for economic interests, but from within the internal history of racial thought as represented by serious scholars like Charles White and Georges Cuvier whose works are discussed later. The view that the main increase in racial consciousness occurred in the latter part of the nineteenth century will be outlined at the end of Chapter 2.

One of the major eighteenth-century changes in the external conditions likely to influence racial thought was the declaration of the independence of the United States in 1776. A majority of the whites chose to break away from the country with which they had previously identified themselves. To create a new state was difficult. To create a new nation to support that state, more so. For what was to bind together the members of the new nation and distinguish them from the British with whom they shared language, religion, culture and physical appearance? They decided, in effect, that it should be their political institutions. They would form a more perfect union to establish a higher standard of justice and insure domestic tranquility, as their constitution was to declare. There are here some connections which may surprise those who expect doctrines of racial inferiority to have arisen from black–white encounters, for the circumstances in which both the French and the English first came to use the word race in a political context were remarkably similar and they had their echo in late eighteenth-century North America.

From the sixteenth to the eighteenth centuries there were historians of France who maintained that their country's history was that of the interaction of two races. At the end of the fifth century, they said, a small Frankish Kingdom had conquered Gaul, but the Franks and the Gauls had remained distinct. The nobility were the descendants of the Franks whose name was supposed to mean 'free' and who derived their claim to privilege from the right of conquest. These claims were contested by other historians who asserted that the Gauls had invited the assistance of the Franks to help expel the Romans. Historians searched the writings of Caesar and Tacitus to see what they had to say about the earliest Frenchmen, as if that would decide the entitlements of their successors. In England, Richard Verstegan opened his book *Restitution of Decayed Intelligence*, first published in 1605, with the proclamation that 'Englishmen are descended of German race and were heretofore generally called Saxons'; he went on to explain why 'the Germans are a most noble nation' and to stress that according to Tacitus the authority of their kings was limited. This Germanic race had settled in England from AD 449. Such a history was advanced to challenge the ambitions of the Stuart monarchs who wanted to weaken the power of parliament and to rule by divine right. It asserted that the royal claims had not been acknowledged in the past and that they ran contrary to the nature of the people. It was suggested that the Anglo-Saxon centuries, before the arrival of Norman rulers in 1066, had been a golden age. An ancestral myth was created which derived the chief English virtues from their Anglo-Saxon forebears. Sir Walter Scott got this idea from a play about Runnymede and used it in one of the best-selling novels of the century, *Ivanhoe*, published in 1820. Its theme is that of the ill-feeling between the resentful Saxon peasantry, whose hero is Robin Hood, and their cruel oppressive Norman rulers. Scott presents it as a struggle between two races. It is probable that no single book or event did more to introduce the word race into popular use than Scott's historical romance (Banton, 1977: 15–26).

By 1776 many whites in the United States aligned themselves with the English radicals who had been demanding constitutional change in order to cleanse their country of religious and political abuses stemming from the Norman Conquest and to restore Anglo-Saxon institutions. This transatlantic affinity is seen most vividly in the writings of Thomas Jefferson, the principal author of the Declaration of Independence and the second president of the United States. He thought the study of the Anglo-Saxon language so important for his fellow countrymen that he wrote a simplified grammar to make it more accessible, and included the subject in the curriculum of the University of Virginia. Like de Tocqueville, later, Jefferson stressed the fundamental importance of a country's institutions; since in his view Anglo-Saxon freedom had been based on the holding of land in fee simple, nothing gave him greater pleasure than his work for the abolition of primogeniture and entail in the law of Virginia (Horsman, 1981: 21). Jefferson is noted for advocating the abolition of slavery but his *Notes on the State of Virginia* (written in 1781–2 though not generally available before 1787) show that he found environmentalist explanations of black–white differences unpersuasive. He noted that slavery among the Greeks and Romans had produced slaves of talent and achievement – but they had been whites. As for Negroes, he concluded, 'It is not their condition then, but nature, which has produced the distinction.' Though uncertain whether blacks were 'originally a distinct race, or made distinct by time and circumstance' the difference between them and the whites was equated with the difference between species (see Jordan, 1968: 429–90).

Such theories evoked the disapproval of the president of what is now Princeton University. Samuel Stanhope Smith published in 1787 *An Essay on the Causes of the Variety of Complexion and Figure in the Human Species, to Which Are Added Strictures on Lord Kaims's Discourse, on the Original Diversity of Mankind*. Though it is the Scots jurist whose doctrines are singled out, Smith had his targets nearer home as well. His starting point was the belief that Christians were not at liberty to question the Biblical account. His principal argument then, as in the second edition of 1810, was that all conceptions of morality would be confused if it were thought that the different kinds of men were different species:

> The rules which would result from the study of our own nature, would not apply to the natives of other countries who would be of different species; perhaps, not to two families in our own country, who might be sprung from a dissimilar composition of species. Such principles tend to confound all science, as well as piety; and leave us in the world uncertain whom to trust; or what opinions to frame of others . . . The doctrine of one race, removes this uncertainty, renders human nature susceptible of system, illustrates the power of physical causes, and opens a rich and extensive field for moral science.

Smith would not accept any division between the reasoning of religion and that of science. As Jordan writes, he marshalled Linnaean classification and the power of environmental influence to support the book of Genesis. Stanhope Smith and Jefferson both started from assumptions of human equality. Smith's assumption came from a religious belief that constrained the significance attributable to physical differences. Jefferson's assumption came from a scientific belief that acknowledged fundamental similarities, allowed for the possibility that Negroes might be unable ever to equal whites, but added 'whatever be their degree of talent, it is no measure of their rights'. Stanhope Smith was

> inclined to ascribe the apparent dullness of the negro principally to the wretched state of his existence first in his original country . . . and afterwards in those regions to which he is transported to finish his days in slavery, and toil . . . The abject servitude of the negro in America . . . must condemn him, while these circumstances remain, to perpetual sterility of genius.

In the twenty three years that passed before publication of the second edition of Smith's book, the objections to the monogenetic explanation of diversity increased. In particular, evidence had accumulated which pointed to inherited differences in the capacities of individuals of different race. Arguments had to address themselves to the nature and significance of those inequalities. One author whose work, though not widely read in the United States, had impressed some influential people, was the Manchester surgeon Charles White. So Stanhope Smith had to study White's slender volume *An Account of the Regular Gradation in Man, and in different Animals and Vegetables; and from the former to the latter* (1799). White had measured the anatomical features of over fifty Negroes,

compared them with figures for whites, and concluded that in respect of
'bodily structure and economy' the Negro was closer to the ape than was
the European. In seeing, hearing, smelling, memory, and the powers of
mastication the European was 'least perfect, the African more so, and the
brutes most perfect of all'. As the title indicated, White's thought was
dominated by the idea of the Great Chain of Being. He wanted to see 'the
pernicious practice of enslaving mankind . . . abolished throughout the
world' and held that 'the negroes are, at least, equal to thousands of Europeans, in capacity and responsibility; and ought, therefore, to be equally
entitled to freedom and protection'. By the same measure they were not
equal to even more thousands of Europeans. Where the line might be
drawn between men and apes needed further investigation and infertility
could not be accepted as a sufficient criterion of species. Stanhope Smith
believed that he must combat this unbiblical notion of a chain of being and
to do so he changed his ground; abandoning his presumption of the unity
of religion and science, he contested arguments from science with counter
arguments from science alone. He made his own measurements of Negro
anatomy and skin temperature, arguing that the American environment
was producing changes, especially among domestic slaves (as opposed to
field hands) and among free Negroes. Among other things, their complexions were becoming whiter. The effect of heat was to thicken the skin
and to free the bile which had deposited a dark residue such 'that colour
may be justly considered as a universal freckle'. If the temperature was
reduced, then complexions lightened; just as the complexions of Europeans varied from the Mediterranean up towards the Arctic, so could
physical differences between Negroes and Caucasians be explained by
reference to universal causes. Stanhope Smith could deny neither the facts
of physical difference nor those of present racial inferiority. His answer to
the measurements of facial angle, for example, was not to declare them
irrelevant but to assert that the Negro form was changing so as to resemble
the higher form of the Whites. As Jordan has observed, 'his whole book
shouted that the Negro was going to be the equal of the white man only
when he came to look like one' (Jordan, 1968: 486–8, 507–17).

Chronology

If all men and women were descended from Adam and Eve, as the Bible
seemed to say, then it was possible to calculate how many generations had
passed from Adam through the line of David down to the period of
recorded history, and discover for how many years humans had lived on
the earth's surface. One who attempted this was a vice-chancellor of

Cambridge University, John Lightfoot, who in 1644 came to the conclusion that 'Man was created by the Trinity about the third hour of the day, or nine of the clock in the morning' in the year now identified as 3928 BC. Six years later Archbishop James Ussher decided that 'the beginning of time fell upon the night before the twenty-third day of October in the year of the Julian calendar 710' which was 4004 BC. Ussher's data was widely accepted and printed in some English translations of the Bible, though there were many other studies that came to somewhat different conclusions. One of the obstacles to any formulation of a theory of evolution was the resulting belief that the earth was only about six thousand years old and that therefore any explanation of change would have to show how the contemporary diversity could have been produced in such a period of time. As late as 1886 Sir Samuel Baker, the African explorer, concluded that there could be no doubt as to the rapidity with which races became differentiated, for the differences between Englishmen and the Africans of the White Nile must have been the work of only 5870 years.

The debates about the age of the earth which started within geology, especially with a paper by James Hutton delivered before the Royal Society of Edinburgh in 1785, were therefore of very wide importance. On the one hand were ranged the Neptunists who held that all rocks were formed as precipitation from the water of a primitive universal ocean which had held in solution great quantities of mineral matter. Granite was one of the oldest of rocks; softer rocks, like sandstone, had been created more recently, but in any event the earth must be of great antiquity. The Neptunists were opposed by the Plutonists (or Vulcanists) who held that many rocks were of igneous or volcanic origin. Hutton's theory was important to the latter school. He maintained that natural agents now at work and within the earth had operated with general uniformity throughout long periods of time. There was also a third position, called catastrophism, which contended that God for his own purposes (such as to punish a sinful humanity) had from time to time caused dramatic changes by ordaining great floods and volcanic eruptions; this was the only doctrine that could easily be harmonized with a Biblical chronology.

If the claim that the earth was of great antiquity was accepted, it became possible to contemplate an evolutionary explanation of natural diversity. The great chain of being could represent a process whereby higher forms had developed from lower. The centre of intellectual advance in this respect was Paris, and the three most important names were those of the botanist Lamarck (1744–1829), the comparative anatomist Cuvier (1769–1832), and the morphologist Geoffroy (1772–1844), whose full name was Etienne Geoffroy Saint-Hilaire. According to Lamarck, all animals could be ordered so as to show a graded series of 'perfection'. There was such an amazing diversity of organisms that 'anything which it is possible to imagine has effectively taken place'. Transformations could occur within lines of descent but change was so slow as to be imperceptible, the evidence for this being available in the fossil record. Evolutionary change explained why some forms had died out, and by studying it scholars could learn more about the harmony of nature and the wisdom of the creator. Since environments change, there must be some process enabling a species to remain in balance with its environment. By introducing a time factor, says Mayr (1982: 349), Lamarck had discovered the Achilles' heel of the old theology. Change occurred because God had given all species the power to develop towards greater complexity and a capacity to react to special conditions in the environment. There was a sequence whereby a changing environment created new needs, which altered the animals' habits and these changed its use of its various parts or organs so that, over time, they changed too. Cuvier (whose influence is discussed in Chapter 2) opposed such theories of organic development. He interpreted the geological record as showing the stability of the major animals over long periods of time, while the drastic breaks in geological strata seemed to support the possibility of rapid change in connection with natural catastrophes. Geoffroy's views were in some ways less sophisticated than Lamarck's, for he thought that the environment might influence the animal embryo directly. Where Cuvier believed that function determined structure, Geoffroy maintained the reverse: 'animals have no habits but those that result from the structure of their organs'. Cuvier stressed correlation, asserting that all herbivores have hoofs and no carnivores have horns. Geoffroy stressed connection and composition, maintaining that all animals were built according to a single plan which could be seen in the relative position of organs: the hoof of the ruminant became the claw of the lion, the paw of the monkey, the wing of the bat, the fin of the sea mammal, and so on. He challenged the conventional distinction between vertebrates and non-vertebrates but could make little impression against Cuvier's more cautious, well-grounded arguments. It was thought unsatisfactory to argue for the unity of composition, as Geoffroy did, by pointing to correlations between the parts of animals; if one form was to develop from another, the intermediate forms had also to be viable creatures who could feed and survive; otherwise they would not be able to pass on their characters. It is doubtful whether Geoffroy is properly regarded as an evolutionist (Mayr, 1982: 362–3, 462–3) but his work added substantially to interest in the ways in which environmental influences might explain variation. Any explanation of racial differences among humans had to be part of a more complex explanation of the origin and nature of species of all kinds. Those who favoured an evolutionary explanation were inclined to see races as inter-grading rather than as distinct, but this still left room for the possibility that some were naturally superior.

There was a striking parallel between an ordering of species from simple to complex and the development of the embryo from its initial simplicity in the egg to its complexity in the adult form. If there was an evolution of species it had to be transmitted through the embryo. This might be the place to look for the 'hidden agency' whereby environment altered species. From the early 1820s it was argued that 'ontogeny recapitulates phylogeny'. According to this view the higher forms had to pass through the earlier phases of evolution before reaching their own stage. None of the earlier stages could be left out. Ontogeny, by which is meant the life history of an individual, had to repeat phylogeny, that is, the evolutionary history which had produced the species to which the individual belonged. It was thought that while in the embryo each individual went through the earlier phases including the adult stages. Every human while in the womb recapitulated the development of a fish, a reptile, a bird, and a mammal, before it emerged as a human. In this form the theory was demolished in 1828 by von Baer, who showed that the embryo of a higher animal is never like the adult form of a lower animal but only like its embryo (Gould, 1977: 52–7). Nevertheless, modified in certain particulars, the theory of recapitulation remained influential throughout the nineteenth century being revived by Ernst Haeckel in 1866 so that it stimulated discoveries which remain important today (Mayr, 1982: 474–5).

Naturphilosophie

While the laboratory work flourished in Paris, German biology succumbed to a romantic movement called *Naturphilosophie* which sought a unification of all knowledge about nature through such transcendental beliefs as that which saw the history of the universe as the history of spirit, beginning in primal chaos and striving upward to reach its highest expression in man. Thus L. Oken in 1847 divided natural phenomena into four categories based on earth processes (nutrition), water processes (digestion), air processes (respiration), fire processes (motion). He classified mammals in varying ways including their sensory systems: so the sense of feeling was represented by carnivores; taste by seals; smell by bears; hearing by apes; and sight by men. Humans could be distinguished as black, yellow and white, but why were there no blue or green races?

Their absence suggested to Oken that colour was an unsatisfactory basis for classifying humans and he advanced a five-fold classification based on the organs of sense, so that there were eye men, nose men, ear men, and so on. This kind of approach reached its highest point in the work of Carl Gustav Carus. To the modern reader his arguments often sound absurd but *Naturphilosophie* was an important influence upon nineteenth-century racial thought.

Carl Gustav Carus (1789–1869) was a man of talents almost as varied as Goethe's. A physician to the royal family, privy counsellor, professor at Dresden, friend of Goethe, art critic and landscape painter, he also published important works on medical topics, on psychology, on the symbolism of the human form and an account of his travels in England and Scotland. In nine of the books he published between 1835 and 1861 Carus had something to say about race but it occupied a relatively small place in the mass of his writing and he is rarely remembered for his racial theory. Carus was impressed by the influence of great men on the course of history and wondered whether their prominence revealed anything about more general differences in human capacity. This explains why his one-hundred-page essay *On the Unequal Capacity of the Different Divisions of Mankind for Higher Spiritual Development* (his chief statement about race) was published as a memorial to Goethe on the centenary of his birth. Carus was acquainted with earlier racial classifications and the work of Klemm and J. C. Prichard, but he was dissatisfied with classifications based solely on external physical form. He thought he had found a better basis in the relation of the divisions of mankind to the earth as a planet, and in particular to the sun. This separated the earth's peoples into those of the day, of the eastern twilight, of the western twilight, and of the night. He referred to a recognized but not yet explained law that progress follows a path from east to west; the great human migrations had gone in this direction and so had epidemic diseases. But no argument was advanced as to how the sun could have had a differential effect upon humans: the terminology was metaphorical. Carus himself represented it on occasion as dealing with symbolic relationships and made no attempt to deal with the obvious difficulties inherent in such a theory. He drew on Morton's measurements of cranial capacity but instead of maintaining that physique determined culture, he regarded them both, physique and culture, as manifestations of the whole entity.

Carus wrote, 'The day peoples, who achieve a specially pure form in the region of the Caucasus, have spread out their type, sometimes in greater, sometimes in lesser perfection, over all Europe . . . ' but this is the only time he used the word 'type'. The Eastern twilight peoples were the

Mongolians, Malayans, Hindus, Turks, and Slavs; the Western twilight peoples were the American Indians; the night peoples were the Africans and Australians. Carus opened his discussion of the day peoples with a statement of the recapitulation theory, listing the most notable twelve: Caucasians, Persians, Armenians, Semites, Pelasgians, Etruscans, Thracians, Illyrians, Iberians, Romans, Celts, and Germans. Apparently the last named recapitulated in their embryonic development not only their eleven forebears but also certain peoples from the other three-quarters of humanity. From this, Carus said, emerged an important phenomenon 'that the big movements in the history of peoples, if they stem from a special stock, always demonstrate the special energy of this stock . . . in the childhood of peoples the material force is dominant but in more developed circumstances the spiritual principle comes to the fore' (1849: 81–2; see also Poliakov, 1974: 250). It was the duty of the day peoples to guide and help the less favoured ones. Though he was not explicit on this point, Carus implied that in the right circumstances a people could civilize itself and in this he provoked Gobineau's dissent.

The other great German racial theorist of this period also lived in Dresden. This was Gustav Klemm (1802–67) who spent most of his life in charge of the royal library in that town. In the years 1843–52 he produced a ten volume study, *Allegemeine Cultur-Geschichte der Menscheit*, synthesizing ethnographic accounts of the peoples of the world; in it he distinguished three stages of cultural evolution: savagery, domestication, and freedom. He divided mankind into active and passive races, stating that peoples differed in mentality and temperament. Much of the argument was summarized in an address of his on the fundamental ideas of a general science of culture (Klemm, 1851). Klemm's conception of culture history was of a philosophy of history of the kind envisaged by Herder and Kant; it emphasized environmental and cultural influences upon human development and was opposed to the more idealistic orientation deriving from Fichte in which different aspects of culture were subordinated to political evolution (Voegelin, 1933b: 159). In politics Klemm was a liberal democrat who found the decline of the ancient regime congenial, while the rise of egalitarian democracy appeared to him as the crowning peak of history.

One problem is to decide whether Carus and Klemm were advancing a conception of races as permanent human types or were using the terminology of race in a metaphorical fashion. There are many passages in the original sources that favour the second interpretation but their intention is often obscure to the modern reader. Moreover, the two leading authorities, Erich Voegelin (the refugee from Nazi Germany) and Hermann

Blome (who wrote in an intellectual milieu sympathetic to the typological conception of race) are not in complete agreement. Blome is adamant that Carus's conception of race had nothing whatsoever in common with those definitions that were rooted in biological categories; his four races were appearances of similarity which existed only as symbolical manifestations of planetary relations. Whereas Klemm's conception of race was free from romantic influences in its ethnological and culture-historical foundation, his theory of race bespoke the romantic spirit and philosophy (1943: 221, 253). Blome wrote:

> Just as Klemm thought it was from the 'marriage of peoples' and from the penetration of the passive by the active peoples that humanity starts upon a general cultural development, so Carus saw the inequality of human races as Nature's summons to interaction, to give-and-take, whereby humanity as a total organism might be served. The tribe of day peoples was 'entitled to regard itself as the true flowers of humanity', but for Carus that signified not only that this tribe was the bearer of civilization but also that, because of its superiority, power, resoluteness and persever-ance, it had the duty to lead the weak and less favoured tribes by lighting their path and assisting them along it; in so doing it would prove true to itself [quoting Carus 1849: 85]. To the question exactly how this task was given to the day peoples or active tribes, both Carus and Klemm give extensive answers. They see the whole of humanity as one great organism; its unequal parts, the races, have to stand in an inter-acting relationship of exchange and progress, so that under the leadership of the white race the 'idea' of humanity can be realized. (Blome, 1943: 254–5)

The pictures of Caucasian and Ethiopian skulls in Blumenbach's volumes were unsatisfying because the author could not say what their peculiarities meant. In the new romantic visions these pictures became alive. Men belonged no longer to abstract categories, but to races whose distinctive physical and cultural characters were related to the basic principles of Creation.

Voegelin also emphasized the way in which Carus's theory brought body and mind together. He believed that in Christian theology there must be a sharp distinction between these two realms and deplored the way in which biological differences could be used to divide the human com-munity. Consequently he looked more anxiously at Carus's basic philosophy and pictured his synthesis as important to the later develop-ment of more ominous racial theories. Voegelin was unimpressed by Klemm's interpretations, describing his racial theory as a rather banal con-glomeration of all the suggestions which an industrious research worker could receive from his generation, but he went on to conclude that Klemm and Gobineau were at one in their major theses, namely: (i) all important cultures in history have as their basis a symbiosis of races; (ii) there are distinct human types called by Gobineau the strong and the weak, by Klemm the active and the passive; (iii) the races migrate, or at least the active do; (iv) migration leads to the conquest of the weak by the strong; (v) as a result of conquest the races enter into a symbiosis which, by mixture or extermination, ends with the dissolution of the active conquering race as a distinct unit; (vi) when the active race dissolves, political tension disappears and an egalitarian society is established (an occasion for Klemm's satisfaction and Gobineau's despair).

This does not do full justice to the differences between the two writers. Klemm did not employ the concept of type; nor is it evident that he did regard racial characteristics as innate and permanent. He wrote of humanity as divided into two kinds of races analogous to the division into two sexes and to the division of the atmosphere into oxygen and nitrogen, so the argument seemed to lie on a metaphorical plane. Though he selected Caucasians as exemplifying the active races, and coloured peoples the passive races, and though he paid considerable attention to the expansion of the former, any conception of them as superior was left implicit. Explicitly he emphasized the complementary nature of the two halves. Active races isolated from their passive partners (like the nomadic Mongols) were incomplete and could not achieve true culture. On occasion he referred to the active and passive castes. 'First through the mixture of the two races, the active and the passive, I would like to say through the marriage of peoples, does humanity become complete; in this way it first springs to life and nourishes the blossoms of culture' (1843 i: 192–204; 1851: 169, 179).

The romantic world-view of a writer like Carus needs to be explored with the care of a social anthropologist trying to discover the conceptual structure of a strange culture. Its representation of race has more in common with the biblical story of the creation than with the approach of the modern scientist. Though Carus clearly formulated a theory of European superiority, it was within a conception of races as forming a symmetrical whole, and led to conclusions about how people ought to behave rather than to interpretations of their actions as pre-determined.

Nature and culture

The most respected writer on questions of race after Blumenbach was an Englishman, James Cowles Prichard (1786–1848). As a boy in Bristol he liked to visit the docks and speak with foreign sailors; indeed he chose medicine for his profession primarily because it afforded him opportunities to pursue his anthropological inclinations. For his M.D. in Edinburgh in 1808 he wrote a dissertation entitled *De Generis Humani Varietate* and he went on to expand this into a book written in English entitled *Researches into the Physical History of Mankind* which in successive editions 1813, 1826, 1836, 1851, expanded from one volume into five. It was complemented by another, *The Natural History of Man: comprising inquiries into the modifying influence of physical and moral agencies on the different tribes of the human family*, which, published in 1843, 1845, 1848 and 1855, expanded into two volumes. The former dealt with man's physical nature, the latter with his culture, but Prichard saw no opposition between the two any more than he could contemplate a conflict between his science and his religious belief. In his first work Prichard was concerned both to defend the Mosaic account by criticizing suggestions that human diversities have been constant from the very beginning, and to argue that there was no good evidence to indicate that acquired characters could be transmitted by heredity to the next generation. Both these arguments returned again and again in his later books. First came the question whether the races of mankind 'constitute separate species or are merely varieties of one species'. Species were to be identified by 'peculiarities of structure which have always been constant and undeviating'. He used race to refer to physically distinctive nations but was equally content to write of 'the tribes of men' (cf. 1826: 90). Faithful to the traditional interpretations of Genesis Prichard believed that the Creation occurred some six thousand years earlier; his problem was to explain the appearance of racial differences within this period by some hypothesis other than that of the inheritance of acquired characteristics, and, in the current state of knowledge he could not do this. Always he was led back to antecedents, as when he wrote, 'in some instances . . . the forms of several animals seem to be so modelled on a particular type, that they have all been imagined to have arisen from the same race' (1826: 91).

While rejecting the claim that acquired characters could be inherited, Prichard was conscious that children do not resemble their parents in any predictable manner; he contended that the more accurate our researches into the ethnography of the world became, the less ground could be found for the opinion that the characteristics of human races were permanent. So he enquired:

> has man received from his Maker a principle of accommodation by which he becomes fitted to possess and occupy the whole earth? He modifies the agencies of the elements upon himself; but do not these agencies also modify him? Have they not rendered him in his very organization different in different regions . . . ? (1843: 3–4)

At one time Prichard came quite close to what we now know to be the answer. He remarked that whole colonies of individuals may perish when moved to climates for which they are not adapted. Horses and cattle when transported to Paraguay and allowed to run wild underwent an alteration, but domesticated breeds did not. Perhaps, he said, there was an analogy with the races of man, and that once varieties were newly established in a stock they might continue there long after the race had been removed from the climate in which they originated (1826: 581–3).

From his anatomical studies Prichard concluded, tentatively, that there were three types of skull: prognathous, pyramidal, and oval. Every type showed deviations and shaded into the others by insensible gradations. All three types of cranium were found amongst Negroes and the types seemed to be associated with degrees of civilization rather than geographical populations. Each species, said Prichard, had a psychological character, but the type was preserved in the individual varieties, so he studied the psychological make up of human races and concluded that this supported the evidence of external characters, and that mankind constituted a single species (cf. Stocking, 1973).

The industry with which Prichard assembled evidence from so many sources, and the sobriety of his judgements, gave his books a special authority, but much turned on the definition of species, which was problematic. Usage varied. In 1826 Desmoulins, a Paris anatomist, was putting forward a classification of man into sixteen species; certain of these were divided into races, which made race a subspecific category. More than two decades later a cautious English ethnologist was writing 'a race is a class of individuals concerning which there are doubts as to whether they constitute a separate species or a variety of a recognized one. Hence the term is *subjective* . . . the present writer . . . has either not used the word race at all, or used it inadvertently' (Latham, 1850: 564).

Implications of error for racial thought

The relevance of the argument which started in embryology is illustrated by some of the fall-out from a controversy generated by Robert Chambers (1802–71). His personal story bears upon his work, for both he and his brother were born hexadactyls, with six fingers on each hand and six toes on each foot. While adolescents, they were operated upon to have the extra fingers and toes removed. Afterwards Robert ailed and may have employed his time while convalescent to read and reflect upon the possible causes of his unusual inheritance. Later he wrote a book *Vestiges of the Natural History of Creation* (1844) in which he set forth the 'Principle of

Progressive Development' as an explanation of evolution. Knowing that it would be regarded as a scandalous work, especially by the religious folk of Edinburgh, he had his wife copy out his manuscript in her handwriting and then sent it to a friend in Manchester who arranged for its publication. It appeared and attracted the very disapproval he had anticipated. The book was widely read and went through ten editions in ten years. His responsibility for the work was not acknowledged until thirteen years after his death but the suspicion that he might be the author was such that when, late in life, he was being considered as a candidate for the post of Lord Provost of Edinburgh, he felt obliged to withdraw for fear of further controversy.

The most distinguished British scientists of the time, including T. H. Huxley, attacked *Vestiges* ferociously, but Ernst Mayr (1982: 383–5) considers that despite all the faults Chambers saw the forest where the others could see only the trees. Chambers marshalled the evidence for a slow and gradual process of evolution in no way correlated with environmental catastrophes, even though he could not explain quite how it came about. Among other things, he drew attention to the reasons for believing that embryos go through stages resembling their more primitive relations: 'in the reproduction of the higher animals, the new being passes through stages in which it is successively fish-like and reptile-like. But the resemblance is not to the adult fish or the adult reptile, but to the fish and reptile at a certain point in their foetal progress' (1844: 212). Later on he came back to the hypothesis of recapitulation in more striking terms:

> Our brain . . . after completing the animal transformations, it passes through the characters in which it appears in the Negro, Malay, American, and Mongolian nations, and finally is Caucasian. The face partakes of these alterations . . . The leading characters, in short, of the various races of mankind, are simply representations of particular stages in the development of the highest or Caucasian type . . . The Mongolian is an arrested infant newly-born. (1844: 306–7)

The notion of recapitulation was widely accepted in the middle and latter part of the century. It appeared in one of Tennyson's poems. It was parodied by Benjamin Disraeli in his novel *Tancred* (1847) when he had Lady Constance say:

> It is all explained . . . First there was nothing, then there was something; then, I forget the next, I think there were shells, then fishes. Then we came . . . And the next stage will be something very superior to us, something with wings . . . This is development. We had fins: we may have wings.

It is not surprising then if it was in the mind of a superintendent of a

London mental hospital when, in 1866, he tried to classify the various kinds of mental disorder among patients in his care. Did some disorders stem from environmental causes, he asked? Has the nurse dosed the child with opium? Has the little one met with any accidents? Did instruments cause injury in childbirth? Did the mental disorder stem from congenital or developmental causes? Those who suffered from the congenital disorders of idiocy and imbecility could be classified by reference:

> to one of the great divisions of the human family other than the class from which they have sprung. Of course there are numerous representatives of the great Caucasian family. Several well marked examples of the Ethiopian variety have come under my notice . . . Some arrange themselves around the Malay variety . . . The great Mongolian family has numerous representatives, and it is to this division, I wish, in this paper, to call special attention. A very large number of congenital idiots are typical Mongols. So marked is this, that when placed side by side, it is difficult to believe that the specimens are not children of the same parents . . . They are, for the most part, instances of degeneracy arising from tubercolosis in the parents.

The superintendent was Dr John Langdon Down and the condition he was describing (Down, 1866: 259–62) is now known to be caused by triploidy of the twenty-first chromosome which prevents the normal development of some organs of the body. For at least a century this condition was called Mongolism, but it is now identified as Down's syndrome. Down thought that his argument told against the contemporary supposition that human races represented distinct and permanent types. If it was the case, as he maintained, that disease could destroy the features which distinguished races, then such examples of degeneracy 'furnish some argument in favour of the unity of the human species'. Down's underlying proposition is that disease causes retrogression to a form occurring earlier in the developmental sequence. Proper development depended on the correct environmental conditions. Thus Down, who favoured the admission of women to higher education, later supported this policy by asserting 'if there is one thing more certain than another about the production of idiocy it is the danger which arises from the culture of only one side of a woman's nature' (1887: 89).

Another example of the implications of error is provided by the history of telegony, the hypothesis that offspring sometimes inherit characters from a previous mate of their dam. It began with a letter written by Lord Morton to the Royal Society in 1820, and published by them. Morton reported that he had mated an Arab mare with a quagga (a now extinct zebra-like creature) and obtained a foal with faint stripes. Later he mated the mare with an Arab stallion, producing three foals, all with rather more marked stripes, presumably as a result of the prior mating. This phenomenon was given the name telegony to denote inheritance from a step father. Darwin in 1868 was prepared to accept that such things could happen and telegony was later debated by such eminent authorities as Spencer, Romanes and Weismann. It was falsified by experiments conducted outside Edinburgh in the 1890s by J. Cossar Ewart, who wrote the article on telegony in the eleventh edition of the *Encyclopaedia Britannica*. The belief in telegony nevertheless lingered. For another fifty years some English sheep-breeders would not allow a pure-bred ewe that had once been mated with a ram of another breed to remain in the Flock Book. Among humans it has given rise to what in the United States used to be called the 'black baby myth': the belief that if a white woman has sexual intercourse with a black man there is always the possibility that any baby she may subsequently bear, perhaps years after the incident in question, will have black physical characteristics. The persistence of this belief in England was investigated by Veronica Pearson (1973). She interviewed two samples of elderly women. Sample A was of twenty-five women, average age 77.4 years, many living in a poor inner city neighbourhood of Bristol with a significant proportion of black residents, Sample B was of twenty-five women, average age 68.8 years, all of whom had previously been school teachers. In Sample A, ten women said they believed that if a white woman had sexual relations with a black man any child she subsequently bore might be black; another woman had heard of this belief but thought it unlikely to be true. In Sample B, four accepted the belief, four thought it unlikely and two had heard of it in connection with animal breeding.

Explanations of physical variation among humans cannot be separated from explanations of similar features among animals. Only in the 1760s did Europeans begin to breed farm animals systematically to produce the characteristics they valued. It was from the study of controlled breeding, or domestication as it was called, that Prichard and Darwin got their ideas about natural selection. It is only to be expected that when people in the twentieth century profess beliefs about inheritance and education among humans, they will be influenced by their beliefs about inheritance among animals and *vice versa*. So the story of telegony teaches a lesson about the dangers of treating beliefs about race in isolation, as well as showing that it can take a long time to overcome the effects of past mistakes.

2

RACE AS TYPE

A new phase in the history of racial thought was inaugurated in the chronologically convenient year of 1800 by Georges Cuvier when he submitted a memorandum for a French expedition to the Pacific, advising on 'the researches to be carried out relative to the anatomical differences between the diverse races of man' (Stocking, 1968: 13–41). Cuvier's career prospered, and under Napoleon he became one of the dominant figures in French science.

Cuvier was a Protestant who accepted the Biblical story of man's common descent but did not believe that Genesis provided a complete chronology. He took up the questions of Creation and classification in a more open-minded manner than his predecessors, believing that a scientist should concentrate on problems where sufficient evidence was available or could be accumulated, and should not concern himself with those that were for the time being beyond reach. Within zoology Cuvier continued Linnaeus' work by compiling a magisterial study of the animal kingdom. He distinguished four principal branches within this kingdom, the vertebrates, molluscs, articulates, and zoophytes, which were further divided into genera and subgenera. Cuvier put great reliance on the concept of biological type, believing that if that had been grasped the essentials of the category could be understood. He emphasized the importance of type in opposition to those who considered that the various forms shaded imperceptibly into one another. Genera and species were both discrete, morphologically stable units, and therefore examples of types. In his extensive study of fishes each volume deals with one genus and the first chapter is devoted to a description of the specimen chosen to represent the type. Cuvier is probably better known, however, for his geological theory that there had been a series of natural catastrophes (such as floods) which had killed off large numbers of species and divided natural history into some eight separate epochs. A recent biographer (Coleman, 1964) has concluded that Cuvier did not believe, as was often very understandably thought, that each epoch began with a new creation. He thought that some individuals survived the catastrophes; migration and the mutual exchange of species between territories could then account for subsequent diversity. In this way Cuvier could accept that all men were descended from Adam, suggesting at the same time that the three major races escaped in different directions after the last catastrophe, some five thousand years before, and had developed in isolation. A variant of this theory, sometimes associated with Cuvier (e.g. Prichard 1843: 133) regarded the three major races as stemming from particular mountain slopes: whites from the region of Mount Caucasus, yellows from the neighbourhood of Mount Altai, and blacks from the southern face of the chain of Mount Atlas.

Lineage and variety confused

For Cuvier *Homo sapiens* was a division of the vertebrates and was split into three subspecies: Caucasian, Mongolian, and Ethiopian. Each of these three was further subdivided on geographical, linguistic, and physical grounds. Malays, Eskimos, and American Indians remained outside these subdivisions, but, being inter-fertile, all mankind was one species. Near the beginning of Cuvier's *Le Règne animal* of 1817 is a section entitled 'Variétés de l'espèce humaine' which starts:

> Quoique l'espèce humaine paraisse unique, puisque tous les individus peuvent se mêler indistinctement, et produire des individus féconds, on y remarque de certaines conformations héréditaires que constituent ce qu'on nomme des *races*.

The italics are in the original. Although Kant and Herder had warned about the dangers of confusing a name for a class and a reference to origin, Cuvier made race and variety synonymous. Cuvier's first English translator took it upon himself to reduce some of the confusion, for in the 1827 London translation the last sentence appears as ' ... which constitute what are called *varieties*'. In several of the passages where Cuvier put race this translator put variety. Yet in the next English translation (published in New York in 1831) the sentence runs ' ... which constitute what are termed *races*' and 'race' is used thereafter.

Prichard regretted any failure to distinguish race from variety, and he may have had Cuvier in mind when he wrote (1836: 109) that:

> races are properly successions of individuals propagated from any given stock; and the term should be used without any involved meaning that such a progeny or stock has always possessed a particular character. The real import of the term has often been overlooked, and the word race has been used as if it implied a distinction in the physical character of a whole

series of individuals. By writers on anthropology, who adopt this term, it is often tacitly assumed that such distinctions were primordial, and that their successive transmission has been unbroken. If such were the fact, a race so characterised would be a species in the strict meaning of the word, and it ought to be so termed. (1836: 109)

This is such an important issue, and the ambiguity in the word race so easily taken for granted, that it seems desirable to pause and use a very simple example of the difference between race as lineage and as variety. Let the reader recall the first use in English of the word 'race' in the sense with which this book is concerned. Foxe referred to 'the race and stocke of Abraham'. A later member of that stock was Moses, who was classified as a Levite. Moses had a brother and sister, Aaron and Miriam. He first married a Midionite woman, Zipporah, who bore him two sons. Gershon and Eliezer. Later he married an Ethiopian woman (Aaron and Miriam 'spoke against him' for this). Imagine that this wife bore him a son. That son would be just as much of 'the race and stock' of Levi as would Gershon and Eliezer. But if some contemporary anthropologist had set out to classify the individuals, Moses would have been accounted a Semite and his son a hybrid; he would not have been assigned to the same race as Levi and Moses. The ambiguity arises because individuals of similar 'race' look alike and similarity of appearance is attributed to common descent. Since the processes of descent are complicated, and were ill understood at the time, it would have been better had the warnings of Kant and Prichard been heeded and the vocabulary of classification kept separate from that of descent.

Two features of Cuvier's conception of human varieties deserve attention. The first was his representation of them as forming a hierarchy with whites at the top and blacks at the bottom. The second was his contention that differences in culture and mental quality were produced by differences in physique. 'It is not for nothing', he wrote, 'that the Caucasian race has gained dominion over the world and made the most rapid progress in the sciences.' The Chinese were less advanced. They had skulls shaped more like those of animals. The Negroes were 'sunken in slavery and the pleasures of the senses' yet they 'were rational and sensitive creatures', while 'slavery was degrading for both slave and master and must be abolished' (Coleman, 1964: 166).

To argue that man was an animal was scarcely daring. The key question was whether he was just an animal. Man could create his own world, could build a civilization, and study himself. Could this be explained by the same principles as those which accounted for his physical being? Cuvier's affirmative answer to this question is one of the biggest steps leading to the doctrine of racial types. It can also be seen as a criterion for distinguishing between two paradigms in the study of man: the anthropological approach which sought to explain both physique and culture in a unified theory that found the causes of differentiation in biological laws; and the ethnological approach which drew a sharp distinction between man's physical nature and his culture, believing that the latter demanded explanations of a different kind (cf. Stocking, 1973: c). This was not the way in which most nineteenth-century writers saw the distinction. Latham, for example, saw anthropology as studying the relations of man to other mammals; ethnology as studying the relations of the different varieties of mankind to each other; both were concerned with physical influences and not with the study of moral causes, which was the province of history (1850: 559). Others drew the dividing line in different places still, but it became ever clearer that the key question was whether culture was independent of physical character, so it is not unreasonable to label the two kinds of answer to it 'anthropological' and 'ethnological'.

The notion of type was a convenient one because it was not tied to any particular classificatory level in zoology, so that it was easy to refer to the physical types characteristic of particular nations, to 'types of cranial conformation', or to say that a skull 'approximates to the Negro type' without having to establish just what that type was. This was appreciated at the time, for W. F. Edwards in his important essay of 1829 observed.

> In identifying a combination of well defined characters as a type – a word which has the same sense in ordinary speech and in natural history – I avoid all discussion about the rank which a group so characterized will occupy in a general classification, since it suits equally well the distinctions between variety, race, family, species, genus, and other categories yet more general. (1829: 125)

As the evidence about the diversity of human forms accumulated, more and more writers tended to refer to various kinds of type, and, indeed, the construction of typologies of various kinds became a characteristic of nineteenth-century scholarship. It was used in the analysis of poetry, aesthetics, biography, personality and culture. In sociology it contributed to the concept of an ideal type. In anthropology and ethnology the concept of racial type was central to the debates about race for more than a century. It appealed to many, like Edwards, because it could be used at any taxonomic level; this was one of the main objections to it from writers like Prichard who believed that the problems of classification were confused by the introduction of a new kind of class which did not have a definite place. Prichard used the word type himself, but he would have been only consistent had he rejected it as redundant. Writers who were impressed by the differences between blacks and whites but were reluctant to call them

separate species sometimes called them races and implied a species difference (see, for example, Jordan's comment on John Augustine Smith in his
introduction to S. Stanhope Smith, 1965: xxxix).

On two counts, therefore, Cuvier must bear a heavy responsibility for
the nineteenth-century confusion about the meaning of the word race.
Firstly, because he blurred the distinction between the earlier sense of race
and the concept of a variety. Secondly, because his use of a concept of type
made it easier for his successors to discuss natural differences without
facing up to questions about whether these were differences at the level of
genus, species or variety.

The American School

The conception of race as type was developed most systematically in the
United States. The external conditions of the society in which the authors
lived and the reasoning internal to their field of study both influenced the
course of the development, but the two kinds of influence cannot be
separated and weighed against one another. Any writings about racial differences were immediately scrutinized to see what implications they might
have for the conflict over Negro slavery. The authors themselves could not
but hold opinions about slavery which were likely to influence any attempt
they made to study human variation dispassionately. Yet at the same time
there were many features of daily life in the New World arising from the
relations between blacks, whites and native Americans which encouraged
genuinely intellectual speculation about the causes of variation. Nor can
there be any doubt that Cuvier's works were studied and that he was
regarded as one of the greatest authorities.

Slave owners had been aware from an early period that it was desirable
for slaves to be allowed a period of acclimatization; they knew, too, that
it took time for a European to adjust to the new conditions. Though
acclimatization might help, it did not confer immunity to new diseases,
and when cholera came to North America in 1832 fear galvanized
Southern planters into seeing that slave cabins were scrubbed and
cleaned, that buildings were white-washed, and that slave bedding was
aired. The following year cholera cost the planters of Louisiana four
million dollars, for the disease hit blacks much harder. In Charleston, for
example, where the population was evenly divided, 80 per cent of the
deaths were of blacks. Medical students were told that slave medicine was
the most profitable speciality because planters were so anxious to protect
their investments. When cholera came to the Mississippi delta in 1849 a
physician could be paid up to $500 a day to remain on the plantation and
attend to slaves (Kiple and King, 1981: 148–66).

Other diseases affected Europeans but not blacks. In the late seventeenth and early eighteenth centuries one half of the English who went to West Africa died in their first year and only one in ten were able to return to England (see Curtin, 1964: 58–87, 483–7). In the late eighteenth-century slave ships more of the English sailors died than did slaves. The slave dealers in Bristol and Liverpool tried to conceal the evidence that about 20 per cent of the crew died each voyage. In West Africa in the nineteenth century white troops died at rates varying between 48 and 67 per cent per annum, mostly from yellow fever and malaria, while black troops, who had some inherited immunity to these diseases, died at 3 per cent per annum. European armies could not fight in the Caribbean. Between 1803 and 1816 white soldiers there died at a rate of 13.8 per cent per annum, blacks at 6.4 per cent. While both blacks and whites contracted yellow fever, the relative immunity of blacks meant that they recovered when whites did not. Thus in Memphis in 1878, 78 per cent of blacks were infected and 9 per cent died as a result, whereas 70 per cent of the infected whites succumbed. These differences (and the susceptibility of Native Americans to smallpox, measles and mumps) can now be explained. In West Africa genes which conferred immunity to the fevers had been favoured by natural selection. The diet of people there was rich in carbo-hydrates but deficient in protein, calcium, iron and vitamins C and D. With plenty of sunlight the lack of vitamin D did not matter; nor did the inability to digest milk products which was associated with a genetic adaptation to that environment. Transported to North America, however, these deficiencies became more important. A slave diet which was good relative to the dietary requirements of whites, did not give the blacks the nutrients they needed; the practice of soil-eating (which slave-owners feared as a cause of death and sought to prevent) may very well have arisen as a response to nutritional deficiencies. Blacks suffered more than whites from tuberculosis, whooping cough, tetanus, scrofula and pellagra (Kiple and King, 1981). These differences could reasonably sustain the belief that there were actual and inherited differences between the people of different races.

White people in the United States met blacks and reds almost exclusively in situations in which whites were the superior party in terms of power and knowledge. In any unequal relationship the superior party is likely to stereotype members of the inferior party, and when inherited differences of outward appearance are added this tendency is all the stronger. So a report from a leading historian, George M. Fredrickson (1971: 43) is of particu-lar interest. He writes that prior to the 1830s, although black subordi-nation was widespread and whites commonly assumed that Negroes were inferior, 'open assertions of *permanent* inferiority were exceedingly rare'.

One of the first such published assertions was a pamphlet by Richard Colfax, published in New York in 1833, which assembled a whole series of negative evaluations of Negro capacity and concluded that their disadvantages were unalterable since despite 'their proximity to refined nations' they had 'never even *attempted* to raise themselves above their present equivocal station in the great zoological chain'. This was, as Fredrickson says, an assertion; it lacked a scientific explanation of the causes of inequality.

The kind of explanation that was to appeal to people who thought like Colfax was already in the making, for in 1830 a Philadelphian doctor, Samuel George Morton (1799–1851), chose to deliver a lecture on the skulls of the five races of Blumenbach's classification. Being unable to buy or borrow any Mongolian or Malay skull, he decided to start his own collection. By 1839 he had enough for him to publish a book *Crania Americana*. As the title indicates, most of his skulls were American, but he found sufficient of other kinds to add a footnote to the last page of his text (see Figure 1). In it he reported the results of measurements of their internal capacity, suggesting that whites had the biggest brains, blacks the smallest, and that brown people came in between. Difference in brain size, he implied, explained differences in the capacity for civilization. This footnote was historically of the greatest importance, for the table was reproduced in 1849 by Carl Gustav Carus, who, while he did not accept Morton's view, regarded both brain size and cultural differences as manifestations of some, as yet ill-understood, law of development. The table was then copied from Carus by Gobineau and given much greater publicity. Can it be said that the course of history would have been much different had Morton's footnote been overlooked? Or would these measurements have been repeated by some other scholar much as, say, Mendel's paper on the genetics of garden peas was overlooked and then its principles rediscovered?

It could be argued that it did not matter very much whether Mendel's laws were discovered in 1866 or in 1900. It was just a matter of time before someone discovered them and the laws would be the same whoever did it. But for Morton's findings, it could be said, matters were otherwise, since Morton's table of measurements was misleading; had the measurements been carried out by someone lacking Morton's racial bias the resulting table would not have seemed to support Gobineau's claims. This argument would make much of the evidence that when Stephen Jay Gould (1981: 50–69) re-examined Morton's skulls in 1977 using better techniques of measurement and better statistical procedures, he concluded that the internal capacity of Mongolian and Modern Caucasian skulls should have

Note. – *On the Internal Capacity of the Cranium in the different Races of Men.* – Having subjected the skulls in my possession, and such also as I could obtain from my friends, to the internal capacity measurement already described, I have obtained the following results. The mean of the American Race, (omitting the fraction) is repeated here merely to complete the Table. The skulls of idiots and persons under age were of course rejected.

Races	No. of skulls	Mean internal capacity in cubic inches	Largest in the series	Smallest in the series
Caucasian	52	87	109	75
Mongolian	10	83	93	69
Malay	18	81	89	64
American	147	82	100	60
Ethiopian	29	78	94	65

1. The *Caucasians* were, with a single exception, derived from the lowest and least educated class of society. It is proper, however, to mention that but three Hindoos are admitted in the whole number, because the skulls of these people are probably smaller than those of any other existing nation. For example, seventeen Hindoo heads give a mean of but seventy-five cubic inches; and the three received into the table are taken at that average. To be more specific, we will give in detail the number of individuals of each nation as far as ascertained.

Anglo-Americans,	6
Germans, Swiss and Dutch,	7
Celtic Irish and Scots,	7
English,	4
Guanché (Libyan,)	1
Spanish,	1
Hindoo,	3
Europeans, nation not ascertained,	23
	52

2. The *Mongolians* measured, consist of Chinese and Eskimaux; and what is worthy of remark, three of the latter give a mean of eighty-six cubic inches, while seven Chinese give but eighty-two.

3. The *Malays* embrace Malays proper and Polynesians, thirteen of the former and five of the latter; and the mean of each presents but a fractional difference from the mean of all.

4. The *Ethiopians* were all unmixed Negroes, and nine of them native Africans, for which I am chiefly indebted to Dr. McDowell, formerly attached to the colony at Liberia.

5. Respecting the American Race I have nothing to add, excepting the striking fact that of all the American nations the Peruvians had the smallest heads, while those of the Mexicans were something larger, and those of the barbarous tribes the largest of all, viz:

Toltecan nations	Peruvians collectively,	76 cubic inches
	Mexicans collectively,	79 cubic inches
	Barbarous tribes, as per Table,	82 cubic inches

An interesting question remains to be solved, viz: the relative proportion of brain in the anterior and posterior chambers of the skull in the different races; an inquiry for which I have hitherto possessed neither sufficient leisure nor adequate materials.

Figure 1. *Morton's footnote*

been reported as 87 cubic inches, Amerindian 86, Malay 85, Caucasian skulls from ancient Egyptian tombs 84, and African 83.

Against this view it could be maintained that Morton's errors were those likely to be made by any scholar undertaking such studies in the 1830s and 1840s. The chief mistake was the failure to appreciate that there is an association between brain size and stature. Big people have bigger brains. Men are bigger than women; men have bigger brains. There are ethnic differences in stature, for reasons of environment and nutrition, and so there are ethnic differences in brain size, but no association between these differences and cultural variation has been established, any more than differences in intelligence between men and women. The association between cranial capacity and stature could have been deduced from Morton's skulls but though he made remarks suggesting a partial awareness of it, Morton never recognized this explicitly or allowed for it. Nor had anyone else at that time recognized it. Morton's partial awareness can be seen in his reference to Hindoo skulls in paragraph one of his footnote. Why include only three of the seventeen in his measure? He gave no proper reason. The effect of his doing so was to make the Caucasian average higher than it otherwise would have been. In paragraph five he remarked that Peruvians had small heads, but he left them out of the average for American skulls in the table, basing this entry solely upon the so-called 'barbarous tribes'. What Morton should have done was to prepare separate tables for male and female skulls and, to allow for his having more skulls from some groups than others, he should have taken averages for each group by sex in order to calculate for each race an average of the averages for the sub-groups. If this is done, the differences between the races turn out to be very small, while the differences within the races are substantial. It will be noticed that in paragraph two Morton attached no significance to the figure for Eskimos being almost as high as that for Caucasians; he failed to observe that some American skulls were large, those for the Iroquois returning an average of 91.5, well above the Caucasian; small errors of measurement and the rounding out of decimal points all seem to have gone in the direction of reinforcing his prior expectation that the skulls of white people would be larger than those of black people. Yet Gould, who is a severe critic, found no evidence of fraud or conscious manipulation. Morton made no attempt to cover up his errors.

Morton's views about racial differences among humans should not be seen in isolation from contemporary attempts to account for variation in forms of life generally. One possible explanation was that which, following Cuvier, emphasized the stability of species over time. Applied to humans it was almost certain to produce a theory that differences in the ways of life and levels of attainment of races stemmed from permanent physical differences. The most obvious and best understood physical differences were the anatomical ones so those, and particularly anything associated with possible differences in the brain, were bound to attract attention. Craniological studies were stimulated by Morton's findings but they were not dependent upon them and they would have flourished in any event. Seen from this standpoint, Morton's errors appear less momentous.

Those who, like Stanhope Smith and Prichard, believed that humans constituted one species stemming from an original pair, had to explain how it was that the descendants of this pair varied in so many ways. Three kinds of explanation were open to them (i) divine intervention, like a curse upon the descendants of Ham; (ii) congenital or accidental variations arising naturally had been selectively preserved (the explanation Prichard entertained in 1826 but from which he retreated); (iii) the effect of climate. The critics scoffed at the first and brought forward persuasive arguments against the second and third. Congenital variations were not uncommon and a parent might transmit one (like, say, being cross-eyed) to a child but thereafter they seemed to die out. Whoever heard of a cross-eyed race? it was asked. Climate could certainly exert an influence, just as Europeans became sunburned, but how could an acquired character be transmitted to offspring? Prichard himself had denied that such transmission occurred. The examples of change he cited all seemed to have happened long ago. Why could such changes not be observed in the present? Prichard acknowledged that many types remained unchanged after centuries in new environments, so why should one stock change and not another? (see Nott and Gliddon, 1854: 57–9). If, on the other hand, the use of fertility as the criterion of species was abandoned, it became possible to regard the various kinds of humans as different species separately created. Diversity could then be regarded as having existed, unchanged, from a much earlier period; perhaps, indeed, from the creation. This led on to the view that each race was adapted to a particular climate and a particular zone of the earth. If that was the case then inherited characters had to be understood in relation to different environments. In this form, the theory of permanent racial differences provided no justification for believing one race superior to another. Each was superior in its own zone or province.

This fourth explanation of diversity can be traced back to the sixteenth century, but it was given new life and persuasiveness by Cuvier, reinforced by Morton, and then developed most explicitly in Nott and Gliddon's book *Types of Mankind* (1854). At much the same time people in France, Britain and Germany were working along similar lines and they produced similar statements, so that racial typology constituted an international school of thought. If Nott and Gliddon had not elaborated upon the Cuvier–Morton line of argument, then someone else would have done. The Typological Theory can be summarized as holding that:

1 Variations in the constitution and behaviour of individuals are the expression of differences between underlying types of a relatively permanent kind, each of which is suited to a particular continent or zoological province.
2 Social categories in the long-run reflect and are aligned with the natural categories that produce them.
3 Individuals belonging to a particular racial type display an innate antagonism towards individuals belonging to other types, the degree of antagonism depending upon the relationship between the two types.

Morton moved steadily towards an acceptance of these propositions. On the first page of *Crania Americana* he declared, 'from remote ages the inhabitants of every extended locality have been marked by certain physical and moral peculiarities, common among themselves, and serving to distinguish them from all other people. The Arabians are, at this time precisely what they were in the days of the patriarchs . . . ' The concept of type did not appear (though he used it in 1841) and he presented races as sub-specific classes. Morton introduced some doubts about the orthodox view, as when he referred to calculations that Noah and his family left the Ark 4,179 years previously whereas Ethiopians were known to exist 3,445 years ago; recent discoveries, he added, made it clear that only by a miracle, could the Negro race have developed out of the Caucasian in the course of 734 years (1839: 1, 88). But the general effect was very restrained. Having obtained a collection of Egyptian skulls, he was willing to go a little further five years later, and in *Crania Aegyptica* (1844: 66) reached the conclusion that 'Negroes were numerous in Egypt, but their social position in ancient times was the same as it now is, that of servants and slaves.' Negroes had a natural social position as well as a geographical position and gave evidence of being a permanent type.

In later publications Morton's attack on orthodoxy became more explicit. He criticized the view that infertility of hybrids was the best test of separate species for creatures that had become domesticated, and emphasized 'the repugnance of some human races to mix with others'. By this time Morton had acquired allies, and they were men of a more combative temperament. The first was George Robbins Gliddon (1809–57), the English-born vice-consul for the United States in Cairo, who collected ancient Egyptian skulls for him. Then came Josiah Clark Nott (1804–73) a physician in Alabama, Ephraim George Squier (1821–88) the first authoritative voice in American archaeology, and Louis Agassiz (1807–

73) a professor of natural history in Switzerland who moved to the United States in 1846 and became a professor at Harvard. Nott was the first of this new school to argue that the various races, being permanent and lacking in adaptability, had been created separately in their several environments. The others followed quite quickly.

All versions of the monogenetic theory depended upon the assumption that human life on earth was to be counted in several thousands of years. Religious orthodoxy presumed a chronology of about six thousand years. The anthropologists gave reasons for concluding that natural causes could not have produced the existing range of racial diversity within so short a time period. They began with the evidence, already mentioned, which, they claimed, indicated that Negroes and Caucasians were as distinct physically 4000 years ago as they were at the present time. Then, with the excavation of Native American burial mounds in the Mississippi valley by Squier, a skull was found which Morton pronounced 'a perfect type' of its race, the race which was 'indigenous to the American continent, having been planted there by the hand of Omnipotence'. To determine the age of the mounds was difficult, but some calculations could be based upon the levels of land which constituted terraces in the valley and testified to a process by which the river had subsided. They proved that the burial mounds were of 'no inconsiderable antiquity'; the reader could deduce that the time period was many times greater than six thousand years. The chronology therefore supported the claim that Native Americans were indigenous to the continent and not the result of some earlier immigration. As Stanton writes in his excellent study (1960: 88), Squier had done for the Indian what Gliddon had done for the Negro. The archaeological evidence contradicted the claims of the orthodox, like Samuel Stanhope Smith, that environmental influence could bring about enough change within historical time to account for the diversity of races. It greatly strengthened earlier criticisms such as that of Charles White, who objected that if the environment could produce different species, then the entire animal kingdom could derive from a single ancestral pair and a more 'degrading notion' could not be imagined. John Augustine Smith, the critic of his namesake, had also objected that if environmental change affected complexion this did not explain why different individuals living in the same environment could have such different complexions. Why, too, if the Creator had originally adapted the Indians for the various American climates, did Morton think there was a single Indian type?

The anthropological school was greatly strengthened by the support received from Agassiz. Before leaving Switzerland he had delivered lectures in which he maintained that 'all organized beings, plants as well as animals, are confined to a special area' but this principle did not apply to humans who could spread across all the regions of the earth. Agassiz had not, apparently, considered the evidence for human diversity with any care. In the United States he encountered Negroes for the first time and his response showed little of the caution to be expected of a scientist. Their appearance shocked him. He wrote home to his mother that the Negro could not be of the same species as the white man. Any one could easily see that the Negro was not the white man's equal, and almost all white men did. Four years later, in 1850, Agassiz declared that the races shared the distinguishing attributes of humanity in differing degrees. Like other animals, the races of men occupied distinct zoological provinces and 'did not originate from a common centre, nor from a single pair'. This became the foundation of the argument underlying Nott and Gliddon's 1854 book *Types of Mankind*. Near the beginning was a nineteen-page 'Sketch of the Natural Provinces of the Animal World and their Relation to the different Types of Man contributed by Prof. L. Agassiz, L.L.D.' with a coloured lithographic Tableau and Map. On the map eight provinces were distinguished: the Arctic, Asiatic, European, American, African, East Indian, Australian, and Polynesian realms. In the tableau Agassiz called the second realm Mongol; he added an extra division after the African to catalogue the fauna of the Cape-lands and its 'distinct race of men, the Hottentots', and left out the races and animals of Polynesia. Agassiz drew attention to flora and fauna characteristic of particular provinces (as, for example, marsupials and Australian Aborigines were distinctive of the Australian realm), but there were many errors in his scheme (see Quatrefages, 1879: 163–7). He wrote, 'I am prepared to show that the differences existing between the races of men are of the same kind as the differences observed between the different families, genera and species of monkeys or other animals' and concluded that there were only two possible explanations of organic diversity. One was that mankind originated from a common stock, which would mean that their present diversity had arisen since the creation and was not part of any plan operating at that time. The other was that diversity was determined by the will of the Creator and the present geographical distribution of animals was part of God's plan, demonstrating the great harmonies established in Nature.

In Part I of *Types*, the hand of Dr Nott is very evident. In 1844 a medical journal had published an article of his entitled 'The Mulatto a Hybrid – Probable Extermination of the Two Races If the Whites and Blacks Are Allowed To Intermarry' in which he testified that mulattoes did not live so long as members of the parent races. The union of mulattoes was less prolific than the union of mulatto with White or Negro. After reading this article, Morton had written to its author and collaboration ensued. In *Types*, Nott repeated his earlier claims. Morton had defined a species as 'a primordial organic form'. There were remote species, of the same genus, among which hybrids were never produced; allied species, which produced infertile offspring; and proximate species which could produce fertile offspring. Nott followed this, but added a fourth category in between the first two: this consisted of those cases in which hybrids could not reproduce between themselves but could do so when mated with the parent stock. Morton had maintained that what at that time were called the five races, could be better designated five groups, each of which could be divided into proximate races. Nott argued that hybridity was not a unitary phenomenon but something to be studied in terms of degrees of hybridity, and that this demonstrated the wisdom of Morton's definitions. The observations in Nott's 1842 article were based largely upon his knowledge of mulattoes in South Carolina. In 1854 he added that further observations in Mobile and New Orleans had introduced some modifications to his views, since he had there witnessed many examples of great longevity among mulattoes and of manifestly prolific marriages among them. His conclusion was that around the Mexican Gulf the blood of the white population was preponderantly drawn from French, Italian, Spanish, Portuguese and other dark-skinned whites. Their blood mixed more easily with that of African peoples than did that of the people of Anglo-Saxon origin on the Atlantic coast of North America. Nott went on to maintain that the smallest admixture of Negro blood conferred immunity to yellow fever; to discuss the evidence for telegony and its implications; and to assert, in an anticipation of Darwin's theory, that 'Nature marches steadily towards perfection; and that it attains this end through the consecutive destruction of living beings'.

At the end of Part I of *Types* is printed a list of 'deductions' or conclusions (reproduced in Figure 2). They show an intellectual commitment to environmental relativism. Elsewhere in the text Nott and Gliddon declared, 'Every race, at the present time, is more or less mixed', but 'there is abundant evidence to show that the principal physical characters of a people may be preserved throughout a long series of ages, in a great part of the population, despite of climate, mixture of races, invasion of foreigners, progress of civilization, or other known influences; and that a *type can long outlive its language, history, religion, customs, and recollections*'.

They could maintain that present-day races were mixed because they distinguished between the type, which was immutable, and the contemporary expression of it in a population which could diverge from that type

1. *That the surface of our globe is naturally divided into several zoological provinces, each of which is a distinct centre of creation, possessing a peculiar fauna and flora; and that every species of animal and plant was originally assigned to its appropriate province.*
2. *That the human family offers no exception to this general law, but fully conforms to it: Mankind being divided into several groups of* Races, *each of which constitutes a primitive element in the fauna of its peculiar province.*
3. *That history affords no evidence of the transformation of one Type into another, nor of the origination of a new and* Permanent *Type.*
4. *That certain Types have been* Permanent *through all recorded time, and despite the most opposite moral and physical influences.*
5. *That Permanence of Type is accepted by science as the surest test of* Specific *character.*
6. *That certain Types have existed (the same as now) in and around the Valley of the Nile, from ages anterior to 3500 years B.C., and consequently long prior to any alphabetic chronicles, sacred or profane.*
7. *That the ancient Egyptians had already classified Mankind, as known to them, into* Four Races, *previously to any date assignable to Moses.*
8. *That high antiquity for distinct Races is amply sustained by linguistic researches, by psychological history, and by anatomical characteristics.*
9. *That the primeval existence of Man, in widely separate portions of the globe, is proven by the discovery of his osseous and industrial remains in alluvial deposits and in diluvial drifts; and more especially in his fossil bones, imbedded in various rocky strata along with the vestiges of extinct species of animals.*
10. *That* Proflicacy *of distinct species,* inter se, *is now proved to be no test of* Common Origin.
11. *That those* Races *of men most separated in physical organization – such as the* Blacks *and the* Whites – *do not amalgamate perfectly, but obey the Laws of Hybridity. Hence*
12. *It follows, as a corollary, that there exists a* Genus Homo, *embracing many primordial* Types *or "Species."*

Figure 2. *Nott and Gliddon's 'conclusions'*

to a certain degree. Their distinction lived on in the twentieth century in the notion of pure types or pure races. The racial thought of the Nazis was close to this way of thinking and when, in the period following upon World War Two, attempts were made to correct mistaken popular beliefs about race, it was common to stress that science offered no warrant for any conception of pure races. Both the first and second UNESCO statements on the nature of race (in 1950 and 1951) included the sentence, 'Vast social changes have occurred that have not been connected in any way with changes in racial type.' Such references to type can still be noticed. In a 1961 presidential address to the American Anthropological Society (Washburn, 1963), the speaker said:

> If we look back to the time when I was educated, races were regarded as
> types. We were taught to go to a population and divide it into a series of
> types and to re-create history out of this artificial arrangement. Those of
> you who have read *Current Anthropology* will realize that this kind of
> anthropology is still alive, amazingly, and in full force in some countries;
> relics of it are still alive in our teaching today.

It is also necessary to look out for occasions on which, though the word
type is not employed, the word race is used in the sense of a pure or permanent type underlying the diversities of modern populations. The sense of
race as type is still significant.

Discussing the Mongolian group, Nott wrote that the facts confirm 'the
only rational theory: viz., that races were created in each zoological
province, and therefore all primitive types must be of equal antiquity'.
Despite this environmental relativism, there are many passages witnessing
to the author's belief in white superiority:

> The higher castes of what are termed Caucasian races, are influenced by
> several causes in a greater degree than other races. To them have been
> assigned, in all ages, the largest brains and the most powerful intellect;
> *theirs* is the mission of extending and perfecting civilization – they are by
> nature ambitious, daring, domineering and reckless of danger – impelled
> by an irresistible instinct, they visit all climes, regardless of difficulties;
> but how many thousands are sacrificed annually to climates foreign to
> their nature!

Caucasians 'have in all ages been the rulers', while 'none but the fair-
skinned types of mankind' have hitherto been able to realize the Germanic
style of democracy described by Tacitus. Dark-skinned races, on the other
hand, were 'only fit for military governments', and Negroes, as Jefferson
said, had never produced a thought above the level of plain narrative (Nott
and Gliddon, 1854: 67, 79, 404–5, 456). In a separate article Nott maintained that race mixture could be beneficial. A 'small trace of white blood
in the Negro improves his intelligence and moral character, and a small
trace of Negro blood, as in the quadroon, will protect the individual
against the deadly influence of climate'. The Caucasian was a happy blend
of the best qualities of several species, a true 'cosmopolite' (Stanton, 1960:
160). It would seem as if Nott was not so persuaded by the typological doctrine of zoological provinces that he felt he should adhere to it consistently
(for a recent assessment of Nott's contribution to medicine, see Sym-
posium: 1974). Nott also collaborated with Henry Hotze (on whom see
Lorimer, 1978: 149–50) in publishing a one-volume edition of translated
selections from Gobineau's *Essay*. Nott testified, 'I have seldom perused a
work which has afforded me so much pleasure'; he contributed a fifty-page
appendix which up-dated Morton's cranial measurements, set out to

correct Gobineau on the matter of hybridity, and observed that Gobineau had been hindered by 'religious scruples'. In reality, wrote Nott, the first chapter of Genesis gave an account entirely in accordance with the teachings of science, but the passage in Acts, 17: 26 misled readers because the translator had taken liberties with the original text.

In 1854 Nott referred to the claim that white Europeans would degenerate in the North American environment, but did not commit himself to it. Three years later in another volume edited by the same authors, Nott reviewed the statistics of mortality and morbidity and concluded 'races . . . have their appropriate geographical ranges, beyond which they cannot go with impunity'. He commented sardonically on man that 'although boasting of *reason*, as the prerogative that distinguishes him, he is, in many respects, the most unreasonable of animals'. One respect was that 'he forsakes the land of his birth, with all its associations, and all the comforts which earth can give, to colonize foreign lands – where he knows full well that a thousand hardships must await him, and with the certainty of risking his life *in climates that nature never intended him for*' (1857: 399–400). If each type was suited to its own province, none could be superior to the others. Unwilling to break with this principle, Nott could not develop his inclination to maintain that the Caucasian was the highest type.

The easiest way of reconciling typology with a belief in white superiority would have been to add an extra proposition to the list set out on p. 42. This might have stated that zoological provinces could overlap, and that where, as in the Valley of the Nile, European and African provinces overlapped, Europeans would rule. Nott and Gliddon never made such a claim though it would have resolved an apparent conflict between their first and sixth conclusions and strengthened the grounds for their statement (1854: 79) that 'no two distinctly-marked races can dwell together on equal terms'. Nor did they, like Knox, identify what later came to be called race prejudice and claim that it was an inbred characteristic of some or all types. This seems not to have been something which they regarded as requiring explanation. Nevertheless their doctrine of race included a theory of race relations, for they asserted that the natural order determined what kinds of social relations would be harmonious. If the permanent types had distinctive attributes then any social relationship which did not permit these attributes to obtain natural expression would eventually fail.

Part I of *Types* was critical of the monogenetic theory, but in Part II Gliddon carried the fight into the critics' camp. Since many who appealed to the authority of the Bible knew it only in the translation authorized by King James, Gliddon stressed that this was based on the Latin and Greek translations of the Old Testament and not on the Hebrew originals. He selected the 10th chapter of Genesis, which lists the generations of Noah, to explain the features of the Hebrew text, and followed an Italian scholar to maintain that the series of names of Noah's descendants could be interpreted as a geographical recital of the various parts of the earth known at the time the manuscript was first prepared. He discussed the structure of the first three chapters of Genesis, quoting the views of some fathers of the church on matters of exegesis, and reviewed some of the 120 or so attempts to calculate the date of the creation using the Biblical evidence. How good his scholarship was would be a matter for expert assessment, but it must surely have astonished those who rejected racial typology on the simple grounds that it was contrary to Bible truth.

It should not be thought that the typological theory was welcomed by Southern whites as a justification for the prevailing pattern of racial inequality. White Southerners were divided along class lines but both sections defended slavery on Biblical grounds, leading Stanton (1960: 194) to assert that 'the South turned its back on the only intellectually respectable defence of slavery it could have taken up'. This requires some qualification. For decades there had been a Southern Bourbon tradition which defended slavery as an institution independently of the question of racial difference. Non-slave holding whites, of course, disliked it. Some aspired to become slave-owners themselves and many were anxious to protect and increase their privileges at the expense of black workers. With the extension of the suffrage in the 1830s to white males by the weakening of property-owning qualifications, the white workers' influence grew and the planter class had to adjust to their beliefs, demands and phobias. The shift in opinion was reflected in the views of George Fitzhugh, a spokesman for the Bourbon philosophy. In 1854 he had declared, 'We deplore the doctrine of the *Types of Mankind*, first, because it is at war with scripture . . . secondly, because it encourages and incites brutal planters to treat negroes, not as weak, ignorant and dependent brethren, but as wicked beasts without the pale of humanity.' Other writers over the decades had equally insisted that the facts of inequality could just as well be taken to indicate that blacks should be treated with extra kindness. Dr Charles Caldwell of North Carolina (on whom see Erickson, 1981), criticizing Stanhope Smith in 1830, maintained that Caucasians were not justified in enslaving the Africans or destroying the Indians 'merely because their superiority in intellect and war enable them to do so. Such practices are an abuse of power.' Sir William Lawrence, lecturing on medicine in London in 1819 declared, 'Superior endowments . . . should be employed to extend the blessings of civilization . . . not as a means of oppressing the weak.'

William Jay, a relatively conservative supporter of abolition in the United States, in 1853 addressed those who favoured sending blacks back to Africa and asked if it was conceivable that Christ would have commanded men to love one another had they not been given the power to do so? Yet the reader is apt to conclude that arguments from physical difference were increasingly being taken as guides to morality. In 1861 Fitzhugh announced his conversion to the view that blacks and whites were separate species and that 'the habitudes, instincts, moral and intellectual qualities and capabilities of all animals are the universal and necessary concomitants (if not the consequences) of their physical conformation . . . ' If the white South had turned its back on racial typology to start with, it soon found a way of accepting (Fredrickson, 1971: 29, 69–70, 73, 84; Stanton, 1960: 194; Curtin, 1964: 239).

France

Though there has been a distinct strain of antisemitism in French writing and politics, relatively few French authors have advanced theories of racial differences. Some might say that one man, Arthur de Gobineau (1816–82) has made up for this, for he has been called the father of racist ideology. Gobineau's influence has often been exaggerated and his outlook misrepresented. He came to the topic of racial differences from a wide reading in German literature, so it should not be surprising to find in his work traces of a similar kind of romanticism. Working on a novel of the kind made popular by Scott's *Ivanhoe*, he had carefully studied the work of Thierry and some of the French authors who interpreted French history as a matter of race. Though he did not stand squarely in that line of debate, being anti-nationalist and pro-European, one strand of the Frankish, anti-Roman, genealogy can be traced through Montesquieu, Boulainvilliers and Montlosier to Gobineau. The novel entitled *L'Abbaye de Typhaines*, dealt with a twelfth-century revolt. Characteristically, Gobineau did not take sides between the peasants, bourgeoisie and clergy. He showed a concern for local liberties but implied that mere love of liberty was insufficient to ensure that people would be able to exercise it.

Gobineau's first significant use of 'race' to account for human nobility appeared in an epic poem and in the *Essay* he made relatively little reference to anthropological authorities for his assumptions. His arguments were less original than he claimed; many of them were expounded by Victor Courtet de l'Isle (1813–67), the Saint-Simonian author of *La Science politique fondée sur la science de l'homme* published in 1837. Courtet was elected Secretary of the Société ethnographique de Paris in

1846 and re-elected in 1848; the following year he published his *Tableau ethnographique* and, as many of his associates were well known to Gobineau, it seems certain that the latter borrowed heavily from him without acknowledgement (Boissel, 1972: 83, 178–80). Courtet identified the Germans as a superior race which had formerly been spread over Europe 'like the oil of the nations'. Where Thierry had stressed the conflict of races, Courtet saw the mingling of blood as having 'chemical' consequences which he thought must ultimately be beneficial. Gobineau disparaged Prichard ('a mediocre historian and even more mediocre theologian') and brought into prominence the table of cranial capacity in different races that Carus had taken from Morton. Though he had not had Klemm's book in his hands, Gobineau had heard of his distinction between active and passive races. When he claimed that human activities had their origin in the 'male' and 'female' currents within humanity and that civilizations were born from the mixing of races, the resemblance was close, but Gobineau believed that if the two of them were travelling along the same paths it would not be surprising if they came upon the same truths.

The *Essay* began with a statement that everything great, noble, and fruitful in the works of man on this earth springs from the Aryan family. It expounded his principles for explaining the rise and fall of civilizations and then showed their operation in a lengthy review of the ten most notable (for a summary, see Biddiss, 1970: 112–31). History began after one of the cosmic catastrophes envisaged by Cuvier: the Aryans were living in small independent communities, unable to see as their equals those other creatures which, with their evil hostility, their hideous ugliness, brutal intelligence and their claim to be the offspring of monkeys, seemed to be falling back into the ranks of animals (1853: 442). From this base the Aryans spread out to create first the Hindu civilization, then the Egyptian, Assyrian, Greek, Chinese, Roman, German,* Alleghenian, Mexican and Peruvian civilizations (how Aryans came to create the last two is never explained). Gobineau considered possible causes for the rise and decline of these civilizations: climate, irreligion, corruption of morals, and bad government. He found none satisfactory, and settled for racial mixture as an explanation of both rise and decline. Societies which were averse from all mixture remained small and stagnant. A little mixture might enable one race, like the Aryans, to grow in power so that its members met members of other races in the relations of masters to servants. Such a relationship led to increased mixture and thus to the decline of the former. Thus Gobineau

* Gobineau wrote of 'les races germaniques' but this should have been translated as 'the Teutonic races' (cf. Chadwick, 1945: 142–9); Gobineau's Teutons were a larger unit than the people who called themselves Deutsch.

celebrated the vigour of the Aryans and asserted that 'the irreconcilable antagonism between different races and cultures is clearly established by history' (1853: 181); nevertheless, in order to avoid disappearing into the masses over whom it ruled, 'the white family needed to add to the power of its genius and courage a certain guarantee of numbers' (1853: 393) and consequently lost some of its potency unless reinforced by further migrations from other Aryan populations. The book's most quoted assertion is:

> Such is the lesson of history. It shows us that all civilizations derive from the white race, that none can exist without its help, and that a society is great and brilliant only so far as it preserves the blood of the noble group that created it, provided that this group itself belongs to the most illustrious branch of our species. (1853: 209)

It appears that Gobineau wished to make use of a version of the typological theory without committing himself to all its constituent parts. There is a chapter entitled 'Racial Differences are Permanent' in which the influence of Cuvier is very apparent. In it Gobineau observes, 'the reader will not fail to see that the question on which the argument here turns is that of the permanence of types'. He used the concept of type in two senses. The first is one that relates to the declaration in his dedication of the book in which he said that he was constructing a moral geology that dealt only in series of centuries, occupying himself rarely with individuals, but always with ethnic units. The geology spans four periods. The type of man first created was the Adamite but it must be left out of the argument since we could know nothing of its specific character. In his earliest stages, man might have assumed unstable forms and change would then have been easier, producing races which differed from their original ancestor as much as they differed from each other. In the second stage three races were present: white, black, and yellow, though 'it is probable that none of the three original types was ever found in absolute simplicity'. Inter-mixture is the origin, he says, of what we may call tertiary types, though 'our knowledge of the life of these tertiary races is very slight. Only in the misty beginnings of human history can we catch a glimpse, in certain places, of the white race when it was still in this stage – a stage which seems to have been everywhere short-lived . . . to the tertiary races succeed others, which I will call "quarternary"' (1853: 155–7). A quarternary race could be further modified by the intervention of a new type. Gobineau wrote of the existing races as being descended from the secondary races, as if present-day populations might represent the second, third, fourth, or even a subsequent stage in the process.

The second use of type is that which became important in anthropological theorizing; the assumption that there was, or had been, a pure physical form behind the appearances of diversity. Gobineau never defined race and made it clear that he regarded all the contemporary groups to which that label was applied as having in varying degrees lost their true character through miscegenation. For example, he wrote, 'As for the Persian race, it no longer exists in the scientific sense of the word, any more than does the French race, and of all the peoples of Europe we are surely that in which the type has been most obliterated. It is even this obliteration which we accept, in physique and in culture, as being our own type. It is the same with the Persians' (Buenzod, 1967: 558 n38).

It seems as if Gobineau was trying to defend a belief in permanent differences of racial type independent of association with zoological provinces and therefore unaffected by environmental relativism. This is the theme of Aryan superiority. But in other parts of his *Essay* a subsidiary theme can be discerned, as Janine Buenzod has demonstrated. This dealt with the contribution that other races can make to the creation of civilizations, the emergence of elites and the inability of the white race to progress in confined environments (like that of Newfoundland). To the 'moral geology' can be added another evocative expression (which also appears in the Dedication), that of 'historical chemistry'. Gobineau did not think of racial crossing in terms of blending inheritance, as if the progeny inherited equally from both parents. Rather, he regarded the superior race, especially the Aryan, as a catalytic agent, bringing out latent powers in others (as yeast makes dough rise), or, if it was too strong, destroying them (Buenzod, 1967: 328, 384). The principles of this mixing were not understood, a conclusion which recalls the author's earlier remark that 'the science of social anatomy is in its infancy' (1853: 58).

The elements that go into the historical chemistry were no longer pure and all the races contained their own differences of quality. 'When it is a question of individual merit', Gobineau writes,

> I refuse completely to make use of that mode of argument which runs 'every negro is stupid', and my chief objection is that, to complete the comparison, I would then be obliged to concede that every European is intelligent; and heaven preserve me from such a paradox . . . I have no doubt that many negro chiefs are superior, in the wealth of their ideas, the synthetic power of their minds, and the strength of their capacity for action, to the level usually reached by our peasants, or even by average specimens of our half-educated bourgeoisie . . . Let us leave these puerilities, and compare, not men, but groups. (1853: 182)

It is from the comparison of groups that Gobineau concluded that the

Aryans had overstretched themselves and that the chemistry had gone wrong. It is not difficult to accept the conclusion that 'the chief element in the *Essay* is the idea of the decadence of civilizations and not that of the inequality of races . . . The explanation in terms of race is a key; but the door which has to be opened – that of understanding history in its broadest dimensions – comes before the key.' It demands much more to assent to the same writer's statement 'the central idea, the truly fertile idea in the *Essay*, is that of the complementarity of races' (Buenzod, 1967: 328–9, 471). If there were evidence that Gobineau saw the chemistry as Carus saw the phases of day and night, as a whole, as part of a meaningful design for the universe, it would be easier to agree.

If Gobineau derived such ideas from Carus and other writers he gave them little emphasis. The principal passage came towards the end of the first book when he wrote about the advantages that had followed from the mixture of blood.

> Artistic genius, which is equally foreign to each of the three great types, arose only after the inter-marriage of white and black. Again, in the Malayan variety, a human family was produced from the yellow and black races that had more intelligence than either of its ancestors . . . to racial mixtures is due the refinement of manners and beliefs, and especially the tempering of passion and desire. (1853: 208)

Elsewhere Gobineau maintained that for the world-wide movement of cultural fusion to stretch out it was not sufficient just that a civilizing milieu should deploy all its energy; it was necessary that in the different regions ethnic workshops should establish themselves to work on their own localities (1853: 867–8). How this fitted with other parts of his vision is problematic. It is also difficult to be sure what he meant when in a discussion of Hindu caste he declared:

> a light admixture from the black species develops intelligence in the white race, in that it turns it towards imagination, makes it more artistic, lends it larger wings; at the same time it weakens the reasoning power of the white race, diminishes the intensity of its practical faculties, delivers an irremediable blow to its activity and physical power, and almost always removes from the group deriving from this mixture, if not the right of shining much brighter than the whites and thinking more profoundly, at least that of contending against it with patience, tenacity, and wisdom. (1853: 346)

At times Gobineau poured the new wine of racial typology into the old bottles of romanticism, but he did not always pour it very straight, and the idea of complementarity was, in a crucial passage, clearly subordinated to that of natural aristocracy.

> If mixtures of blood are, to a certain extent, beneficial to the mass of mankind, if they raise and ennoble it, this is merely at the expense of mankind itself, which is stunted, abased, enervated, and humiliated in the persons of its noblest sons. Even if we were to admit that it is better to turn a myriad of degraded beings into mediocre men than to preserve the race of princes whose blood is adulterated and impoverished by being made to suffer this dishonourable change, yet there is still the unfortunate fact that the change does not stop here. (1853: 209)

He then went on to sketch the way in which the unions of the degraded lead societies into the abyss of nothingness.

It is remarked time and again that those who write the history of distant periods regularly do so from the standpoint of their own generation. They interpret ancient disputes in the terms that are alive as they write. This observation is particularly relevant to Gobineau and his *Essay*. Joseph Arthur de Gobineau (1816–82) was born into a bourgeois family with aristocratic pretensions that had been devoted to the Bourbon dynasty and completely opposed to the aspirations of the French Revolution. His experiences of family life, with both his mother and his wife, included much that was unhappy. Gobineau earned a living mainly from journalism until the Revolution of 1848, after which he obtained a succession of diplomatic appointments up to 1877. In 1855, when he first came into contact with a black people, the Somalis, he wrote home saying that never before had he seen 'creatures so beautiful and perfect', so personal experiences did not have the influence upon him that they did on Agassiz. Gobineau's short stories about the Middle East reveal an impressive ability to interpret everyday life as it might have appeared to people brought up in the local cultures. A major theme in them and the novels is the existence of an aristocracy of spirit to be found in men and women of different nations, and which is not necessarily displayed by people of great wealth or gentle parentage.

The *Essay* began with a reference to the revolutions of 1848 which Gobineau saw as symptomatic of the decay of European civilization and he continued to write from the perspective of a man out of harmony with his time. He thought it unnecessary to provide evidence to support his views that the Aryans were degenerating and that there could be no new civilization (had he known that in 1944 German troops would dynamite a museum created in his honour he might have thought it evidence in favour of the former proposition). As Michael Biddiss explains, his hypothesis was founded in the contemporary world; it was social and political rather than properly biological (1970: 132). Unlike most of those with whom he can be compared, Gobineau did not expound a theory to press a particular solution on his readers. He had no solution, and in his thought the theory worked towards the annihilation of political will and purpose. Though his belief in natural aristocracy, and race as one of its forms, ran through other writings, not one of the seventeen books he wrote after the *Essay* developed his comparison of the major races. It is the history of one race that concerned him and his books about it were a very personal declaration.

That Gobineau's use of the conception of type was in accordance with contemporary French scientific usage is suggested by an essay published in 1859–60. In it Paul Broca, founder of the Paris Anthropological Society, criticized the view 'that the crossing of races constantly produces disastrous effects'. This was far too general, for under certain circumstances it had favourable results. Broca insisted on the importance of distinguishing between race and type. The popular view that people with hair of different colour did not belong to the same race seized the true meaning of the term race, whereas only the scientist, studying the ensemble of characters common to a natural group, could constitute the type of that group (1864: 8). Human types were abstractions and were not to be confused with actual groups of men. The use of 'race' as if this denoted a pure category was to be avoided. 'Every confusion in words', Broca sternly warned, 'exposes us to errors in the interpretation of facts.'

Britain

The pioneer of racial typology in Britain was Charles Hamilton Smith (1776–1859), a disciple and friend of Cuvier who saw military service with British troops in West Africa, the West Indies, and 'on both portions of the American continent' between 1797 and 1807, later translating the works of the master while on manoeuvres. In 1848 he published *The Natural History of the Human Species* which built on Cuvier's foundations a speculative superstructure about man's origin in three aboriginal normal types springing from a common centre near the Gobi desert 'for this was, approximately, either the seat of Man's first development . . . or the space where a portion of human beings found safety, when convulsions and changes of surface, which may have swept away a more ancient zoology, had passed over the earth and were introductory to a new order of things' (1848: 169). Smith maintained that zoology limited the possibilities of colonization. A race could have only provisional tenure of a region until the indestructible typical form appeared to take over the territory assigned to it by nature. Conquest entailed extermination unless it was one of the great typical stocks effecting an incorporation of its own affiliates.

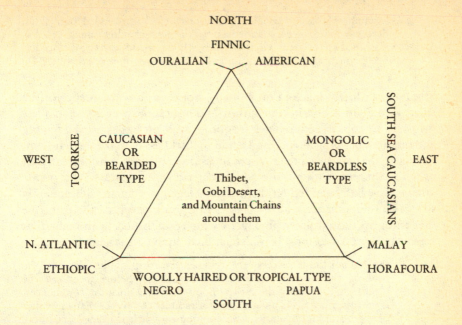

NORTH

FINNIC

OURALIAN AMERICAN

SOUTH SEA CAUCASIANS

WEST

TOORKEE

CAUCASIAN
OR
BEARDED
TYPE

Thibet,
Gobi Desert,
and Mountain Chains
around them

MONGOLIC
OR
BEARDLESS
TYPE

EAST

N. ATLANTIC MALAY

ETHIOPIC HORAFOURA

WOOLLY HAIRED OR TROPICAL TYPE
NEGRO PAPUA
SOUTH

Figure 3. *Charles Hamilton Smith's view of the primaeval location of mankind and the three typical stocks*

Mulatto strains were eventually infertile. For Smith the three types were the woolly-haired or Negro; beardless or Mongolian; and bearded or Caucasian.

This argument was a development of the views expounded by Cuvier. On the question of whether man was one species Smith equivocated. He wrote that this 'is assumed to be answered in the affirmative', but his whole text was built round the view that man was one genus with three species, and that the variety of types of humans resulted from different mixtures between the original three kinds (see Figure 3).

Environmental relativism was weaker in Smith's scheme than in Nott's. He allowed more scope for the superior Caucasians to settle outside Europe, while claiming that in extremes of temperature they could maintain their numbers only by further immigration. The Caucasian was described as a veritable paragon, able:

> to endure the greatest vicissitudes of temperature in all climates; to emigrate, colonize, and multiply in them, with the sole exception of the positive extremes . . . he alone of the races of mankind has produced

examples of free and popular institutions . . . he has ascended to the skies, descended into the deep, and mastered the powers of lightning . . . He has instituted all the great religious systems in the world, and to his stock has been vouchsafed the glory and the conditions of revelation. (1848: 371–2)

The Negro's lowly place in the human order was a consequence of the small volume of his brain (the author had noticed how even the smallest British army caps issued to black troops in the West Indies proved too big and required padding an inch and a half in thickness to make them fit, but, he added, the caps fitted the non-commissioned officers, who were in part of white descent, without any additional aid; he also stated that white infants who had been fed on the milk of Negro wet nurses subsequently suffered in appearance and temperament). Smith accepted the principle that ontogeny recapitulated phylogeny which established, he thought, that cerebral progress was most complete at birth in the Caucasian type:

> the human brain successively assumes the form of the Negroes, the Malays, the Americans, and the Mongolians, before it attains the Caucasian . . . One of the earliest points where ossification commences, is the lower jaw. This bone is therefore sooner completed than any other of the head, and acquires a predominance which it never loses in the Negro. (1848: 125–7, 159–60)

As in other versions of typology, Smith's formulation contained the beginnings of a theory of racial relations, since he referred to 'the deep rooted hatred of the Caucasian races towards the typical Negro'. As in Gobineau, though several years earlier, there was also a subsidiary and undeveloped theme which found in the mixing of races something important to the creation of civilizations. Thus he wrote of the 'amalgamation of the typical stocks, without which no permanent progress in the path of true civilization is made'. The black stock had nothing to contribute since 'the good qualities given to the Negro by the bounty of Nature, have served only to make him a slave'. Thus, 'No people of the typical stocks could arrive at a progressive social existence, without intermixture of one or more branches of the homogeneous nations of the bearded and beardless forms; and through these, such rudiments of advancement as can be traced among the woolly haired, were likewise engendered' (1848: 334, 120, 197, 179). Here, then, in lectures originally given to the Plymouth Institution between 1832 and 1837, was most of the theory that occasioned the controversies of the 1850s.

A more pugnacious propagandist for typology was Robert Knox (1791–1862), the son of an Edinburgh school teacher who graduated in medicine in 1814, and served as an army surgeon in Belgium and for three years in

South Africa. He studied in Paris and then went on to establish himself as a very successful lecturer in anatomy in his native city. In 1828 misfortune struck him. Medical teachers in Edinburgh, as elsewhere, needed cadavers for teaching purposes and often had to obtain them from disreputable sources. Two men, Burke and Hare, who were convicted of murder, had sold the body of their victim to an agent acting on behalf of Dr Knox. Though Knox was formally cleared of liability for the actions of Burke and Hare, his position in Edinburgh became untenable. Thereafter he held only occasional medical appointments and maintained himself for some periods by writing and lecturing. The unhappiness he must have experienced may help to explain the disjointed and dogmatic nature of his pronunciations upon race when they appeared in 1850 as a book of lectures entitled *The Races of Men*. A second edition, with a new appendix, was brought out in 1862.

W. and R. Chambers, the Edinburgh publishers already mentioned, arranged for the publication in 1842 of Quetelet's *A Treatise on Man*. Knox was responsible for its translation from the French and he added an appendix, partly on the pulse rate and partly on the effects of climate. In it he explained that the various climates could be classified as two zones (inter- and extra-tropical, the latter being subdivided into two or three regions). The tropical regions of the Old World had been inhabited from the earliest historic period by the Negro and other dark-coloured races; the temperate region of the extra-tropical zone had been held by the Celtic and Saxon races. Celts and Saxons when living in the tropics, unless at great elevation, suffered greatly from fevers and did not live long. Knox reviewed the evidence suggesting that neither temperature nor humidity was the cause. He contributed his own observation that 'when our troops occupied Walcheren and Flushing, during the deplorable scheme of invading Europe, the mortality assumed a most alarming character'. Fevers killed the French and the British but not the Dutch. Since the English and the Dutch derived from one parent stock he concluded that acclimatization must take several generations, during which relatively few might survive. The Dutch had survived, even prospered, at the Cape, presumably because they had never laboured. If the Celt and the Saxon were to maintain their populations in other zones they required a slave population of native labourers. Knox concluded that when these matters had been more fully investigated, and fitting remedies discovered, Europeans would be able with confidence to emigrate to Canada and certain other regions. This opinion he subsequently modified.

In *The Races of Men*, Knox elaborated upon what he called 'transcendental anatomy' an expression used by Geoffroy but which Knox said was coined by his esteemed friend and teacher (and Cuvier's successor) H. M. D. de Blainville. Knox described it as originating from South Germany and from a mixture of the Slav and Gothic races. Its object was 'to explain in a connected chain the phenomena of the living material world'; to show that 'all animals are formed upon one great plan'. ' "There is but one animal, not many" was the remarkable expression of Geoffroy; it contains the whole question. What was, now is, under other forms; but the essence is still the same.' As there was only one creation, 'in time there is probably no such thing as species' but 'for a few centuries organic forms seem not to have changed'. This theory had been popularized in Britain (and, according to Knox, misstated) by the anonymous author of a best-selling work *Vestiges of Creation*. Geoffroy claimed that the unity of animal forms could be proved by the examination of embryonic forms. Knox also started from the recapitulation theory: 'whatever is irregular in man is a regular structure in some lower animal and was in him a regular structure during his embryonic life. This law . . . is the basis of the law productive of irregular form in man – the law of deformation.' Variety was deformity. It was balanced by 'the law of unity of the organization' (Knox, 1862: 167, 175, 477). Knox summarized his argument as follows:

> The races of men differ from each other, and have done so from the earliest historic period, as proved –
> 1. By their external characters, which have never altered during the last six thousand years.
> 2. By anatomical differences in structure.
> 3. By the infertility of the hybrid product, originating in the intermingling of two races.
> 4. By historic evidence, which shows that no distinct hybrid race can ever be shown to exist anywhere.

But his summary is scarcely complete, for elsewhere Knox insisted on including in his typology of races not only their external characters, but their internal ones as well. He believed that men differ more in their intelligence than their physique. By intelligence he meant what is now called culture, for he included religion, literature and morale in the characteristic of a race. One consequence was his readiness to include racial attitudes among the criteria of classification. This can be noticed in his discussion of 'Hottentots or Bosjemen':

> Did the Dutch, the Christian Dutch, consider these races to be men and women? I scarcely think so . . . The coloured men the Dutch called boys, and the coloured women they called maids . . . *De facto*, then, the Dutch did not hold these races to be the same as their own. (1862: 503, 233)

Like Smith (and, before them both, Cuvier) Knox did not distinguish clearly between type and race but used the latter synonymously with species. Perhaps he was the more inclined to do so because of the popular character of his lectures. As Michael Biddiss has observed, Knox's chief concern was to awaken his contemporaries to the fundamentally racial nature of the chief political conflicts within Europe at mid century. Four main races were the parties to these conflicts. The first was that of the Scandinavians who were naturally democratic but refused to extend to subordinated peoples their own principles of freedom and justice. Second came the Celts, who were notable warriors but had less understanding of liberty, being incapable of implementing ideas of freedom in government. Third were the Slavonians who had great intellectual and political potential. Had they a leadership conscious of the racial nature of their problems they might yet liberate themselves from the Habsburg, Brandenburg and Romanov tyrannies. Fourth came the Sarmantians or Russ, who were incapable of real achievement in literature or science. Their blind obedience to despots made them a threat to liberty (Biddiss, 1976: 249). Knox never drew attention to intra-racial differences or attributed to race any variations within countries, though his vocabulary was often lacking in precision. Thus he wrote: 'The really momentous question for England, as a *nation*, is the presence of three sections of the Celtic race still on her soil.' He referred to the Scots, Welsh, and, of course, the Irish: 'The source of all evil lies in the race, the Celtic race of Ireland . . . *the race* must be forced from the soil; by fair means, if possible; still, they must leave. England's safety requires it. I speak not of the justice of the case; nations must ever act as Machiavelli advised: look to yourself' (1862: 378–9). Knox did not explain why the soil of Ireland belonged to the English, for though he wrote at times as if each race had its particular province, and though he could assert that a race could not be changed 'so long as they occupy the soil on which nature first placed them', he suggested no principles for mapping the natural zones of races (as Agassiz had done).

Nevertheless, Knox adhered fairly closely to all three distinguishing tenets of the typological school. As to the first, he maintained that 'human character, individual and national, is traceable solely to the nature of that race to which the individual or nation belongs' and went on to explain that while there was a process of biological development 'organic forms seem not to have changed . . . for a few thousand years'. Concerning the second, Knox wrote 'I feel disposed to think that there must be a physical and, consequently, a psychological inferiority in the dark races generally.' The third proposition of the typological theory is evident in passages such as 'The various species of Men constitute one great natural family. Each species or race has a certain degree of antagonism to the others, some more, some less.' Of the darker races, 'Furthest removed by nature from the Saxon race, the antipathy between these races is greater than between any other: in each other they perceive their direct antagonists.' Knox stated explicitly that 'Climate has no influence in permanently altering the varieties or races of men' and that hybrids were ultimately sterile. He subscribed to the same kind of environmentalism as Agassiz and Nott and was ready to draw the conclusion that racial superiority was limited by natural boundaries; thus, remarking on the inordinate self-esteem of the Saxon, he insisted,

> his race cannot domineer over the earth – cannot even exist permanently on any continent to which he is not indigenous – cannot ever become native, true-born Americans – cannot hold in permanency any portion of any continent but the one on which he *first* originated. (Knox, 1862: v–vi, 53, 224, 449; 1863: 254)

When he wrote a text-book for medical students, Knox was much more cautious. He stated that the human species was 'composed of a number of distinct races, which are usually called varieties, the extent and origin of which, have not as yet been determined' though 'they are of vast antiquity'. After listing some, he wrote 'these races differ from each other in their intellectual characters and physical structure; but it is probable, and as regards structure, it is certain, that the differences are to a great extent, unimportant'. The most remarkable differences were those to be found among the Bosjeman (or Hottentots). Races 'thrive best in the land on which they were originally found'. In apparent contradiction to his popular lectures Knox testified, 'Man is everywhere the same; actuated by the same feelings, passions and desires.' He though it 'by no means improbable' that each race could produce its own kind of civilization, like the Coptic, Phoenician, Persian, Saracenic, Etrurian, Mexican, Peruvian and Chinese. 'The present forms of European civilization, using the term in its most extended sense, are modelled on these, for it does not appear that any form of civilization ever originated with the western European races' (Knox, 1857: 168–71).

Politically, Knox was a radical who sympathized with the French revolution, a man who dismissed stories of cannibalism as 'a romance invented by Catholic missionaries' and declared that 'as a Saxon I abhor all dynasties, monarchies and bayonet governments'. His radicalism and his belief in racial zones came together in his criticism of imperialism and 'that den of all abuses, the office of the Colonial Secretary'. Writing about racial antagonism in South Africa, he declared that there the Anglo-Saxon and Dutch Saxon:

so debase the coloured races as to deprive them for ever of all chance of recovering that inestimable treasure beyond all price or value, freedom of speech, thought, and action; in a word, the rights of man. How has this antagonism of race arisen? The truth is, it has always existed, but it never appeared in its terrible form until the Saxon race began to migrate over the earth, to establish free colonies as they are called – free to the white man and their own race – dens of horror and cruelty to the coloured. (Knox, 1862: 27, 222, 470, 546)

Knox's influence was considerable. One of his biographers (Lonsdale, 1870: 292–3) testifies, 'Previous to his time, little or nothing was heard about Race in the medical schools: he changed all this by his Saturday's lectures, and Race became as familiar as household words to his students, through whom some of his novel ideas became disseminated far and wide, both at home and abroad.' Knox's influence was the greater because he attracted an energetic disciple, James Hunt (1833–69). Hunt inherited from his father the ownership of an establishment for the cure of stammering, on which he wrote an authoritative textbook. Hunt graduated D.Phil from the University of Giessen (with which he had a family connection) in 1856 and was awarded an honorary M.S. from the same university in 1867. He was a man of great energy who led a breakaway from the Ethnological Society to found the Anthropological Society of London (Stocking, 1971). In his presidential address to that society in 1865, Hunt declared that 'the Negro belongs to a distinct type. The term species, in the present state of science, is not satisfactory.' He ended with six conclusions much like Nott's, but including

4. That the Negro becomes more humanized when in his natural subordination to the European than in any other circumstances.
5. That the Negro race can only be humanized and civilized by Europeans.

Quite how this humanizing and civilizing was going to take place was by no means clear, for in a paper published just after his death Hunt (1870: 137) asserted that races could not long survive outside their natural zones. In transmitting the lessons of his science Hunt affected the same tones of Olympian disdain as characterized the prose of Knox, Gobineau and Nott:

Anthropological science cannot consent to consult the wishes or prejudices of the subjects with which it has to deal. Whilst, therefore, fully admitting the powers of civilised men to struggle for a time against the decrees of nature, we must yet venture to point out even to the boastful Anglo-Saxon, that the world is not for him; and that although his skill in war and chicanery may exterminate native races, it will yet be demonstrated that in the New World the almost exterminated savages will be amply revenged by a slow gradual degeneracy, and perhaps final extinction, of their conquerors.

Hunt was an effective publicist but no original contributor to his chosen field. In his short and fairly spectacular career he seems to have had no experience outside Europe and to have been motivated primarily by his enthusiasm for a theory which he believed of the greatest relevance to the problems of his age.

The typological school

From the time of Richard Colfax onwards there were authors, especially in the United States, who elaborated upon the alleged deficiencies of Negroes by comparison with Caucasians. Such attempts to explain the differences between two groups were less convincing than theories which recognized variations between a larger number of races and claimed to account for them all in terms of general principles. The Typological Theory was of the greater power because, in the eyes of some people at least, it seemed able to do this. The view which sees typology as the development of trends inherent in pre-Darwinian biological thought is strengthened by its independent appearance in the United States, France and Britain. Because of the tradition of *Naturphilosophie*, Germany did not contribute on the same scale, but there was a distinct echo from the ebullient Karl Vogt (1817–95), or 'monkey Vogt' as he was called when he took up Darwinian doctrine. Vogt was a professor of anatomy at Giessen, a radical and militant materialist, who also occupied a parliamentary seat and participated in the revolutionary movements of his time. He was the subject of Marx's diatribe, *Herr Vogt*. Dismissed from his chair at Giessen, he obtained another in geology at Geneva. Vogt was first a follower of Cuvier who translated *The Vestiges of Creation* into German while standing aside from its evolutionary speculations. His materialism was evident in his *Lectures on Man* (1863) which maintained that the cultural development of races corresponded to variations in their cranial capacity. He asserted that 'the differences in the human genus which we may designate either races or species . . . are original'. Negro intellectual development was arrested at puberty. Vogt quoted 'the general rule of the slaveholder' that Negro slaves 'must be treated like neglected and badly brought up children' (1863: 440, 191–3 and on typology, 214–21). Yet in contradiction of his own arguments he drew attention to measurements reporting a lower cranial capacity for Negroes in the United States than in Africa and asked 'is this the effect of that cursed institution which degrades men to the condition of chattel?'. His radical spirit rising, he remarked that as slavery exercised an equally injurious influence on the master it would be worth collecting the skulls of the Civil War dead to test the hypothesis that the cranial capacity of white Southerners had been reduced below that of Northerners. By the end of the book he had grasped the significance of Darwin's message about the mutability of types and was speculating about man evolving from multiple origins to interbreed: 'the innumerable mongrel races gradually fill up the spaces between originally so distinct types, and, notwithstanding the constancy of characters, in spite of the tenacity with which the primitive races resist alteration, they are by fusion slowly led towards unity' (1863: 92, 448, 468).

It is also worth noting a passage in which Vogt bade his hearers look westwards:

> the Anglo-Saxon race is itself a mongrel race, produced by Celts, Saxons, Normans and Danes, a raceless chaos without any fixed type; and the descendants of this raceless multitude have in America so much inter-mixed with Frenchmen, Germans, Dutch, and Irish, as to have given rise to another raceless chaos, which is kept up by continued immigration. We can readily believe that from this chaos a new race is gradually forming. (Vogt, 1864: 433)

Yet it would not include the German Saxon race, for that had become a fixed type which had not changed, even in America. The notion of a 'race-less chaos' was later perverted and popularized by his one-time pupil Houston Stewart Chamberlain. But Vogt's book is more interesting as an example of a scientist's inconsistencies as he comes to accept a new theory; the author's combination of political radicalism with the assertion of racial inferiority is also worth some attention as a pointer to the differences in the intellectual scene of his day and our own.

Unlike Darwin, who led a secluded life and avoided political issues, those who expounded the typological doctrine responded wholeheartedly to the movements of their time. They were also less ethnocentric than most of their contemporaries. For most of them it was important to resist the representatives of organized religion who claimed to determine the proper scope of scientific research. After religion, the main external influence upon their work derived from the political struggles within Europe. In explaining how he came to write his *Essay*, Gobineau referred explicitly to 'the great events, the bloody wars, the revolutions', referring to the upheavals of 1848. That year was described by T. H. Hodgkin as remark-able 'for the savage atrocities which have signalized those wars of races which have disgraced it'. He must have supposed that there were racial divisions within national populations or between them and their rulers.

The 'great events' began in the February when the French king was forced to abdicate. In March the population of Vienna revolted and drove out Metternich, the famous Austrian state chancellor. A new constitution was promised. Five days later there was a revolution in Berlin. The king surrendered to the people and it was agreed that an assembly of representatives would meet in Frankfurt. Schleswig-Holstein claimed independence from Denmark. The Italians drove the Austrian garrisons out of Milan and Venice, and nationalist secessions were threatened throughout the Austrian empire. The Csechs took the first steps towards home rule. In April there were riots in London and the government had to bring in troops, barricade the bridges, and garrison many public buildings. All Europe was affected. The uprisings were popular movements directed against hereditary wealth and power. Social and economic changes, which some see as the signs of an expanding industrial capitalism, broke the traditional structures in favour of social mobility and parliamentary democracy. In the long-run, the greater competition for status probably made people more conscious of status distinctions, such as those linked with racial differences; the typologists, however, thought that the upheavals demonstrated the power of underlying racial forces. Knox and Vogt, the radicals, welcomed these changes; Gobineau thought they justified his pessimism.

Events overseas probably gave the typological theory an extra plausibility when they appeared as conflicts between Europeans and members of coloured races. The China war, the Crimean war, the Indian 'Mutiny', the civil war in the United States, the Jamaican uprising of 1865 could all be seen as matters of race, but the 1860s were not an expansionist age and Gladstone's cabinet of 1868 is sometimes considered as marking the high point of *anti*-imperialist sentiment. Imperialism was in no sense a popular political idea before Disraeli's second premiership of 1874–80 and there is no clear evidence that British imperialism and Victorian ideas of race are linked in any causal way (Watson, 1973: 213, 215). Certainly the climate of opinion in Britain was changing at this time. The opportunities for schooling were being extended. Literacy was growing rapidly and there was a burgeoning popular literature. More men were being given the vote. The prospects of greater social mobility increased status consciousness. Douglas Lorimer, an author sensitive to the possible influence of external conditions upon racial thought, and one who has looked closely into the Victorian debate on what was sometimes called 'the Negro Question', has concluded that changes in English society were the main influences responsible for an increase in racial sentiment. The doctrines counted for less. He dates the more strident racialism from the 1850s but believes that it did not materialize before the 1870s and 1880s, so it cannot have exerted much influence upon the writers of the 1850s. Lorimer refers to a 'transition in racial attitudes from an earlier ethnocentric response to a more openly racist one' as reflecting not the 'needs of Empire' but 'new attitudes towards social status emerging within English society' (Lorimer, 1978: 15–16, 208).

To notice the respects in which the typological theory grew out of earlier reasoning about differences between species and varieties is to examine it in terms of the internal history of racial thought. That perspective surely shows that however prejudiced the writers may or may not have been, their arguments were constrained by the available evidence and their need to persuade their audience that their explanations were to be preferred to others. Their arguments needed to be studied in the context of their external history also, but no one can assess the significance of the external influences unless their bearing upon the intellectual enterprise of trying to discover new knowledge can be ascertained. Discoveries require hard mental labour and are never the simple product of circumstances.

There was a division within the typological school. Charles Hamilton Smith and Gobineau followed Cuvier in favouring the catastrophic view of geological change; they were correspondingly less inclined to associate racial types with zoological provinces or to stress acclimatization as a constraint upon European expansion. They allowed for hybridization among humans and found some complementarity between races. Gobineau in particular left room for major differences of ability within racial groups. This first version of typology could more easily be reconciled with the book of Genesis. By contrast, Nott, Gliddon, Knox and Hunt were more committed to the postulate of permanent types adapted to particular zoological provinces, suggesting that a limited number of racial types (perhaps eight, perhaps more) had existed from the beginning of human life. This version went with the beliefs that racial hybrids were eventually sterile and that races could not acclimatize to new environments. It left less room for intra-racial differences, though Morton thought that some cranial variability might be associated with differences between the social rank of the individuals in question. Those who represented this division within typology expressed themselves forcefully on matters of national politics but were more decidedly critical of imperialism.

It also reveals something of the scientific temper of the typologists to consider how they reacted to Darwin's *Origin*. Knox died only three years after its publication but there is no reason to believe that he had any sympathy for the new theory. His disciple Hunt (1866) published a paper on the application of the principle of natural selection to anthropology which did little more than reiterate old and by then irrelevant opinions in favour of polygenesis. Gobineau seems not to have understood that Darwin had changed the nature of the debate. He thought he could select from Darwin's work the elements that suited him and was attracted to his idea that 'some of our present mongrelized races' might be descended from certain beings intermediate between man and the monkey' (Biddiss, 1970: 248). Nott, however, told a friend that he would not have published *Types of Mankind* 'if the prehistoric period of men had been so firmly established as it is at the present day'. He knew that his explanation depended upon a shorter time-scale and that once this assumption was changed, the whole structure was undermined. Another friend also testified that Nott 'was broad enough . . . to accept to the full all of Darwin's views and conclusions' (Stanton, 1960: 186, 237).

This connection between racial typology and seventeenth-century chronology helps illustrate the backward-looking nature of this school of thought when seen within the history of science. Addressing the question, 'Why are they not like us?', the typologists answered, 'Because they have always been different.', but they could not explain how it was that each generation of 'us' and 'them' looked like its ancestors. They stressed continuity but could not account for it. Like the eighteenth-century naturalists, they assumed that to classify was to explain.

3

RACE AS SUBSPECIES

In the 1850s two views of human diversity were in contention. The first was associated with a conception of race as lineage and with the ethnological approach. It assumed that all humans had descended from a single ancestral pair and had since diversified, so that it offered a theory of change in which a major influence was exercised in some as yet mysterious way that seemed to be tied to environmental circumstances. The second view was associated with a conception of race as type and with the anthropological approach. It assumed that racial differences had existed from some very early period of prehistory when different stocks had been created either by God or by some natural catastrophe. It offered a theory of continuity based upon the evidence of inheritance. The achievement of Charles Darwin (1809–82) was to subsume these two theories within a new synthesis which explained both change and continuity.

Darwin's method

Darwin utilized a concept of race somewhat obliquely in the fourth edition (1866) of his book *On the Origin of Natural Selection or the Preservation of Favoured Races in the Struggle for Life* (1859). He quoted the reference, in one of A. R. Wallace's papers about butterflies in Malaysia, to 'geographical races, or subspecies' as 'local forms completely fixed and isolated'. Because they were isolated they did not inter-breed, and so 'there is no possible test but individual opinion to determine which of them shall be considered as species and which as varieties'. He must have meant that there was no independent test of whether the forms were subspecies, since their geographical isolation prevented any observation of whether they were able to inter-breed. As Darwin was attempting to explain the way living things changed, questions of classification at moments of time were not of central importance. If the general changes in biological thought which he introduced are considered first it should be easier to understand what was entailed in this reference to 'geographical races'. Only now that more than a century has passed since the publication of *The Origin* is it possible fully to appreciate the astonishing range and complexity of Darwin's contribution and the inter-relations between the research he undertook in different fields.

As described by Michael T. Ghiselin (1969: 9–12), Darwin's research and publications can be grouped in six major divisions. The first was that of natural history, in which he assembled observations and gathered specimens more or less as opportunities arose. His years as companion to the captain on the voyage of H.M.S. Beagle exploring the coastline of South America (1831–6), provided many occasions for this kind of natural history. The second division was concerned with geology; it overlapped with the first and was exemplified by three books deriving from that voyage. The third represents his zoological work, such as his studies between 1846 and 1854 on the classification of barnacles. The fourth, or strictly evolutionary, division could be dated from 1837 when Darwin opened the first notebook in which he started to record materials relating to the transmutation of species. In the following year, as a result of reading Malthus' essay on population, it struck him that under conditions of 'struggle for existence . . . favourable variations would tend to be preserved and unfavourable ones to be destroyed. The result of this would be the formation of new species. Here, then, I had at last got a theory by which to work.' In 1842 and 1844 he drafted essays in which he analyzed evolution as the outcome of variation, heredity and the struggle for life. In 1858 as a result of the news that A. R. Wallace had independently reached very similar conclusions (also after reading Malthus!) Darwin was impelled to return to this work. A paper under the joint names of Darwin and Wallace was presented to the Linnaean Society. Darwin set about preparing a book that would give a simple account of the views to which he had been led, and this was published as the *Origin*. He later wrote two other books on evolution: *The Variation of Plants and Animals under Domestication* (1862) and *The Descent of Man* (1871). The fifth division of Darwin's work included six major botanical studies, written after the *Origin*, while the sixth division was research of a psychological character dealing both with humans and with earthworms.

There has been no greater scientist than Charles Darwin, and yet there was nothing in his formal education that foreshadowed his later eminence. What enabled him to do such outstanding work? Ghiselin (1969: 4) has no doubt about the answer: his method.

Unless one understands this – that Darwin applied, rigorously and consistently, the modern hypothetico-deductive scientific method – his accomplishments cannot be appreciated. His entire scientific accomplishment must be attributed not to the collection of facts, but to the development of theory.

All the time Darwin worked to gather evidence that bore upon critical hypotheses and he seems to have been puzzled that others should not do likewise, for he wrote to a correspondent, 'How odd it is that anyone should not see that all observation must be for or against some view if it is to be of service.' Again, he wrote that:

> False facts are highly injurious to the progress of science, for they often endure long; but false views, if supported by some evidence, do little harm, for every one takes a salutary pleasure in proving their falseness; and when this is done, one path towards error is closed and the road to truth is often at the same time opened.

The finding of the bones attributed to Piltdown Man was a false fact that set anthropologists on a barren trail for decades; the misleading evidence suggesting that Lord Morton's arab mare had borne foals with stripes deriving from a previous mating was another that took longer to put right; Samuel George Morton's misleading presentation of his measurements of cranial capacity was accepted by other people as factual. That the error in the second and third cases arose because someone fitted facts to a mistaken hypothesis shows that it is often difficult to disentangle fact and opinion, but this only reinforces the main argument that research workers need to make their hypotheses explicit and to collect evidence which can effectively test them.

In support of his interpretation Ghiselin asks why, when Darwin had formulated his theory of natural selection, he should have put this work aside to devote eight years to a taxonomic revision of the barnacles? Ghiselin's answer (1969: 113–21) is fascinating. Nothing in evolution is more important than sexuality, for the presence of two sexes produces more genetic variation and permits more rapid natural selection. Darwin had worked out his theoretical views on the evolution of sexuality before undertaking his studies on barnacles. Intending simply to write up some of the work deriving from his South American expedition, he discovered that barnacles furnished evidence bearing upon his theories and so he decided to follow the trail. Some barnacles are hermaphrodites; sometimes there are female barnacles accompanied by dwarf males; Darwin found an intermediate condition in which hermaphrodites were accompanied by dwarf males. This interested him because, as he wrote, 'my species theory convinced me that a hermaphrodite species must pass into a bisexual species by insensibly small stages; and here we have it for the male organs in the hermaphrodite are beginning to fail'. Darwin had devised a comparative method by which he analyzed vestigial structures to test his hypotheses about the route by which species had evolved. The example shows how he worked out the best questions to ask and then set out to obtain evidence pointing surely towards the answers.

Even so, it was difficult to win other biologists round to his way of thinking. When the President of the Linnaean Society reviewed the work of the society during 1858 he declared that, 'The year . . . has not been marked by any of those striking discoveries . . . ' Although the *Origin* made an immediate impact, the theory of natural selection did not win quick or widespread approval. Even Darwin's friends had difficulty understanding it. Thus T. H. Huxley, the man who did most to popularize and defend the theory, and who is reported to have said he was very stupid not to have thought of it for himself, had to struggle with the new perspective. Huxley lectured about it in 1860, yet Darwin wrote that, 'He gave no just idea of Natural Selection' and 'as an exposition of the doctrine the lecture seems to me an entire failure'. One of the reasons why it proved so difficult is that Darwin was advancing not one new theory but several related theories. Ernst Mayr (1982: 505–10) distinguishes five.

Darwin's theories

The first theory, which was the least contentious as far as the scientists were concerned, was that the world was not constant but evolving. The second was the theory of evolution by common descent, which stated that all organisms have descended from common ancestors by a continuous process whereby parental species have split into daughter species. The third was the theory that evolution occurred gradually. This was an argument which those who held an essentialist concept of species could not easily accept, for all their work was built upon the analysis of differences between species. Darwin may have been helped to his views on this matter by his experience on the Galapagos Islands where certain kinds of birds and turtles differed slightly from one island to another. Scientists who worked from fossils could often find no intermediate forms so they deduced that there had been sudden changes and were sceptical of the gradualist view. The fourth theory was that of populational speciation, which held that there was sufficient genetic variability for new species to emerge by a purely random process. This is now known as genetic drift. Two identical populations in similar but separate environments could become distinct without being subject to any external influences. For a

long time many evolutionists could not accept this and it
debate. The fifth theory was that evolution occurred by
features which did not help an organism survive in an
progressively eliminated.

According to Mayr (1982: 487–8), the single most
enabled Darwin to revolutionize biology was the change 'from
to population thinking'. He was led to it by the realization, stimulated
Malthus, that the struggle for existence due to competition was a struggle
between individuals rather than between species. Those who operated
with essentialist concepts assumed that all individual members of a species
were fundamentally similar, whereas every animal breeder knew well that
no two animals were identical and that by controlling the mating of
animals in the herd he could gradually change its composition. Darwin
seems to have learned a lot from animal breeders. The essentialists concentrated upon what they regarded as the type or typical form; they regarded
varying characters as accidental deviations from the type and as being of
no intrinsic interest. Darwin, and those who, after a significant interval,
followed him, regarded individual variations as more rewarding of study
than the similarities between members of the same class. Population thinking, as Mayr has presented it, requires an understanding of a genus, species
or variety as consisting of individuals that are similar in some respects and
dissimilar in others. The most generally used criterion to distinguish a
species is still that of fertile mating. A subspecies – which is the name now
given to what used to be called 'variety' – is defined as a subdivision of a
sexual species with all the attributes of a species except that reproductive
isolation is partial rather than complete. In other words, *Larus fuscus
britannicus* and *Larus fuscus antelius* are subdivisions of *Larus fuscus*
which maintain their distinctiveness because they do not share any territory in which they might mate (*Larus fuscus antelius* being found in
Siberia) though even if they do meet they may fail to mate, apparently from
choice. Gulls belonging to a subspecies may imprint upon parental features
like bill, eye colour, eye-ring etc., and mate only with birds possessing the
same features. In this way they can transform themselves into a distinctive
species. Among humans, West Africans and Norwegians maintain their
distinctiveness because mating is overwhelmingly within the group and
there are so few matings between these groups. It is possible that if they
shared territory, most individual West Africans and Norwegians would
for a time prefer to mate with others of the same appearance as themselves,
but their choices would be culturally conditioned since there seems to be
little or no imprinting in the human species. Moreover, humans differ in
many social attributes, like wealth, which can easily outweigh preferences

or physical features. These examples make it easier to appreciate the significance of the conception of a geographical race or subspecies as a distinct local form which maintains its special characteristics; it can evolve to a point such that it is no longer able to inter-breed with other forms that have split off from the same stock. *This* is the origin of species.

Thus Darwin worked with a new conception of species as a genealogical entity. He did not believe, as did the essentialists, that the similarity of species members derived from their common inheritance of a distinctive essence. Nor did he believe, with one school of nominalists, that a species was simply a class consisting of specimens which met chosen criteria of similarity. He saw it as a class which was distinctive because its members inherited common characters but inherited them in different combinations which were subject to continual modification. The grouping of specimens into a species was therefore a matter of judgement, and to this extent arbitrary; but in another sense species were also real entities since their common features derived from the real processes of inheritance and set limits to the exercise of judgement. As Ghiselin (1969: 54–7) writes, this new manner of thinking entailed a concept of population as a system of interacting individuals. The pattern of interaction, by its influence upon reproduction, influenced the nature of the individuals which constituted it. This relates to the definition above of a subspecies as a subdivision of a sexual species, because the patterns of reproductive interaction are different in sexual and asexual species.

The implications of sexuality for the evolution of species are developed in Darwin's book of 1871 entitled *The Descent of Man, and Selection in Relation to Sex*. Its central theme is sexual selection as a special case of natural selection. As the sociobiologists have recently emphasized, a male has sufficient sperm to inseminate numerous females, so his investment in a single copulation is usually small. Males are therefore ready to mate with any female and quite often do not even discriminate between females of their own and other species. A female, however, often produces relatively few eggs and may make a big investment in developing the embryos and taking care of the brood after hatching. If she mates with an unfit male or one of the wrong species she may produce an inferior or sterile brood. So it is in her interest to be selective. In some species, therefore (and the peacock is the most obvious example), males compete with one another to develop the sort of appearance which will give them an advantage in obtaining a mate. Darwin observed that just as the poultry breeder can develop the features of his birds which he thinks beautiful, so female birds in a state of nature have, by a long selection of the more attractive males, added to their beauty; the beautiful ones have thus been able to reproduce more than the ugly ones. Selection, whether artificial (by a human breeder) or natural, or sexual, is a matter of differential reproductive success and in the short run at least it may have nothing at all to do with adaptation to the environment. When male birds with beautiful tails obtain a better chance of securing a mate, the population to which they belong has become a system of individuals interacting in a manner that influences the population's evolution. This illustrates Ghiselin's argument.

By the time he came to write *The Descent*, Darwin was willing to follow Francis Galton and W. R. Greg in underlining the importance of natural selection as a process affecting the civilized nations and in calling for eugenic measures. He wrote 'the wonderful progress of the United States, as well as the character of the people, are the results of natural selection; for the more energetic, restless, and courageous men from all parts of Europe have emigrated . . . and have there succeeded best'. A few pages later there was an implicit comparison as he wrote about the declining fertility and likely extinction of savage races – with their smaller brains – unable to change their habits when brought into contact with civilized races. At the same time it would be misguided to attribute Darwin's over-emphasis upon the importance of selection in social change to the temper of his times. Darwin's theory does not depend on any analogy with the kind of social struggle supposed to be responsible for nineteenth-century progress. In the study of evolution something corresponding to 'struggle' occurs when one species uses energy to prevent another species feeding on its territory or otherwise competing for resources. This direct competition is contrasted with indirect competition, in which two species feed off the same scarce resource and whichever can feed faster has the advantage. Indirect competition is usually the more important.

The student of evolution is concerned with fitness not in the sense that the medal-winning athlete is fitter than the person who is overweight, but with fitness as an ability to survive and reproduce. The essential element is differential fertility: those populations which are able to reproduce and multiply in successive generations are fitter than those which cannot. Darwin emphasized selection the more heavily in that part of *The Descent* which seems to have a racialist flavour because he subscribed to a blending theory of inheritance according to which an inherited character appears as a compromise between parental attributes (to over-simplify, a black-haired man and a blonde woman will have brown-haired children). He did not know, as Mendel did, that inheritance was particulate. According to a blending theory, if a clever person married someone stupid, the capacities of the former would all be lost in the next generation (a stimulus to eugenic proposals). As the effects (whether beneficent or undesirable) of a new variant would disappear so quickly, selection would have to be drastic to be effective. The cause of variation was not central to Darwin's problem and his mistaken presentation of it has sometimes led to misinterpretations of his argument.

The changes to prevailing modes of thought which Darwin introduced were revolutionary in many respects. Ernst Mayr (1982: 501) lists six in particular:
1 The replacement of a static by an evolving world
2 The demonstration of the implausibility of creationism
3 The refutation of cosmic teleology
4 The application to man of the principle of common descent
5 The explanation of the natural world in terms of natural selection
6 The replacement of essentialism by population thinking.
The readjustments that had to be made were therefore far more extensive than those entailed by the scientific revolutions in the sphere of physics which are most frequently utilized in undergraduate teaching about the philosophy of science. As was only to be expected, they occasioned long and bitter controversies. Darwin himself did not resolve all the difficulties in the new approach or see all its implications. Other scholars, try as they might, often had great difficulty applying the new principles.

Attempted applications

The year 1859 was also notable for the founding of the Société d'Anthropologie de Paris. For the next twenty years or so scholars elsewhere looked to Paris for the most authoritative declarations about racial classifications. The Parisian school was led by the craniologist Paul Broca and its main basis was in anatomy, so it had some difficulty in coming to terms with the new Darwinian interpretation of evolution. A. de Quatrefages, a monogenist, accepted most of Darwin's arguments but objected that Darwin had no clear conception of species: 'he often opposes *species* and *race*, which he also calls *variety*, but without ever stating clearly what he understands by one or the other'. If species were distinct because they could not inter-breed, what explained the emergence of sterility between units that previously had been inter-fertile? Any conception of gradual and progressive evolution was in conflict with 'the isolation of specific groups from the earliest ages of the world, and the maintenance of organic order through all the revolutions of the globe' (1879: 95–102). Darwinian doctrine generated a host of problems. Physical anthropologists were ready to agree that the groups designated races in popular speech were usually political units of mixed origin, but they were reluctant to abandon the polygenetic idea of underlying differences, particularly those associated with the cranium, for they might one day explain much that was puzzling.

For a time, therefore, the idea of race as type persisted alongside that of race as subspecies. The change-over to a Darwinian mode of explanation was neither simple nor straightforward. This may be illustrated by a consideration of the work of someone who occupied only a minor place in the history of science but was much respected in his own generation. John Beddoe (1826–1922) was a president of the Royal Anthropological Institute, Fellow of the Royal Society, Fellow of the Royal College of Physicians and honorary doctor of laws of the University of Edinburgh. He was honoured by anthropological and scientific societies in Belgium, France, Germany, Russia and the United States. Beddoe was an extraordinarily assiduous collector of information about eye and hair colour and of measurements of peoples' heads; yet he did not accept Darwin's view that progress depends upon an investigator's collecting the sort of observation that tells for or against a theory. Beddoe set out to test, not theories, but the reliability of the material with which theories were, one day, to be constructed (1885: 299). His biggest book, *The Races of Britain* (1885), like some of his articles, consists of as many pages of tables as of text.

Beddoe's belief that problems were to be solved by patient labour did not protect him from confusion. He terminated a series of lectures in 1891 by stating three main conclusions. The first was that, 'We have fairly satisfactory proof that under ordinary circumstances the physical characteristics of well-defined races of men, such as form, colour, and even size, are absolutely permanent.' The second, that 'Natural selection may alter the type'; and the third that acquired characters are not inherited. The first two of these conclusions are contradictory. If natural selection alters the type, there can be no permanence of type. Beddoe called himself an evolutionist; he accepted the theory of natural selection; but he had not eliminated from his explanatory scheme a set of typological assumptions that he probably acquired in the years before he became acquainted with Darwin's theories. At one point he declared, 'The rule is that an anthropological type once in possession of the ground is never wholly dispossessed or extirpated.' At another he told his Scottish audience that Sir Walter Scott was 'the product of the Scottish border, and could not have been born anywhere else' (1912: 53, 188), pronouncements which could have come from Knox or Nott. The question to which he led up was, 'To what races or types is the future to belong?' although he had no technique that would enable him to extrapolate from the past to the future. Among humans, he said, natural selection was complemented by conjugal selection. He had checked the hair colour of 524 Bristol women, to find that among those with red or black hair 76.2 per cent were married; among those with fair, brown or dark hair 86 per cent were married (from which it might be inferred, in the phrase of a later generation, that gentlemen prefer blondes). Beddoe also described processes of social selection. He had the greatest respect for Scotsmen and for fair-haired, long-headed, races, but doubted if the future world would belong to them because their birth rate was low. Blond children needed fresh air and abundant food. They did not adapt well to city life and were more likely to die from rheumatism, scarlatina and throat infections. Because of urbanization England was experiencing a reflux migration: the Gaelic and Iberian races who had earlier been pushed westwards were moving back and tending to swamp the blond Teutons.

Some of Beddoe's statements sound inexcusable to a modern reader (like his observation that Jews are gradually attracting to themselves the whole moveable wealth of the world) but he did not subscribe to the typological thesis that race determined history. His interest was in the way history – especially because of migration and marriage – was changing the old pattern whereby the peoples of different regions each had their distinctive appearance. He wanted to record what remained of the races of Britain before railways and other contemporary changes mixed them up. Beddoe's objection to such mixing was not racialist, but aesthetic, for he feared that if present trends were to continue 'we should have a general prevalence of dull shades of brown to the confusion and despair of artists'. He concluded his lecture:

> finally, there are assuredly diversities of gifts pertaining to diverse breeds of men; and unless we are all reduced to the dull dead level of socialism, and perhaps even in that case, for the sake of relief, we shall continue to stand in need of all these gifts. Let us hope, then, that blue eyes, as well as brown eyes, will continue to beam on our descendants, and that heads will never come to be framed all upon one and the same pattern. (1912: 189)

Most physical anthropologists of Beddoe's generation were interested in craniology and there was no reason in principle to suggest that the enormous labour that went into this research would prove of very little long-term value. It was a blind alley in science, but no one could know that at the time. The really difficult question is to decide what an anthropologist of Beddoe's generation should have been studying instead. If Beddoe was biased, what was he biased away from? In retrospect it can be seen that the years from 1859 to 1930 were a dead period for physical anthropology as a generalizing science. No progress could be made in solving the central problems until work in other fields – mainly in genetics but also in the study of human development – had reached the point where they could bear effectively on questions about variation in the shape of skulls, and so on. It was a period when physical anthropologists might have been better employed cultivating their links with archaeologists and developing their subject's historical dimension. Had Beddoe and some of his contemporaries appreciated that 'observation must be for or against some view if it is to be of service' they might not have misdirected their energies into such unprofitable channels.

Other anthropologists who tried to apply ideas of natural and social selection to the human species, and particularly to race relations, were less cautious. The three who are often grouped with Beddoe as representatives of an anthropo-sociological school were Otto Ammon in Germany, Georges Vacher de Lapouge in France and G. C. Closson in the United States. The 'laws' postulated by the two first named have been conveniently summarized by Sorokin (1928: 233–51). Vacher de Lapouge was particularly pessimistic, maintaining that natural selection operated to the advantage of the worst elements in the population. In war-time it was the patriots who were killed, not the cowards. In democratic societies the demagogue and trickster triumphed over the honest man. Charity preserved the weak, capitalism destroyed natural aristocracies and the poor had most children. 'I am convinced [he wrote in 1887] that in the next century millions will cut each others' throats because of one or two degrees more or less of cephalic index. This is the sign which is replacing the Biblical *shibboleth* and linguistic affinities, and by which people will recognize one another as belonging to the same nationalities and by which the most sentimental will assist in the wholesale slaughter of peoples'. De Lapouge was a socialist who sought to revise Marxist doctrine to accord with what he considered Darwinian principles (Thuillier, 1977: 53–61).

Much of the literature of this period about physical and social differences has been classed by later commentators as social Darwinist, but this is misleading since it is difficult to find among the various authors any group who shared a common set of principles, apart from those who were supporters of the Eugenics Society (Halliday, 1971). There were writers who subscribed to some theses that can reasonably be described as social Darwinist but were fundamentally opposed to other important elements in this same outlook: such was the case of Herbert Spencer (Freeman, 1974). There were other writers, like William Graham Sumner who wrote in a social Darwinist vein at one stage of their careers and then changed their approach (for a critique of the loose use of the term, see Bannister, 1979). In Mayr's view (1982: 883) social Darwinism 'praised struggle for existence, unmerciful competition, and social bias under the excuse that this was what Darwin taught. Unfortunately the historiography of this subject is as biased as was the movement itself.' 'Social Darwinism' is a label applied by its critics to the lines of argument they criticized. If the views of the authors themselves are to be appreciated properly their various arguments need separate examination.

The belief in white racial superiority appears to have reached its highest level in Western Europe in the two decades preceding World War One, yet in that time there was no publication which set out succinctly a theoretical justification for that belief comparable to the set of propositions featured in Nott and Gliddon's *Types of Mankind*. The most systematic theorist was Vacher de Lapouge, but it is improbable that he and other theorists contributed as much to the belief in white racial superiority as the literary and historical tradition which had equated race with nation. Soon after his appointment, in 1895, as the British Secretary of State for the Colonies, Joseph Chamberlain proclaimed his belief that 'the British race is the greatest governing race that the world has ever seen'. The theorists would have ridiculed the notion of a British race; they saw the British population as forming a political unit composed of peoples of different race. Chamberlain and those who, like him, talked of race in the context of empire, probably regarded race as a synonym for nation. They may have been content that their claims appeared to be supported by biology, but it is doubtful if their use of the word race had the biological connotations a modern reader might assume. Nor did they necessarily believe that hereditary qualities would overcome adverse environmental conditions. The historian J. A. Froude had concluded (1894: 7–8) that 'the experience of all mankind declares that a race of men sound in soul and limb can be bred and reared only in the exercise of plough and spade, in the free air and sunshine, with country enjoyments and amusements, never amidst foul drains and smoke blacks and the eternal clank of machinery'. The anthropo-sociologists were not the only commentators who thought that city life destroyed the distinctive characters of the finer races. Whites might be superior for the time being but their position was precarious. Parents in the higher and more intelligent classes had fewer children; ill-educated Irish Catholic parents contributed disproportionately to population growth; eugenic measures were necessary if the national stock was not to decline. Thus in the early years of twentieth-century Britain 'racial hygiene' became a slogan for a campaign to persuade people to wash themselves properly and to lead a healthy life. The confidence about the British race expressed from public platforms by speakers like Chamberlain and Lord Rosebery was therefore only one aspect of a more complex mood.

Popular beliefs in white superiority were probably conditioned by the success of Britain and other European countries in extending their influence over so much of the world. Since the theorists were members of societies in which such beliefs were widespread they were no doubt influenced by them, but the rise in Germany's power and the growing tensions within Europe exerted restraint. Nor was there any close fit between doctrine and practice in countries where whites were in close contact with blacks. A comparison between East Africa and Nigeria in the period 1880–1914 suggests that the stereotype of African inferiority which emerged in Kenya was a European creation deriving from the social and political desires of the white settlers and not from either genuine observations or from European doctrines (Perraton, 1967: 242). In view of the readiness with which some authors have linked social Darwinist ideas with colonial settings it is also notable that a study of the British in Central Africa comments on the absence (at least up to 1890) of any mention of such doctrines in discussions of racial relations or as a justification for imperial control (Cairns, 1965: 237–8).

In the development of sociological explanations a key figure was William Graham Sumner (1840–1910), who became Professor of Political and Social Science at Yale in 1872. He taught there the first college course in the United States to be entitled 'Sociology'. Coming upon Spencer's work and plunging into Darwin, Haeckel, and Huxley as well, Sumner saturated himself with evolutionism (Hofstadter, 1955: 51–66; Bannister, 1979: 97–113). As a social critic, Sumner's sympathies were with 'the forgotten man' – the middle-class citizen who went quietly about his business, providing for himself and his family without making demands upon the state. Society was a super-organism changing at a geological tempo in accordance with natural laws. Socialists and other social meddlers who ignored those laws and engaged in 'the absurd effort to make the world over' were foolish romantics unwilling to learn the lessons of history.

As his teaching became more systematic Sumner regretted the lack of a suitable textbook; he sat down to write one of his own, which became *Folkways*, one of the most influential works of early twentieth-century sociology. Apart from his own ideas, his inspiration came from Herbert Spencer and two Europeans, Julius Lippert and Gustav Ratzenhofer, though he also borrowed the concept of ethnocentrism without acknowledgement from Gumplowicz (1881: 71) and has been credited with its invention by generations of American sociologists who did not read the classics. In *Folkways* Sumner presented a panorama of human customs, interpreting them as instinctive responses to the stimuli of hunger, sex, vanity, and fear, selectively guided by pain and pleasure. His emphasis was upon the limited ability of 'stateways' and legislation to change behaviour with its deep physical and emotional roots. This shifted the stress from the efficacy of competition to the stability of social forms. It is evident in the book's most influential innovation, the concept of *mores* (the plural form of the Latin *mos*, meaning custom).

Folkways is subtitled 'A Study of the Sociological Importance of Usages, Manners, Customs, Mores and Morals'. It brings together reports from different times and different parts of the world concerning such topics as slavery, abortion, infanticide, cannibalism, marriage, incest, kinship, primitive justice, sacral harlotry, and so forth. Sumner begins with the remark that 'the first task of life is to live. Men begin with acts, not with thoughts.' From man's solutions of problems arise customs. From customs and instincts arise folkways which gradually become arbitrary, and imperative. They are seen as 'right' and 'true'. When they are developed into doctrines of welfare they become mores; this leads to the definition, 'The mores are the folkways, including the philosophical and ethical generalizations as to societal welfare which are suggested by them, and inherent in them, as they grow.' Later comes a chapter entitled 'The Mores Can Make Anything Right and Prevent Condemnation of Anything'. This proposition was demonstrated by examples of modes of punishment and courting customs formerly acceptable in Europe which an American of Sumner's generation would have thought contrary to human feeling.

When he came to discuss blacks and whites in Southern society Sumner maintained that prior to the Civil War relations were based on legal rights and the races lived in peace and concord. The war 'was due to a great divergence in the mores of the North and the South' and afterwards blacks and whites were left to find a new basis for living together. Because the whites had never been converted from the old mores they and the blacks had not at that time made new mores.

> legislation cannot make mores. We see also that mores do not form under social convulsion and discord . . . The two races are separating more than ever before . . . It is evidently impossible for anyone to interfere. We are like spectators at a great natural convulsion. The results will be such as the facts and forces call for. We cannot foresee them. They do not depend on ethical views any more than the volcanic eruption on Martinique contained an ethical element. (1906: 81–2)

There were powerful forces in the United States in favour of a do-nothing policy with respect to Southern race relations. Sumner's presentation of the problem and his use of the concepts of folkways and mores were widely followed by social scientists, particularly to imply that legislation on inter-racial behaviour would be in vain. If he accepted the mores as a homogeneous, unproblematic, and a fairly static social entity, the observer was likely to underestimate the differences between individuals and groups and the changes in time. In the present connection, however, it is important to note that Sumner's conceptions of the 'struggle for existence' and social selection, though inspired by Spencer and Darwin, were not really Darwinist, and that his concepts of folkways and mores bore little relation to the elements of social Darwinism in his earlier essays.

An important study which cast doubt upon the value of craniological studies was conducted by Franz Boas of Columbia University on behalf of the United States Immigration Commission. Concern had been expressed that the United States was admitting immigrants of inferior stock. Boas examined the hair colour, height and weight, head length and breadth, and face breadth, in European-born Americans and their American-born children. In 1911 he reported important differences, particularly in the cephalic index (relation of the breadth of the head to its length, seen from above). The figures suggested that the round-headed East European Jewish children became more long-headed in the United States, whereas the long-headed South Italians became more short-headed. Both were approaching a uniform type. Moreover, the influence of the American environment made itself felt with increasing intensity the longer the time elapsed between the arrival of the mother and the birth of her child. The significance of this finding was negative. 'I find myself unable to give an explanation of the phenomena' wrote the author. Though the changes were small, the findings were in conflict with prevailing expectations and, because they arose within barely a single generation, it did not appear that they could be explained as an outcome of natural selection. Boas concluded 'as long as we do not know the causes of the observed changes, we must speak of a plasticity (as opposed to a permanence) of types' (see 1940: 71). Subsequent research has shown that there was nothing unusual about the changes reported and that, being small, they could be attributed to environmental influences like that of diet (see also Stocking 1968: 161–94).

Darwin's work destroyed the notion of racial types without replacing it with a concept that could easily be grasped, even by those specialists who were interested in racial variation among humans. Only in the 1930s did the various new lines of research start to come together again in a synthesis which has enabled the student to appreciate why the replacement for the concept of racial type was that of population. The foundation of this synthesis was population genetics, the branch of genetics which investigates the changes in gene frequencies. According to Mayr (1982: 553–6), it consisted of two largely independent research programmes: mathematical population genetics and ecological genetics. The former was a development of the Hardy-Weinberg equilibrium principle established in 1908. Sir Ronald Fisher and other mathematical geneticists extended the statistical analysis by treating the gene as the unit of selection and attributing to each gene a definite fitness value. Fitness was defined as the contribution a given gene makes to the gene pool of the next generation. Mayr (1982: 588–9) remarks that some, if not most, of the current criticism of the theory of selection consists of attacks on the un-Darwinian assumption that genes instead of phenotypes are the units of selection. Ecological genetics, by contrast, deals with the actual populations of living organisms studied in the field and in the laboratory. Selection favours certain qualities but it cannot simultaneously improve all of them to the same degree. A bottom limit is set by the principle that can be traced to Cuvier, that at all stages of evolution an animal must remain able to feed itself, reproduce, and evade predators.

Between 1936 and 1947 biologists from several specialized fields and various countries achieved a consensus which Sir Julian Huxley named the evolutionary synthesis. According to Mayr (1982: 567) they accepted two major conclusions:

> (1) that evolution is gradual, being explicatory in terms of small genetic changes and recombination and in terms of ordering of this genetic variation by natural selection; and (2) that by introducing the population concept, by considering species as reproductively isolated aggregates of population, and by analyzing the effects of ecological factors (niche occupation, competition, adaptive radiation) on diversity and on the origin of the higher taxa, one can explain all evolutionary phenomena in a manner that is consistent both with the known genetic mechanism and with the observational evidence of the naturalists.

Many of the objections that have been raised against the Darwinian view of evolution turn upon gaps in the fossil record. For example, it has not been easy to show how reptiles could have evolved into mammals. To take a detailed point, the former have a single earbone and at least four bones in the lower jaw, whereas mammals have two further earbones but only one jawbone. Yet fossil finds in England now constitute an almost perfect transition, enabling the palaeontologist to explain how the forces on the jaw joint change and how the auditory perception was improved. Other finds have pointed the way to more satisfactory explanations of the evolution of the eye, of flight, and comparable problems. Viruses and bacteria can be traced back to pre-Cambrian times, while laboratory experiments can provide accounts of what must have been the earliest self-replicating systems that must have been close to the origin of life itself.

Reductionist explanations

The debate about whether human races were distinctive species or subspecies was a dispute about classification. Darwin upset that debate by advancing a convincing theory which showed that species and subspecies were evolving. It might be convenient for some purposes to have snapshots of what they were like at particular moments in time, but that only distracted attention from the invisible influences which were determining the ways in which they changed. These influences were numerous, and their inter-relations complex: on the one hand was the genetic material of inheritance, which though divisible into an extraordinary number of elements, was, in a sense, of a general or standardized character; on the other hand was the innumerable collection of particular circumstances affecting the ways in which different populations in different environments were organized and interacted with their genetic inheritance. Darwin himself gave an illustration of the way different species could be dependent upon one another when he explained how a particular kind of clover could be fertilized only by a bumble bee because honey bees were not heavy enough to make an entrance to the flower. One of the circumstances determining the availability of bumble bees was the vulnerability of their nests to field mice. There were fewer field mice where there were many cats, and many cats where there were human habitations. So the clover could survive more easily near villages.

To account for the various species and subspecies of clover, bees, mice and cats, and the directions in which they were evolving, was hard enough. To do the same for humans was immensely more difficult for a variety of reasons including the special character of the human species, sometimes called its plasticity or adaptability, and its possession of the special attribute of consciousness. Humans can be aware of themselves as individuals belonging to groups, having a place in the natural world, and utilizing particular means to attain their goals, in ways that other animals cannot. They have the power to discover the natural influences that bear upon their evolution and to modify these influences, striving for ends that otherwise would not be achieved. To account for the evolution of a species which possesses this kind of consciousness is more difficult than accounting for one without it (Crook, 1980).

This problem may be seen as a special case of the more important problem of differing levels of complexity which has occasioned arguments about reductionist explanations.

They often start from the probability that the world has evolved from inorganic to organic material, and from forms of life without consciousness to those distinctive of humans. For this reason it is appropriate to count the level of human culture as uppermost. It is then maintained that the objects of study at each level are composed of elements found at the level beneath and that they can, in part, be explained by reference to the same principles as are used when accounting for observations on the lower level. The disputes centre upon what is called the 'remainder', those observations which are not accounted for by an explanation in terms of the next level down. Sometimes the issue is put the other way round. It is said that as life evolves, whenever it reaches a new level, new and previously unpredictable characteristics of organization emerge. To discuss levels in terms of reduction is to look at them from a standpoint often used in the philosophy of science. To discuss them in terms of emergence is to follow the course of evolution. By way of illustration it may be helpful to consider courtship. In many human societies certain kinds of behaviour can be identified as courtship, but they vary from one society to another and change over time. The patterns of behaviour are socially or culturally conditioned by the expectations each generation learns from its predecessors and, in industrial societies, by the advertizing of goods as likely to impress the people who are the objects of courtship. Seen from a distance, courtship reveals features which may not be in the minds of the people who engage in it. People tend to court others of similar socio-economic status and people who live close enough for frequent contact. Patterns of expected behaviour differ for males and females, and vary according to their ages. It can nevertheless be argued that under these differences lie biological influences, like sexual drives, and personality compatibilities, so that human courtship can be explained in the same terms as the courtship of other species and be the better understood for being located in human evolutionary history. It might be claimed that no explanation of why, among humans, males take the more active part in courtship, can be satisfactory unless it forms part of such a wider account. Yet the process of reduction does not stop with such an explanation. Courtship behaviour is built up out of locomotion, energy utilization, metabolic processes, and so on, which can be seen as questions of physiology, and these in turn as the expression of molecular genetics and then, perhaps ultimately, as chemistry or physics. The organization of scientific activity reflects, if only for convenience, such a series of levels in the complexity of phenomena, though the theories of the basic subjects like physics are no simpler than those of the subjects at the other end of the scale.

The reductionist approach draws attention to certain inter-relations between scientific disciplines but some research problems are not usefully formulated in this way. It may be better to regard courtship behaviour as suggesting different questions to the sociologist, geographer, psychologist, ethologist, evolutionist and physiologist. Each kind of specialist seeks to answer his or her own special questions and these sometimes include questions about the relations between the modes of explanation characteristic of different disciplines.

Discussions of the philosophy of social science have been dominated for a whole generation by the work of two men, Sir Karl Popper and T. S. Kuhn, who have been concerned with the growth of knowledge about the natural world and have taken nearly all their examples from the history of physics. This has had the unfortunate effect that many sociologists have defined their subject in terms of what differentiates its methods and approach from that of physics. They have overlooked the important differences between the biological and physical sciences and the argument (set out by Mayr, 1982: 77) that evolutionary biology can be a bridge between the physical sciences on the one side and the social sciences and humanities on the other. According to Mayr's argument there have for thousands of years been two biologies. One, which used to be practised under the name of medicine or physiology, has been an attempt to discover proximate causes or to answer 'how?' questions. The other, which has been known as natural history, has studied ultimate or evolutionary causes by addressing 'why?' questions. For example, at certain times of the year particular bird species migrate. The first kind of biologist, whom Mayr calls a functional biologist, explains the migration as a response to photoperiodicity: the bird is ready to migrate once the number of hours of daylight falls to a particular level and it leaves as soon thereafter as weather conditions are favourable. The evolutionary biologist explains why birds of this species but not of other species migrate, by referring to a genotype acquired through selection over millions of years of evolution. In evolutionary biology almost all phenomena and processes are explained through inferences from comparative studies. These depend upon careful and detailed descriptive studies which often have to be carried out in difficult conditions. To study the behaviour of the nocturnal mouse lemur of the Madagascan forests required unusual patience and fortitude. This research proved important because it showed that at the very root of primate evolution there was an extremely loose kind of relationship between the sexes, and so it supported the theory of sexual selection mentioned earlier. Scientific research of this kind is unable to manipulate the variables, but depends upon good field work. It is not much concerned with formulating laws, and such laws as have been advanced are mostly probabilistic statements which are not falsified by a single contrary instance. The growth of knowledge in this field, as in much sociology, consists in the development of new concepts and the repeated refinement of definitions by which these concepts are articulated.

In the latter part of the twentieth century it is taken for granted that the processes of socio-cultural evolution occur on a higher level than those of biological evolution. In biological evolution, information is transmitted from one generation to the next through people's genes. In socio-cultural evolution, information is transmitted by teaching of either an explicit or an implicit character. In modern society people learn a great deal from attending school, reading, watching films and so on. A library represents a store-house of information available to people when they want to use it. As a process for transmitting the results of learning, this is infinitely more powerful than the passing on of information by inheritance. Of course, some authors argued this a hundred years ago too, but the differences were not always clearly expressed and others were inclined to insist that though there might be a remainder when social phenomena were explained in biological terms, that remainder was neither very large nor very important. It was therefore a significant achievement when social scientists first described the emergent phenomena and showed how they necessitated new socio-cultural processes of evolution. One influential statement of this kind was the paper by the United States anthropologist A. L. Kroeber (1917) in which he distinguished between organic evolution and what he called superorganic evolution. A parallel declaration was that of the sociologist Robert E. Park when he wrote:

> The individual man is the bearer of a double inheritance. As a member of a race, he transmits by interbreeding a biological inheritance. As a member of society or a social group, on the other hand, he transmits by communication a social inheritance. The particular complex of inherit-able characters which characterizes the individuals of a racial group constitutes the racial temperament. The particular group of habits, accommodations, sentiments, attitudes and ideals transmitted by communication and education constitutes a social tradition. (1921: 140–1)

The levels of complexity are distinguished by the mode of inheritance, either biological or biological plus social.

It is not always so easy to distinguish one level from another. Questions arise as to how many levels can usefully be identified, and about the relations between them. Lower levels may set limits to what can be done on higher levels, but do they exercise a continuing influence or an occasional one? Do not the higher levels sometimes influence what happens on the lower levels? One use of the notion of levels that has been much discussed in social science, is that of Karl Marx. In the preface to his *A Contribution to the Critique of Political Economy* (1859) Marx stated that the foundation of social life consisted in the material productive forces (the ways in which humans win a living from nature) and in the relations of production necessary to the harnessing of these forces (e.g. the social organization used to herd the cattle, till the fields or fish the waters). Upon this infrastructure arose a legal and political superstructure conditioned by the mode of production. The technology for utilizing the material productive forces developed; every now and then it reached a point at which its further development was restricted by the superstructure which conditioned the ways in which humans thought about their societies. At that point the productive forces broke the restraining bonds and forced through a revolution in which the superstructure was brought into line with the form that the process of production had assumed. In this vision, the lower levels dictated to the higher ones though in between periods of revolution the superstructure might develop in independent ways. It was a scheme for interpreting history.

The element of reduction in this kind of argument differs from that mentioned earlier. Marx did not maintain that the activity of people engaged in the productive process was to be explained in terms of their physiology and then as a product of their genes. Nor did he claim that the legal and political superstructure differed from the relations of production in the sort of way that human social organization differed from that of apes, or animal society from plant society.

The notion of levels can be used in varying ways for varying purposes and as many levels can be distinguished as is useful to an argument. For example, it could be argued that with the growth of cities men have competed more fiercely for ownership of the land in the centre than for land on the outskirts because possession of the former confers greater advantages. Such competition occurs on the ecological level and can be compared with the competition of animals for territory within which to forage or nest. Among humans it gives rise to differential land prices. Since land in the centre is expensive it is used more intensively. The buildings in the city centre become multi-storey office blocks. Only very rich people can afford houses in this zone. Thus economic and social patterns are determined by ecological ones. These patterns have their own dysfunctions in the form of congestion and pollution. With technological advance and higher living standards, more people have their own means of transport. Shopping centres and new businesses are then located away from the centre and relative land prices change because new economic and social relations have affected ecological ones. In such an argument it is unwise to push the claim that changes on the lower level determine changes on the upper one because many variables are involved and technological innovation is usually an extraneous factor. Yet the notion of levels is useful because it can be used in a way that, by drawing attention to new parallels, suggests novel questions to ask. In this manner it can open fresh and illuminating perspectives.

Social ecology

The pioneer of ecological analysis in sociology was Robert E. Park (1863–1944). His pupil, Everett C. Hughes, wrote in 1973:

> Park was interested in human ecology as early as 1913 and '14 and tried to persuade his son to become a human ecologist starting with the study of biology of the new ecological sort. When he came to Chicago [in 1913] there was such an interest in the city and the things that were happening to the immigrants there, that he fell in with that project and devoted himself to it rather fully for quite a long time. In 1925 or so, he first gave a course in 'Human Ecology'. I was in it. The emphasis was on large scale human geography; the development of navigation, of world-wide insurance, and news-gathering, and all those devices which made it possible to colonize and to establish economic enterprises at a great distance . . . Park was interested in smaller scale problems but that was only a phase, and not the major one of his thought and career. After he left Chicago at the end of the 1920s, he began his more serious writing on human ecology, considering it as the competition and accommodations made by human beings in their occupancy of the whole of the earth's surface. In his later papers he is interested in the division of labor between the races and the nations. He sees migration as the great process; that and competition are very important in bringing about whatever kinds of communities there are in the world.

Park's conviction that something new was to be learned about human society by noting the features it shared with animal and plant society can be seen in the very influential textbook written by him and his colleague Ernest W. Burgess. Entitled *An Introduction to the Science of Sociology*, this appeared in 1921 and contained 174 passages extracted from the works of a variety of authors but bound together in a distinctive synthesis. A prominent place was given to ecological concepts, for Park sought to utilize accounts of the lives of plants, ants, pigs, and so on, both to bring out that which was distinctively human and to uncover patterns of unconscious relations. Modern sociologists may recognize concepts of adaptation, colonization, commensalism, dominance, invasion, isolation, migration, parasitism, segregation, succession, and symbiosis, even if they do not use these themselves. They may forget that all of them are ecological concepts that can be applied to plants as well as humans. Plant life, wrote Park, offered the simplest examples of communities that were not societies. Anyone who has tended a rock garden has seen how some species spread at the expense of others, acquiring a monopoly over a territory. Some plants live together in peace. Others migrate or invade and establish their dominance. Sometimes one species gives way to a series of others, establishing a natural succession. Such concepts the Chicago school of sociology afterwards used in their studies of the natural areas of the city.

When using ecological concepts it is often helpful to distinguish different levels of organization. In 1921 Park and Burgess described competition as the most fundamental of four such levels, relating them to different types of interaction: the most fundamental type of interaction was competition, which gave rise to ecological organization. This represented human individuals and groups as competing for territory and resources in a manner comparable to animals and plants. On the second level was economic organizations, manifested in the division of labour produced by competition. This was the level on which racial and other forms of group consciousness appeared. The third level, that of political organization, was a means of dealing with the crises generated by economic organization. At this level three new types of interaction, conflict, accommodation and assimilation, appeared. Then came the fourth level of social organization (to give it the name proposed by Frazier, 1957: 34). In 1921 Park did not separate this from the third level, though in 1939 he called it the level of the personal and cultural, maintaining that 'one may think of these different levels as constituting a hierarchy of relations of such a nature that change upon any one level will invariably have repercussions, not immediately, but finally, upon every other' (1950: 107).

The ecological perspective explains why the Park and Burgess *Introduction* gives space to many matters foreign to modern textbooks and neglects some topics that now feature prominently. The chapter on competition includes a famous passage from Adam Smith on the natural harmony of individual interests, explaining how by pursuing his own interest a man is led as by an invisible hand to promote the common good in the most effectual manner. Park did not regard this proposition as necessarily applying outside the economic sphere, yet it is striking that the chapter on conflict includes no discussion of conflicts of interest (indeed the notion of interest appears chiefly in a psychological sense, 'an unsatisfied capacity, corresponding to an unrealized condition'). Conflict is presented only as a feature of collective behaviour without mention of the way conflicts are structured or individuals coerced. It is said that 'the psychological bond of the class is community of interests' but there is no discussion or proper definition of class. The unity of the social group among humans is described in terms of shared social tradition without mention of external oppositions. 'All social problems turn out finally to be problems of social control' (1921: 785), yet there seems to be no place for a conception of power in the elucidation of these problems! Nowhere in the book is there reference to such matters as the inheritance of social inequality. Valuable as was Park's use of the ecological metaphor it may have contributed to some blind spots in his analysis of types of interaction as forming the superstructure of social patterns. The study of collective behaviour needs to be complemented by the study of social structure.

The direction of Park's personal interests may explain his description of Sumner's *Folkways* as 'the most subtle analysis and suggestive statement about human nature and social relations that has yet been written in English'. Park not only included selections concerning folkways, mores, and the in-group/out-group distinction, but adopted in his commentary some of Sumner's basic assumptions. 'As members of society, men act as they do elsewhere from motives that they do not fully comprehend, in order to fulfil aims of which they are but dimly or not at all conscious . . . Under the influence of the mores men act typically, and so representatively, not as individuals but as members of a group.' Park distinguished the political from the cultural process. Politics were concerned with matters in regard to which there was division and difference, but 'the political process, by which a society or social group formulates its wishes and enforces them, goes on within the limits of the mores' (1921: 30, 52–3). This meant that every time a Negro appeared in an unaccustomed situation it provoked comment as something contrary to the mores. Though Park might himself have acknowledged that this was a facet of the relations of power between black and white he did not say so and his writing, like that of most of his contemporaries, neglects this dimension in a fashion that must astonish a later generation.

The chapters in the *Introduction* dealing with race relations, like those reflecting the ecological approach, were mostly Park's work. Ecology was rarely absent from Park's view of race relations; it underlay his conception of prejudice which he defined as 'a spontaneous, more or less instinctive, defence-reaction, the practical effect of which is to restrict free competition between races'. Prejudice was an attempt to restrain competition, to establish a monopolistic hold over a particular social territory (1921: 623). On another, later, occasion, Park asked why anyone should expect racial peace before there was racial justice but the difficulty with his early formulation was that it left no place for such considerations. Park observed that caste, by relegating the subject race to an inferior status gave it a monopoly over the unattractive roles at the same time as it gave the other category its monopoly. He went on 'when this status is accepted by the subject people, as is the case where the caste or slavery systems become fully established, racial competition ceases and racial animosity tends to disappear. This is the explanation of the intimate and friendly relations which so often existed in slavery between master and servant.' Slavery was discussed in the chapter on accommodation, not in that on conflict. There was no mention, for example, of slave revolts, suicides, or escapes. If conflict, accommodation, and assimilation were types of interaction which were acted out on a basis of the more fundamental phenomenon of competition some means had to be found for analyzing monopoly power and the processes by which part of the population was reduced to inferior statuses. This Park did not achieve. He saw the process of competition as resulting in an economic equilibrium on which a political order was built, and did not consider the ways in which political considerations dictated the terms on which individuals could compete (1921: 510). Racial conflicts sprang from the unwillingness of those of superior status to compete on equal terms with those of inferior status (1921: 578). The aggressive aspects of prejudice were not mentioned; nor were ways in which unwillingness to compete was translated into political action and that action then intensified the original unwillingness.

In 1921 it was not generally appreciated, even among social scientists, that racial prejudice was a disposition towards other groups that children learned as they grew up. Perhaps only a minority claimed explicitly that prejudices were biologically inherited characteristics of a group, but many more took racial prejudice for granted as something scarcely requiring investigation. This was the background to the discovery of stereotyping. In the early 1920s an American educational research worker gave some classes of school children the following silent reading test:

> Aladdin was the son of a poor tailor. He lived in Peking, the capital city of China. He was always lazy and liked to play better than to work. What kind of boy was he: Indian, Negro, Chinese, French or Dutch?

To his amazement, he found that many children in the border states were so impressed by the statement that the boy was lazy that they answered that he must be a Negro (Lasker, 1929: 237). From his, and others' observations grew a series of enquiries into the promotion and function of set ideas, followed later by psycho-analytic studies of prejudice. They were intellectually exciting developments that transformed the understanding of race relations. Park is not to be criticized for a failure to utilize perspectives that had not been opened up, though, in retrospect, it does appear as if he failed to appreciate to the full all that W. I. Thomas had written about the social factors influencing the expression of racial prejudice as early as

1904. Park's tendency to see prejudice from the standpoint of the more powerful group was also evident in his description of it as a 'phenomenon of the group mind', presenting prejudice against the Japanese as a reaction to their having the wrong skin colour and not as a consequence of white prejudgements which themselves require analysis (1921: 623–5, 760–1). It is important not to pillory an author by picking out passages that convey an untruthful impression. Park's statements about prejudice are all of them defensible and many of them draw attention to aspects of these phenomena previously neglected. Most of the criticism must be about the inadequacies of his presentation arising from what he failed to say. His pioneering interest in collective behaviour proved valuable for the development of American sociology but a critic must insist that collective behaviour cannot be understood in any depth if it is isolated from the structures that can mould it just as much as the instincts and other qualities of human nature to which Park and Burgess devoted so many pages.

After the publication of the textbook some signs appeared of Park's broadening his approach to these questions. Offering suggestions as to the material needed for a survey of race relations on America's Pacific coast, Park in 1923 opened his remarks with the statement, 'Race conflicts have their biological and economic aspects but it is the attitudes they express and provoke which are of first importance.' He went on to develop an alternative to the earlier view of attitudes as biologically determined, taking from W. I. Thomas and F. Znaniecki the notion that 'personality is the subjective aspect of culture' and that cultures develop their own patterns. The book which these two authors wrote on *The Polish Peasant* was the first, or almost the first, to call attention to the way the situation of the European immigrant in the United States could be defined in terms that implied its logical relation to that of the Negro, although the Negro had been settled in the New World for three centuries (Park, 1950: 159, 358, 198–9). The recognition of this 'logical relation', obvious though it may now seem, was of fundamental significance for establishing a sociology of race relations.

The most mature statement of Park's views in this field was the essay 'The Nature of Race Relations' published in 1939 (reprinted in Park, 1950). This put forward a more complex scheme for examining inter-action. In one sense, said Park, race relations were not so much the relations that existed between individuals of different races as between individuals conscious of these differences. From such a standpoint it would appear that there were no race relations in Brazil because race conscious-ness was absent from there. From another standpoint, however, race relations included relations that were not at that time conscious or personal though they had been in the past. Race problems, he believed, had invariably arisen in response to the expansion of European peoples; this could be seen as a historical extension of European domination accompanied by an increasing integration of, and intimacy with, the races and peoples affected. But he preferred to regard it as a succession of changes connected with, and incidental to, the expansion and integration of a vast and new social organism. The succession ran from trade to political domination, missionary activity, and then, 'the final stage' when 'Europe begins to export not goods but capital' to finance mines, rubber plantations, and eventually factories 'to employ native laborers in the manufacture of commodities which are then sold not only in the colonies, but, as in the case of Japan, in Europe and in competition with European products'. Other features of the succession were the appearance of hybrid peoples, port cities to service world trade, and then the growth of nationalism among both majorities and minorities. This last development was evidence that 'we are at the end of one epoch in human and racial relations and at the beginning of another'. Contradicting some previous writers, he predicted that race conflicts 'will be more and more in the future confused with, and eventually superceded by, the conflicts of classes'. Returning to his opening problem of what precisely distinguished race relations from other fundamental forms of human relations, he offered a further formulation:

> it is the essence of race relations that they are the relations of strangers; of peoples who are associated primarily for secular and practical purposes; for the exchange of goods and services. They are otherwise the relations of people of diverse races and cultures who have been thrown together by the fortunes of war, and who, for any reason, have not been sufficiently knit together by inter-marriage and interbreeding, to constitute a single ethnic community, with all that it implies. (1950: 100, 107–16)

Any assessment of Park's contribution to race relations studies must give a high place to his leadership in formulating an alternative to prevailing conceptions of racial relations as biological relations. For example, the lengthy review *Contemporary Sociological Theories* published by the Harvard professor Pitirim Sorokin included a substantial chapter on the 'Anthropo-Racial, Selectionist, and Hereditarist School' which concluded with the judgement that it 'has been one of the most important and valuable schools in sociology' (1928: 308). Park rejected the theories which defined culture as a racial trait; he saw the backwardness of human populations as a result of their geographical and cultural isolation. Equally, he dismissed the psychological mode of explanation favoured by F. H.

Giddings at Columbia, maintaining 'the thing that distinguishes a mere collection of individuals from a society is not like-mindedness, but corporate action . . . sociology . . . may be described as the science of collective behaviour' (1921: 42). By developing his ecological perspective Park was able to break away from a folk conception of race to a degree that Durkheim could never attain (Fenton, 1980). He explained the various aspects of the relations between people belonging to different races in terms of processes influencing all forms of life, human, animal and plant. It was of particular importance that he moved the emphasis in the expression 'race relations' from the first word to the second. He questioned the assumption that race relations and ethnic relations were fundamentally different. The effect of his teaching was to situate race relations in a context of urban sociology and the power relations stemming from the expansion of the capitalist economy.

One of the sharpest criticisms of Park's approach was that of the black Trinidad-born sociologist Oliver Cromwell Cox (1901–74) who considered the analysis of political organization seriously inadequate. Stanford H. Lyman has also objected to what he sees as an assumption that the place of the black man in United States society will be determined by processes within the white sector of that society. In his view Park 'systematically presented the stages through which the black would pass on the way to his eventual assimilation in a racially homogeneous world' (1972: 121). Park was surely a white liberal critic of prevailing assumptions about race, and yet, equally certain, he accepted other assumptions of his generation which are evident only in the light of hindsight. As Cox charged, Park did not identify with sufficient clarity the special characteristics of racial conflicts. Nor did he work out all the implications of the approach he pioneered. When he moved to the view that race relations are defined by present or past consciousness of racial differences, what did this imply for his theoretical framework? When men were conscious of such differences, what form did that consciousness take? Many of the beliefs white Southerners held in 1921 about racial differences are now known to have been false. If what distinguished these relations was a false consciousness and the falsity was eliminated, then unless there was some intervening variable, nothing substantial would remain to divide blacks from whites. Assimilation was the implicit outcome. An author who, like Lyman, criticizes this in 1972, has the advantage of more hindsight than one writing in 1948 or in 1939. It is easy now to observe that there was an intervening variable of a kind having something to do with nationalism. Park worked in an intuitive manner and did not reason in terms of independent and dependent variables. If he had done so, he would have been no more likely to predict this. It is striking how many of his contemporaries and even most later critics failed to foresee the kinds of change that occurred in American race relations around 1960. When he criticized Park, Cox was no more prescient, for he testified that the solidarity of Negro Americans was not nationalistic (1948: 545). It is fairly clear that Park did not regard racial conflicts as a special kind of conflict, but tended to emphasize what they had in common with other sorts of conflict. He wrote that the growth of nationalism was changing the consciousness of peoples in the colonial world and therefore changing the character of the conflicts. Race conflicts were giving way to class conflicts, and though Park would not have accepted Cox's conception of class, his view that racial conflicts do not have any special characteristic that distinguishes them in the historical dimension was of great importance to his generation and can easily be defended against criticism today.

Genetic explanations

The course of human evolution has entailed changes both in physical structure and behaviour. The structure of the human body evolved from that of some ape-like ancestor because of the way human ancestors used their arms and legs. Particular kinds of behaviour, among humans, as among animals, could have increased fertility and thus conferred greater fitness in the struggle for survival. If some animals or humans were more successful in competition on the ecological level, this may have been because their genetic inheritance enabled them to behave in particular ways; relative success would then have influenced the size of populations in the next generation. So an approach which sees race in terms of population has to consider the ways in which behaviour on the ecological level can be explained in terms of processes on the genetic level.

A pioneer of this line of argument was Sir Arthur Keith (1866–1955) who started to publish about the time when it was discovered that glands in the body produce hormones which regulate the normal growth of the various parts of the body. He inferred that the division of mankind into races had been brought about by the action of hormones, for if a group were isolated from others for a long period they would be unable to develop new characters. Groups could acquire a culture that encouraged self-isolation and thus reinforce physical difference. Among the kinds of behaviour that kept populations distinct one of the most salient was warfare. This led him to the view that human evolution was controlled by two processes, one operating on the physiological level and the other on the cultural, but nature had organized the physiological one 'to serve her ulterior object – the production of higher and better races of mankind'. Racial prejudices served her purpose by keeping populations separate so that they could control their own breeding and develop their genetic potential. The spirit of unrest which afflicted the modern world arose because humans were struggling to adapt their biological inheritance to the requirements of international economic organization. To attain world peace it would be necessary to control that inheritance more strictly: 'peoples of all countries and continents must pool not only their national interests, but they must also pool their bloods'. He told his Scottish audience that the price of such a peace 'is the racial birthright that Nature has bestowed upon you'. Yet even if, recognizing the arguments on the cultural level, people were willing to pay that price, Keith believed that Nature would prevent their doing so, because 'without competition Mankind can never progress'. 'This antipathy or race prejudice Nature has implanted within you for her own ends – the improvement of Mankind through racial differentiation' (Keith, 1931: 20, 47–8). Three points should be noted about this theory. Firstly, as an explanation of the patterns of racial prejudice in the modern world it is very weak. The variations in the intensity of prejudice from one set of circumstances to another, and from one individual to another, can be accounted for more satisfactorily by sociological and psychological theories. If any component is explicable in genetic terms it seems relatively small. (For a contemporary criticism of Keith's argument see the lecture reprinted in Boas, 1940: 8, 16–17.) Secondly, to establish that something has an evolutionary function is neither to justify it nor to account for it. War and prejudice may have functions but they also have dysfunctions. If prejudice keeps populations separate the separation is a consequence of the prejudice and therefore cannot be a cause of it. Thirdly, it is not necessarily the case that the biological improvement of mankind depends upon racial differentiation. Much depends upon preventive medicine and the improvement of the environment. In so far as humans have evolved beyond their ape-like ancestors it has been by the development of plasticity, or the ability to prosper in varying circumstances and environments.

Most physical anthropologists were unwilling to speculate in the way that Keith did. The direction in which their subject developed is illustrated by the introductory textbook *Genetics and the Races of Man* published by William C. Boyd in 1950. After summarizing Keith's views, it pointed to the difficulty in extrapolating from the breeding of domesticated animals. A cattle breeder might believe that when he had obtained cattle that produced more milk he had improved his stock; but by what criteria was the improvement of humans to be determined? (After all, cows with a higher milk yield might be less fit in a wild environment.) In more recent years it has also become apparent that there is a risk in plant and animal breeding unanticipated by Keith. It is best illustrated in cereals. A high-yielding cereal may be adopted by almost all the farmers in a region with excellent results for a time. It may then become subject to a particular disease so that a new variety has to be bred. The ability of the breeders to produce a new, disease-resistant, strain may depend upon the availability of wild strains with different properties that can be bred into the previous strain. Strains that appeared unproductive may turn out to be very valuable. This surely reinforces the conclusion that it is difficult to draw, from animal and plant breeding, any lessons for human breeding. No one can tell what the future holds.

Boyd set out to show that racial differentiation could result from causes which definitely did not improve the stock. He started from an exposition of the principles of genetics and made hardly any mention of craniology. Indeed, he summarized Sir Ronald Fisher's criticisms that even if precise and reliable measurements were available of skulls from different places and times, craniologists could still not determine which were the important measures or the causes of variation. Boyd went on to observe that, 'The difficulty which we experience in trying to classify man, or any other species, into races is quite different from the problem of classifying organisms into species.' Races were more or less genetically open systems whereas species, which did not regularly exchange genes, were genetically closed systems. A race could become a species. It was 'a population which differs significantly from other human populations in regard to the frequency of one or more of the genes it possesses' (Boyd, 1950: 198, 207). Any research worker analyzing, say, the incidence of a genetically based disorder, had to refer only to a population. The word 'race' became redundant. Populations were defined by the procedures of the research workers themselves in drawing samples. Those readers who believe that Prichard was right in 1836 when he warned of the confusions that could result from using the word race as a classification, might say that if a word was needed to identify a set of individuals among whom there was a given frequency of a particular gene, the word 'set' would have been sufficient. Old habits of thought were not so easily shaken off, and some anthropologists who well understood the principles Boyd expounded, nevertheless used the word 'raciation' to identify the process by which sets of individuals became genetically distinctive.

Three senses of the word 'race' have now been distinguished. To start with it was used to identify a lineage, a set of individuals of common descent who, because of out-marriage, could well be of varied appearance. When race was used in the sense of type, this was to identify a set defined by their phenotype, or appearance. Human characteristics change in the course of evolution. Once this was understood, a set of individuals of similar phenotype were better called a subspecies, a class created by shared descent. The boundaries of such a class had to be defined by the classifier. Increasingly, however, research moved away from problems of classification. Research workers drew their own samples without having to consider whether their populations were representative of the sets that other people regarded as races, nations, or social groups. Physical appearance was a preliminary indicator of how an individual might stand in relation to what was known about the frequencies of particular genes. Were it not that so many members of the general public still thought in terms of race, it would by this time have been possible to dispense with the word.

Population genetics shifted the level of interest from that of the species to that of the genes which made the species what it was. Yet when they produced organic change the genetic determinants always influenced existing organisms and did not start from the beginning again. Since a species had to be able to survive in its environment while changing, it could evolve in only a limited number of directions. There is a model here for arguments about reductionism in the study of human society. Social continuity and change result from the actions of individuals just as organic continuity and change result from the combination of genes. Social changes are brought about by changes in individual behaviour but the likelihood that any particular individual change will lead to a social change depends upon the organization of the society in relation to its historical environment.

Keith's argument that human inter-group social behaviour could usefully be seen as, in part, an expression of genetic determinants, was revived in the 1960s and 1970s in connection with the study of what is now called sociobiology. Early formulations of the theory of natural selection presented biological fitness as dependent not upon the physical and mental powers of an individual but upon the number of offspring he or she left. Fitness was a matter of differential reproduction. But, since a person's brothers and sisters have many of the same genes, these can be passed on as well through one sibling as another. Fitness had to be measured inclusively to estimate the ability of a small population to propagate its genetic characteristics. The inclusive fitness of an individual was increased by kin selection and reciprocal altruism. He or she was more able to transmit his or her genes if members of the kin group (who shared those genes) assisted one another; that assistance might be expected to vary in accordance with the degree of their genetic closeness, though the individuals were

unlikely to be conscious that their behaviour was so motivate
behaviour could then be explained as the product of natu
favouring cooperation between individuals of common desce

This theory has been applied to racial relations by Pierre
Berghe (1981) who proposes that such relations be seen as th
influences upon three levels: cultural, ecological, and genetic. He acknowl-
edges that much behaviour cannot be explained in terms of the next level
down, but contends that group behaviour is powerfully affected by an
unconscious tendency to favour people with whom the actor shares a
common genetic inheritance. A different physical appearance is a sign that
identifies a competing population whose members will try to spread their
genes to the disadvantage of members of the first population.

The ecological approach was of great importance in the history of
sociology because it enabled sociologists to break away from the assumption that racial relations had to be explained in biological terms. By con-
ducting field research and actually observing inter-group relations instead
of staying in their studies, sociologists developed new concepts and refined
their definitions in the way that, according to Mayr, underlies the advances
in evolutionary biology. They found the ecological perspective stimulating
as an analogy but inadequate as a total theoretical scheme.

Immigrant groups come to new societies bringing with them the
products of their previous social evolution, which may well include skills
that are of particular value in the new environment. How their social life
develops in that environment may depend upon whether they are able to
establish themselves in an ecological niche and turn a monopoly of some
resource to their shared advantage. It is possible to compare the relative
success of immigrants from the same part of China, Japan or the Indian
subcontinent in various countries of settlement. The immigrants took with
them the same skills but the use they could make of them depended upon
the socio-economic ecology of the receiving societies. For example,
Chinese were recruited as indentured workers for plantation labour in the
Caribbean. In Jamaica, once they had escaped from the plantations, they
moved into retail trade. They reinforced their economic position by con-
solidating as an ethnic group, often sending their children back to Asia to
receive a Chinese upbringing. After 1949 China was Communist and
Jamaica moved towards independence. The younger generation of
Jamaican Chinese determined to be Chinese Jamaicans instead, and pulled
their elders with them, so that the Chinese are now an integral section of
the island's bourgeoisie. Since they seek to conserve their wealth they will
marry their daughters only to members of their own groups, so a Chinese
ancestry, plus Chinese physical traits, distinguishes an ethnic subdivision

of a class. Orlando Patterson (1975) contrasts this with events in Guyana where the Portuguese had captured the retail trade sector before the Chinese were in any position to challenge them for it. Since no avenue of opportunity was open to them as a group, the Chinese there entered a variety of occupations and identified themselves as individuals with the developing Guyanese Creole culture.

Other immigrant groups in industrial societies have found their own niches: Jews in Britain became tailors and later taxi-drivers; one Native American group in the United States became specialists in steel erecting work at great heights, and a host of groups started restaurants offering a distinctive cuisine. The ecological analyses of the Chicago school stimulated a comparable study by John Rex and Robert Moore of the patterns of immigrant housing in Birmingham (see Rex 1968 for a good summary). These studies attest to the continuing value of an ecological perspective but they have also to be related to one or both of the two more comprehensive intellectual traditions discussed in the next two chapters.

4

RACE AS STATUS

In its application to human society, evolutionary theory drew attention to the way in which physical differences served as signs of membership in competing groups and called forth reactions at the level of unconscious behaviour. It also had two particular weaknesses. Firstly, it was unable to do justice to the complexities of behaviour on the conscious level. Secondly, it could not account for the importance of power relations in human society and especially for those associated with social stratification as a form of inequality persisting from one generation to another. These weaknesses started to be remedied once social scientists began to undertake empirical studies of the behaviour of people involved in inter-racial relations. An entirely new phase opened in the early 1930s when two people carried out research in Indianola, a Mississippi town with a population of about 3,000, that served as a centre for a rural county in which about 70 per cent of the population was black. The first research worker was an anthropologist, Hortense Powdermaker, who aimed to present a portrait of the town as a functioning community with particular reference to the Negro population. She was followed by John Dollard, a psychologist who had undergone psycho-analysis in Berlin.

Dollard's most striking contribution to knowledge about racial relations was his exposition of what I have elsewhere (1983: 82–4) summarized in propositional form as the Freudian Theory of Racial Relations. Whereas most whites took their prejudices for granted as the expression of human nature, Dollard showed how these were fashioned to meet emotional needs. In presenting his portrait of the town Dollard was influenced by the caste and class mode of analysis then being developed by another anthropologist, W. Lloyd Warner. Introducing his use of it, Dollard (1937: 61) asserted that what he had seen in the Deep South was not the white racial soul or genius defending its heritage, but 'a moral and status order . . . whose operators safeguard and perpetuate their position in it'. Rather than following Dollard's psychological interpretation, I shall concentrate upon this conception of a status order and describe the gradual construction, over a period of some forty years, of a distinctive theory which has one of its starting points in Dollard's analysis. The field studied and the conceptual work which made these advances possible were nearly all carried out in the United States and were motivated by the whites' concern with what many called 'the Negro problem'. That there was a problem few could contest. The main arguments were about what kind of problem it was, and the priority given to this question meant that theoretical development occurred within a framework constructed by what Americans considered democratic ideals, rather than within abstract categories of scientific reasoning.

Lloyd Warner's conceptions of caste and class were two such categories. Both have been vigorously criticized. To call black–white relations caste relations has suggested to some writers a parallel with the Hindu caste system which they believe quite inappropriate since the latter has religious justifications of an anti-democratic character. Warner's view of class corresponded to what many sociologists would now identify as social status: it was a more systematic formulation of the United States folk concept of class as a rank order based upon wealth and style of life. Debate about the best definition of class continues. One way of reducing some of the confusion is to distinguish between a weak sense of class (e.g. as a set of individuals standing in a common relationship to the labour market) and a strong sense (e.g. as a set of individuals standing in a common relationship to the means of production who will in due course be brought to a consciousness of their position in the process by which capitalism develops). When a weak conception is employed class is one among several dimensions along which individuals are differentiated, and it corresponds to the use of the word in much everyday language where it designates socio-economic status. When a strong conception of class is employed, differentiation by class is a long-term determinant underlying other kinds of social differentiation. This chapter discusses theories which use weak concepts of class; the next one considers what theories using strong concepts of class add to the sociological understanding of racial relations.

Structure and function

In the 1930s it was quite common to regard the social system as a machine with its members interacting with one another in historically defined ways. 'This machine has inertia and goes on working according to its traditionally prescribed pattern. The societal unit continues to function until it is in some manner disorganized; it then goes through a cycle from disorganization to reorganization, and orderly life continues.' This explanation did not satisfy Dollard who thought it plain that powerful pressure was constantly exerted on Negro people to make them display submissive attitudes. The system was maintained not by inertia but by active pressures, social and physical. To identify these pressures it was necessary to discover the differential advantages of membership in particular classes and colour-castes and find out how these advantages were translated into personal, ultimately organic, gratifications (1937: 97, 178).

Dollard's answer to this problem was to describe three kinds of gain which middle-class whites derived from their social position at the expense of blacks and to some extent of lower-class whites. There were economic, sexual and prestige gains. The first of them he documented by reference to occupational rewards. The back-breaking and ill-rewarded nature of some jobs was epitomized in cotton-picking; middle-class whites picked very little cotton. Relatively, middle-class whites got much higher returns for their work than did the lower-class groups who performed the more laborious tasks. This might well have been the case, but it is not an easy matter to prove. In effect, Dollard asserted that whites used their political power to get greater rewards than would otherwise have come to them. The difficulty in this argument is that without additional information about what happened in other circumstances there was no way of deter-mining how much of the 'great favorable differential' in income resulted from the exercise of power and how much was a return for special talents. Whites were immigrating into the area, which suggests that it offered them economic opportunities. Dollard also contended that the social position of middle-class whites entailed certain costs and that they were imprisoned within an inhospitable socio-economic situation as much as any other category, but he asserted that they gained more than they lost by it, and that they therefore had a vested interest in maintaining that system (1937: 98–115). He described the poverty of most Negroes and the incidence of pellagra, a disease caused by dietary deficiency. He also provided plenty of examples of the ways in which white power was used to prevent black workers getting their just reward, or forming labour organizations, and in controlling the jobs that were available to them (on the exploitation of tenant farmers see Dollard 1937: 120–4; Powdermaker, 1939: 86–94). The distribution of rewards in the labour market was clearly determined by the mobilization of white power as well as by the market value of indi-viduals' skills. To this extent at least it may be agreed that one factor in the maintenance of the social system was the economic gain that whites derived from it.

The second kind of gain was sexual, and in its simplest terms consisted in the way white men had access to Negro women as well as to white women. It will not escape notice that, among whites, this was a gain for men only. Dollard remarked that Negro women also had an advantage in that they might receive the attentions of men from both racial categories. In so far as this was a gain for Negro women it was balanced by a loss, in that this situation meant the degradation of the Negro male and that in turn reduced in many ways the satisfactions that Negro women could obtain from married life. The same situation reduced the satisfactions of white women. Dollard conjectured that they were idealized in such a way that white men felt it unbecoming to regard them as sexual objects, feeling guilty and restrained in sexual relations with them and finding black women better sexual partners. White women unconsciously envied the greater sexual freedom of black women (1937: 135–68). In such circumstances the calculation of sexual gain seems a dubious exercise, but one can go along with Dollard in accepting that the patterning of sexual attitudes was a factor important to the motivations which maintained the social system.

The third kind of gain was what Dollard called prestige but would now be called deference. He had in mind the features of Negro behaviour which in inter-personal relations tended to increase the white man's self-esteem. It was illuminating for the traveller to compare the experience of having his bag carried at the Grand Central Terminal in New York and at a railway station in the Deep South. In the former, 'the Negro is a mechanism for moving weight from one point to another . . . in the South he is this, and something more. The Southern porter is extremely nice about it to boot and does various things that are flattering and exhilarating.' Dollard was clear that, first, deference behaviour was something used by Negroes to manipulate whites, and, second, that it had functions in respect of social control. Deference was demanded by whites and any Negro who would not accord it was defined as 'uppity', threatening, and in need of correction. But nevertheless deference was psychologically rewarding to the recipient; it seemed to prove that the Negro was not hostile and to allay the anxiety among white people provoked by the fear that the racial situation engendered in them. The crucial feature for the white man was that he was receiving deference in advance of demand; it appeared as a submissive affection freely yielded, suggesting that his aggressive demands were being passively received and giving him a gratifying sense of mastery over others (1937: 173–87). In non-Western cultures it often appears from the studies of anthropologists that the highest category of economic values is that which brings command over people, while the disparagement of the role of personal servant in industrial societies suggests that deference is a service commanding a high price in the eyes of both the one who pays it and the one who receives the service. The very substantial white deference gain in the South was therefore an index of how much white power affected the bargaining relations of the two racial categories.

The gains were not exclusively on the white side of the colour line. There were many ways in which blacks were able to gratify their impulses, though, as Dollard points out, this was often at an appreciable long-term cost. Negroes had greater sexual freedom among their own number; greater freedom of aggression; and the psychological luxury of a dependent relationship in respect of whites. Whites had the satisfaction that went with mastery, superiority, control, maturity, and duty well-fulfilled. They had the pleasure of despising blacks. Negroes were permitted slack work habits, irresponsibility and, within limits, more personal freedom than is possible in a competitive, economically progressive society. This helped explain why they did not try harder to change the system. The 'tolerant' attitude of whites towards crime in the Negro quarter and their acceptance of slack work habits further weakened Negro resources for mobilizing pressure against white demands (1937: 393, 431–3, 282).

Implicit in Dollard's concept of gain as an instrument for clarifying what was entailed in caste and class relations was the idea of exchange between two partners to a trading relationship. The Negro traded deference for reward. Thus, 'the "Sambo" or "Rastus" type of Negro takes his hat off, grins, strikes the boss for half dollar, and often gets it in exchange for his submissiveness'. Sometimes the Negro traded his labour power in return for his employer's protection. Thus a particular Negro had been known to threaten to kill some other man, saying that he knew he would not be punished for it; 'he will "farm another acre" that is, do extra work for his boss in exchange for the protection'. Not all blacks were willing to trade on these terms. Some 'local Negroes who had been away to school' were offish, cool, and kept to themselves; they would hardly speak to whites in public and were reluctant to speak first. Their experience of life elsewhere had caused them to set a higher price on their pride. The positions occupied by black people varied in the extent to which they made it desirable for them to have a white protector or patron. A black school teacher, for example, had concluded that the only way to get along was to have a white patron because improvements to school buildings could not be obtained in any other way (Dollard, 1937: 179, 282, 185, 263).

The central feature of Warner's analysis was the presumption that two systems, one of caste and the other of class, existed side by side. The caste system ranked whites above blacks, prohibited inter-marriage and placed the offspring of inter-caste sexual relations in the lower category. The class system ranked everyone, blacks and whites, in terms of their entitlement to deference deriving from wealth, education, social origin, style of life, etc. This meant that while all blacks were socially inferior and categorically subordinate to all whites in colour-caste, some were superior and superordinate to many whites in respect of social class. The two systems would have come into conflict more often had there not been a clear understanding that some kinds of social relationships belonged in the one system and other kinds in the second one. Anything relating to sexual relations between blacks and whites, and particularly anything involving black men and white women, was to be regulated by caste norms. Anything of a commercial character was regulated by class norms. It was the whites who decided into which category any incident fell, and often it was the lower-class whites who were first on the scene. They had the greatest interest in enforcing caste norms since these norms were so important to them in reducing the effects of competition from blacks.

The process by which a situation was defined as being of a particular character entailed many risks for the blacks. Dollard described the situation of a Negro landowner who had five white people picking cotton for him. Three of them were women. If one of them had alleged that he had 'shined up' to her it might have cost him his life, though in the book *Deep South* an incident is described in which a lower-class white woman alleged that a black processional man had struck her but failed to get her definition of the situation accepted. Nor did the norm concerning inter-racial sex always protect white men. In Indianola a black man beat a white man for pestering his girl friend; the black man had to leave town after a white posse went after him, but this may have been only temporary. A black tenant who shot a white plantation manager who consorted with his sister was allowed to return to the plantation by the landlord. A black shopkeeper obtained a court order against a white customer requiring him to pay for goods he had taken. The customer regarded this as an intolerable affront and came to beat the shopkeeper, but he lost the fight and other whites refused to aid him. A black man, gun in hand, angrily threatened his white neighbour for repeatedly letting horses loose in his corn. A lynching party assembled at the white's house later the same day but the owner of the horses stopped it 'on the grounds that the Negro did not really know what he was doing'. Automobile accidents in which a black driver killed or injured a white person could also be tricky. A young black driver had his car sideswiped by another so that it was thrown against a white worker in the road, causing him slight injury. The black driver was convicted of an offence and sentenced to serve thirty days at the county farm, where he was badly whipped. A middle-class black driver who had white patrons once hit a car driven by a white woman who happened to be pregnant, an especially unfavourable detail; the police officer abused him and was about to put him in jail when the chief of police declared the matter to have been an accident and ordered his release. In another case a black professional man when driving his car killed a drunken lower-class white man. He was not arrested. Local white bankers offered to lend him money for his defence while a group of upper-class white women called upon him at his place of business to assure him that they considered him a 'great influence for good in the community' and that they intended to see that no harm came to him (Dollard, 1937: 165, 292–3, 288, 92; Davis *et al.*, 1941: 477, 337).

Dollard presented Indianola society as constructed round the inter-locking categories of caste and class: 'they organize local life securely and make social cooperation possible . . . Caste has replaced slavery as a means of maintaining the essence of the old status order in the South. By means of it racial animosity is held at a minimum' (1937: 61–2). This statement is worth notice for its demonstration of the weakness of functionalist explanations. Caste and class were equally responsible for the *in*security of local life and for lack of cooperation. By means of caste racial animosity was evoked and heightened. Any community has a degree of integration, the component parts being to some extent interdependent. Every relation between them is therefore to some degree functional and to some degree dysfunctional. To point to a connection between colour-caste and animosity says nothing about whether animosity would be higher or lower if relations between blacks and whites were regulated in some other way.

The structural interpretations Dollard borrowed from Warner's scheme were much more valuable. He argued that in relations with middle-class blacks, middle-class white people combined class loyalty and caste hostility. Situations of economic position and advantage called forth class-based patterns of behaviour whereas situations of social, and ultimately sexual, contact evoked caste-based patterns. The former was not difficult to account for since the middle-class Negro bought more gasoline, better groceries, more insurance, more medical services, engaged a lawyer more frequently, and was in general a good customer. Whites would bid for the custom of such Negroes and found it worthwhile to persuade Negro land-owners to offer workers the same conditions of service as those offered by white employers. One such landowner said the whites put pressure on him to treat his tenants as they did theirs. Another used his influence to dis-suade some of the local Negroes from bringing a potentially costly suit for damages and had been given special favours in return. Educated Negroes

often found themselves the objects of a more respectful and friendly attention, provided nothing happened to evoke caste differences. These signs of
inter-racial class sympathy were to be set alongside the striking evidence of
hostility between middle-class whites and lower-class whites. A landlord,
for example, deplored the meanness and spitefulness of his white tenant
farmers stating that next year he would replace them with Negroes. Poor
whites were intractable and undeferential but there were Negroes who
'knew their place'.

Caste and Class in a Southern Town was complemented by *Deep South:
A social anthropological study of caste and class* (Davis *et al.*, 1941). This
was a study, directed by Lloyd Warner, of Natchez, a town of over 10,000
persons located on the Mississippi river not far away. Both books describe
a social system that had continually to adjust to changing circumstances.
In 1936 cotton yields increased and there was a shortage of agricultural
workers such that 10–15,000 cotton pickers had to be imported into the
region. Law officers dragged tramps from railroad box cars and hobo
colonies, and rounded up vagrants for work in the fields. Landlords had
earlier competed with one another for good tenants and had much preferred black tenants to white, but with better yields competition in areas
around Natchez became acute. In such circumstances it might have been
expected that dissatisfied Negroes would emigrate and that competition
between whites would result in a diminution in discrimination. How then
was the system maintained? Davis and his colleagues concluded that by far
the most important element was the face-to-face relationship of landlord
and tenant. Intimidation and legal subordination had bred in the black
man a habit of dependence on the landowner. He had become accustomed
to a low standard of living such that he left the system only in periods of
destitution or at times, such as during the war, when conditions were
generally disturbed. Standards were kept uniformly low by upper-class
white pressure on industrial concerns able to pay blacks wages higher than
those conventional in other kinds of employment (Davis *et al.*, 1941: 401,
378, 261). To examine properly the hypothesis of black dependence it
would have been necessary to study perceptions of emigration opportunities; this was neglected, while there is sufficient evidence in the book
itself to evoke the reader's doubts about the adequacy of this explanation.
Other doubts arise with respect to political relations. The authors describe
the antagonism between upper- and lower-class whites. They state that
political power was exercised by a 'ring' which was dependent on the
support of rank and file middle- and lower-class voters, nearly all of whom
were white. Independent organization by lower-class whites was frus-
trated. Instead of the system's being maintained by inertia and psycho-

logical relations like dependence and habituation to low standards, it seems to have rested on the continual use of governmental power to balance lower-class whites and blacks. *Deep South* very properly emphasized the importance of white power to the maintenance of the system and its authors recognized that 'since political control is vested in the upper middle class of the white caste, it is not surprising that there is a close connection between political power and the control of the economic system, which is also in the hands of this class' (1941: 491), but did not relate this as well as they might to the political history of the state or to the explanation of the distinctive features of the social system.

The research of Dollard, Lloyd Warner, and their associates, provided a basic understanding of a two-category social system in which membership of either category was defined in what the participants called racial terms. Their analysis can be strengthened by considering the position in such a system of intermediary groups like Native Americans and Chinese who could possibly be regarded as constituting a third category (Banton, 1977: 169–71). Lloyd Warner stated that community studies must be conducted within the general framework of comparative sociology, placing the study of the Deep South alongside reports from inner Tibet or the Andaman Islands in the Bay of Bengal. This was a commendable aspiration, but it was swamped by one of the dominant characteristics of the culture in which the research workers had themselves been brought up. Citizens of the United States have believed, since their country's independence in 1776, that what most distinguished it was the national commitment to democratic values. The belief that the sharing of values was the most important attribute of a society influenced the form taken by sociology in the United States. It can be seen in the theories of Talcott Parsons which dominated the discipline from the late 1940s until the mid-1960s and which are often designated structural-functionalism. Parsons' approach was introduced to a wider audience through Kingsley Davis' text book *Human Society* (1947) in which he presented human behaviour as chiefly governed by the efforts of individuals to gain their objectives. This might involve the rational utilization of means which could help them towards their goals (the means-end relation) but it did not exclude considerations which could not be rationally justified (such as the value placed in Europe upon gold, pearls and diamonds). Each individual pursued his or her own ends but society came about because these ends were fitted into a common pattern (the cooperation associated with the division of labour) and because individuals share common values (the beliefs that murder should be punished and that pearls are more valuable than cowrie shells). The conception of societies as founded upon the sharing of common ultimate ends introduced an element of relativism: social activities had to be interpreted in terms of the value structure of the society in which they occurred. Thus questions of racial discrimination, of assimilation, and of the legitimacy of a minority identity had to be viewed against the background of United States political principles. As a means of educating readers about the injustices of discrimination, this had its merits, but it erected obstacles to the comparative study of racial relations. It implied that what distinguished racial relations from other kinds of inter-group relations were the values of the dominant group alone, and it failed to follow up the suggestions of Park and W. I. Thomas for comparing those majority–minority relations which were defined as racial with those defined in ethnic terms.

The use of democratic values as a framework within which to conceptualize racial relations was explicit in Dollard's (1937: 60) discussion of the 'conflict between the dominant American mores, which are expressed formally in the Declaration of Independence and the regional mores of the South . . . Two different and contradictory conceptions of human worth as are operating in one social field.' He called it a dilemma, and this formulation provided the main organizing principle for Gunnar Myrdal's *An American Dilemma* (1944), a massive collaborative study which owed a great deal to the structural-functional theory. Another such principle was what was called 'the white man's rank order of discrimination'. Myrdal said that this was observed by nearly all whites in the South and he described it as follows:

> *Myrdal's rank order of discriminations*
> 1. The bar against intermarriage and sexual intercourse involving white women.
> 2. The several etiquettes and discriminations, which specifically concern behaviour in personal relations (dancing, bathing, eating, drinking together, handshaking, hat lifting, use of titles, house entrance and so forth).
> 3. Segregations and discriminations in use of public facilities such as schools, churches and means of conveyance.
> 4. Political disfranchisement.
> 5. Discriminations in law courts, by the police, and by other public servants.
> 6. Discriminations in securing land, credit, jobs, or other means of earning a living and discriminations in public relief and other social welfare activities.

The Negro's own rank order was said to be just about parallel, but inverse, to that of the white man. Being in desperate need of jobs and bread, even more than of justice in the courts or the vote, the Negro was most strongly motivated to resist discrimination on the economic level and least concerned about 'the marriage matter' (Myrdal, 1944: 60–1). A subsequent study of black attitudes in Columbus, Ohio, confirmed this conclusion, but one of black and white attitudes in Texas and Oklahoma questioned whether discrimination in public services did not belong higher in the list. Research in a small industrial town in Connecticut in 1950–2 found that the separation of blacks from whites was most marked in housing, and then, in decreasing order, in social and religious activities, in the more desirable jobs, in public facilities, politics, and education (Lee, 1961: 74). Research at much the same time covering a sample of 248 cities showed considerable variation. In eight cities out of ten it could be taken for granted that Negroes might use the same public rest rooms as whites; but in only four cities out of ten could the same be said for Negro customers in white restaurants, while in less than one in ten could a black man reckon on service in a white barbershop (Williams, 1964: 124–9). Nevertheless, there was a 'strikingly clear unidimensional order' determining the situations in which whites accepted blacks, which did not rest on any single set of economic, political or social interests. It appeared to be the product of 'functionally arbitrary historical circumstances'.

Any analysis that started from values needed to be complemented by one that started from structures. The first sociologist to provide an example of how this might be done in a small-scale study was Everett Cherrington Hughes in his 1946 article on 'The Knitting of Racial Groups in Industry'. Hughes set out to demonstrate that 'a fruitful way of analyzing race relations in industry is to look at them against whatever grid of informal social groupings and of relations within and between such groups [as] exists in the industries, departments and jobs in which Negroes or other new kinds of employees are put to work'. He showed how in the canteen, the fixing room, and the polishing room of a particular factory, patterns had been established of labour–management relations, informal seniority among employees, and group control of individual productivity. New employees had to conform to the existing practices or be subjected to heavy informal pressure. Black female workers were accorded a limited degree of acceptance by white female workers but were not admitted to the friendship cliques of the white women. Since the black women were only partly accepted they were not subject to the full pressure to conform to the established output norms, and some of them had high production rates. Management insisted that workers would be hired, retained and promoted strictly according to their individual merits. This had the effect of making all the workers, but particularly the blacks, feel very much on trial, so that 'the Negro worker apparently feels and is made to feel in some situations that he [or she] has to dissociate himself from others and be a "solitary" in order merely to keep his job' (Hughes & Hughes, 1952: 157). This essay discussed circumstances in which an industrial 'colour line' was being breached; some black workers disliked the pressure and left; others stayed, but did not behave in the same way as most of their white peers. To understand this, wrote Hughes, the sociologist had first to understand the factory and then discover in what ways customary attitudes were changed by the introduction of black workers. It examined one kind of cooperation and looked towards the possibility that racial distinctions might some day lose their social significance in the factory setting.

Sociologists were slow to follow Hughes's lead. The 'race problem' was perceived as a problem of conflict. When, in 1948, Herbert Blumer reviewed the research on racial relations in the United States carried out since World War Two, he concluded that it had been shaped by an underlying interest in bringing these relations abreast of democratic ideals. Had it been under the influence of a different ideology, such as one directed to the maintenance of the *status quo*, other topics would have been studied. The issues on which it had concentrated, the theoretical leads it had followed, and the analytical schemes which it had employed, had not grown out of progressive scientific study of a distinct field of human behaviour. The need for a clear definition of what was meant by racial relations had been disregarded. Most of the research had been devoted to problems which lay along what he termed the 'prejudice–discrimination axis'. It rested on a belief that the nature of the relations between racial groups resulted from the feelings and attitudes which these groups had towards each other. Feelings and attitudes were therefore the chief objects to be studied. They might be the easiest ones to examine, but in Blumer's view they were not the most important ones. Racial relations in his view consisted of the actual behaviour towards one another of peoples in different racial groups. Because this had not been appreciated research had been chaotic and lacking in scientific rationale.

Kinds of system

The inter-war period was one of great intellectual progress in the study of racial relations. By its end the nature of one variety of such relations, that which had been established in the Deep South, and had spread in diluted form to other parts of the United States, was much better understood. The next step was to discover how far that variety was representative. What other varieties were there and how did they differ?

In this connection a particularly influential study was Donald Pierson's

Negroes in Brazil (1942), an account of 'race contact at Bahia' as it was in 1935–9. Of all the regions in Brazil, the province of Bahia and its capital city Salvador (often called Bahia also!) was the one best suited to provide a contrast with the United States. It was not representative of Brazil, but was a good locale for the study of a social system in which physical appearance had quite a different significance from Mississippi. In the United States any outward sign of African descent served to assign an individual to the category black or Negro. It was the basis for a categorical distinction. In Bahia an appearance suggesting more or less African inheritance had an effect similar to the difference in Mississippi between an expensive house and a poor one, an elegant costume or a shabby one, a cultured mode of speaking or bad grammar. It was a basis for a difference of degree, like the calculation of social status. It applied when comparing people whom North Americans would assign to different races, as well as when comparing people assigned to the same race. Pierson mentioned his intellectual obligations to Robert Park, who read the manuscript and then the proofs of the book. As Park did so he came to the conclusion that 'Brazil has no race problem'. The realization that people of different origin could relate to one another unaffected by race prejudice in the sense in which that term was used in the United States, was of fundamental importance. It proved that racial problems could be solved. Pierson (1942: 331) explained that 'such prejudice as does exist is *class* rather than *caste* prejudice. It is the kind of prejudice which exists *inside* the ranks of the Negroes in the United States, the amount and intensity of which is actually very great.' Class prejudice existed in the ranks of white people in the United States too, but because of that country's definition of 'white', Pierson had to look to the black population for a continuous pattern of variation in complexion comparable to Bahia's. He thought that Brazilian whites did not express racial prejudice because they had never experienced a categorical opposition in which blacks or mixed-bloods offered a threat to their own status.

Subsequent research in Brazil during the 1950s – much of it initiated by UNESCO – was discussed in the 1967 edition of Pierson's book. It confirmed the claim that physical differences had a quite different social significance in Bahia from that in most parts of the United States – up to the 1950s at least. There was a Brazilian pattern in which signs of African ancestry constituted one element in a continuous scale of social status. Their effects could be counterbalanced by the effects of other bases for attributing status such as wealth and education. Though there was a profusion of terms for describing differences of complexion, hair, etc. there were no racial categories in the social structure. The darker-skinned people tended to be low down the status scale and the lighter-skinned people to be high up, and inequality was transmitted from one generation to the next, but the association between colour and status was statistical and not categorical. How different this pattern was from that of the United States is still not appreciated by some writers. As Pierson (1967: xxvi) wrote, to call Brazilians of African descent Negroes, blacks or mulattoes is quite misleading.

Another example suggesting that racial contact need not necessarily give rise to a 'race problem' was furnished by the islands of Hawaii. By the early 1960s their population was comprised by five major groups: Caucasians, 32 per cent; Chinese, 6 per cent; Filipinos, 11 per cent; Hawaiians, 17 per cent; and Japanese, 32 per cent. Processes of assimilation or integration had been delayed by the entry of new groups of workers who still retained some of the distinctive characteristics of their homelands. Nevertheless the tendency to assign individuals to distinctive racial categories was diminishing. Over 46 per cent of all marriages were either unions crossing ethnic lines or involved persons who were already of mixed racial ancestry (Lind, 1966). Hawaii seemed to be setting a pattern for changes in other parts of the Pacific too.

Hawaii was therefore an appropriate location in 1954 for an international conference designed to lay the groundwork of social knowledge that could inform political and social policies. No one claimed that this knowledge had reached the point at which it could be synthesized. Indeed Blumer, in his introductory essay to the proceedings (Lind, 1955), maintained that there was little likelihood that any body of theory about race relations could be assembled that would comprehend the diversity of the subject matter. Racial experts might contribute to the devising of social policies, but explanations of inter-racial behaviour had to be sought in social and historical circumstances; these were too diverse to permit the formulation of universal propositions. Blumer went on in subsequent essays to argue that the sense of social position emerging from the way in which people characterized their own and others' groups provided the basis of race prejudice (see Killian, 1970). This was an application of what is known as the perspective of symbolic interactionism. In a later publication he and Troy Duster (1980: 222) outlined a 'theoretical scheme' to try and grasp the phenomena of 'collective definition' which they considered central. It entailed a focus on the ways in which people came to see members of their own and other racial groups, how they defined and interpreted their experiences of one another, and how racial categorization affected their disposition to behave towards members of their own and other groups. Equally important to their conception of racial relations was the assumption that they entailed the superordination of one group and the subordination of another. Around this division four major forces were said to interact. Within the subordinate group there were the assimilationist and separatist orientations: the former was displayed in the intention and effort to gain adjustment inside established institutions; the latter, in the intention and effort to develop a separate institutional world. Within the superordinate group there were the exclusionary and gate-opening orientations; the former was manifested in the intention and effort to hold onto – and sometimes increase – social advantages; the latter, in the intention and effort to extend them to members of the other group. The pattern of relations between the groups took different turns as one or other of the orientations became dominant. This happened as a result of changes elsewhere in society which needed to be explained in terms appropriate to the nature of those changes (e.g. economic theories to explain changes in economic conditions). Useful as a study of the processes of collective definition may be, this is a very limited perspective that has not yet been formulated in properly theoretical terms.

Group relations in places like Hawaii could develop towards the Brazilian pattern rather than towards that of the Deep South, and in places where more than two groups were involved the simple superordination–subordination model was inadequate. Another possible variety of race relations was that denoted by the concept of the plural society as this had recently been employed to analyze relations in Burma and Java between Europeans, Chinese, Indians and various native groups. J. S. Furnival had distinguished between a plural society and a society with plural features. The plural society was associated with the modern tropical economy and arose 'where economic forces are exempt from control by social will' (1948: 306). In its political aspect it had 'three characteristic features; the society as a whole comprises separate racial sections; each section is an aggregate of individuals rather than a corporate or organic whole; and as individuals their social life is incomplete'. (By incomplete he meant that the life of the sections was self-centred or oriented to its homeland rather than to the plural society.) The modern tropical economy was an imperial creation that drew upon both the western principle of freedom and the tropical system of compulsion.

Imperial rule was extended over regions that were already subject to disruptive changes. Thus proposals for the Uganda Railway were approved by the British Parliament on the argument that activities against the East African slave trade must be extended to the interior. Slaves were used as carriers or porters, but porterage was costly both in money and human life so that railway transport could be seen as an immense benefit to the peoples freed from the scourge of porterage. Furnival cites this as an example of the arguments in favour of compulsion. At times people must be obliged, in their long-term interest, to work for ends they do not understand. The western principle of freedom was subject to qualifications which liberal economists in Europe had no reason to explore since they took for granted a sharing of common objectives and values. The most disruptive changes were those that arose from contacts between peoples with different values. Far from regulating these equitably, colonial governments often exacerbated them. Thus in all sections of the nineteenth-century Burmese timber trade Burmans found employment. But Indian convict labour, hired from the government, was cheaper and more docile so it was used to displace free Burmese labour. As Furnival (1948: 46) noted, 'if convicts had not been available, Europeans and Burmese would have learned to work together . . . and the people of the country would have been developed at the same time as its natural resources. The importation of convicts . . . erected a barrier between Burmans and the modern world that has never been broken down.' The entry of Chinese and Indian free workers erected further barriers. The inability of the native peoples to control immigration, and the short-term view of policy taken by the imperial powers, has been in many regions a major cause of racial tension. As Furnival remarks with gentle irony 'the Fiji chieftains invited British protection, and one result has been that half the inhabitants are immigrants from India'. Substantial numbers of 'coolies' were brought from Madras to Burmese towns where they were housed in the worst conceivable conditions, no one counted how many of them died, but the death rate was very high. Burmans were thereby driven out of the towns into the country districts. The one urban occupation open to Burmans for a time was in the printing trade, since, thanks to the monastic schools, almost every Burman had learned to read and write. Yet eventually they were driven even from this trade by cheaper Indian labour. Burmese hostility towards the Indian presence grew steadily; marriages between Indian men and Burmese women came in for particular criticism. The Indian minority, hardworking and increasingly prosperous, did not support the Burmese nationalist movement but tried to preserve a distinct identity. They paid a terrible price. Hundreds were slaughtered in the riots of 1930 and 1938. With the Japanese invasion of 1941, all 900,000 took to flight and very many died on the roads to India (Chakravati, 1971).

One of Furnival's central concerns was with the economies of welfare, and therefore with the analysis of what would now be called public goods. He stressed the distinction between economic progress and welfare. The former consisted in raising production and reducing costs; it was measurable. The latter was largely subjective. 'Order and security are good things, but under foreign rule their value as elements of welfare is debatable; after all, they could be achieved under slavery'. The Burman had his own goals and his own ideas of how much leisure he would forego to attain them. Production was a social function and welfare a social attribute. Burmese society inculcated in its members norms which enabled everyone to increase their welfare, but these norms were neither observed nor recognized by the immigrant groups. The economic aspects of the plural society were therefore revealed in the weakness of the social regulation of demand and supply. Taking a very basic example, Furnival observed that 'sometimes a patch of scrub jungle round a village is reserved as a public convenience and it is closed to fuel cutting'. The social demand for a public good prevailed over any temptation to individuals to fell the trees in this area for firewood. But when they came to Rangoon, Indian immigrants saw in these patches of woodland a way to make easy money and cleared them to sell as fuel in the market. A public good was virtually destroyed. The European, Chinese, Indian and native groups all had their own norms of right conduct in business affairs, based upon relations in their own group, but these norms varied. One employer might be unwilling to employ sweated labour but find he was competing against another producer whose norms allowed him to employ men on terms the first one would consider unfair. The first employer might then reduce his standards. In this way the social controls upon the supply of commodities were reduced to the lowest common factor amongst the various sections.

Other societies might be divided into a variety of groups with distinctive cultures, like South Africa, Canada and the United States (and, indeed, Burma prior to British rule) but Furnival did not count them as plural societies because their population shared norms which allowed them to control the economic forces. He considered them societies with plural features. Sociologists declined to follow this sort of distinction. Furnival had stated a persuasive case for regarding Burma and Java in the first half of the twentieth century as examples of a special kind of society. They could be differentiated from other kinds on several dimensions: control of the economy, separate racial sections, a coercive social framework, relations to the means of production, and so on. For Furnival's purposes the first of these was the most important. Sociologists of inter-group relations recognised the Burma-Java instance as a form of 'race contact' quite different from the two-category system of the Deep South and the continuous gradation of colour and status reported from Bahia. They were more interested in the parallels with other societies in Africa and the West Indies which had been influenced by European imperialism; some of them generalized Furnival's insight by writing of pluralism. Thus M. G. Smith stressed the second and third of the dimensions, defining pluralism as 'a condition in which members of a common society are internally distinguished by fundamental differences in their institutional practice'. Leo Kuper kept closer to the assumption that plural societies were a special kind of society, one in which it was 'the political relations which appreciably determine the relationship to the means of production, rather than the reverse, and the catalyst of revolutionary change is to be found in the structure of power, rather than in economic changes which exhaust the possibilities of a particular mode of production' (Kuper, 1974: 226). He saw the social will in political terms and related it to generalizations about how societies change.

The claim that plural societies are a distinct kind of society brings up the philosophical problem discussed in Chapter 1 as an opposition between realism and nominalism. Those who considered plural societies distinct, presumed that there was a significant difference in the objects of study which should be reflected in the student's conceptual armoury. Critics of this position maintained that Burma and Java differed from one another and from all the other possible examples in many ways, and, indeed, that each society was different at one point in time from all other points in time. The complexity could be mastered only if the student developed his or her own set of categories and used them to organize observations about a large range of societies. The analysis of plural societies was the more attractive in the late 1950s because more scholars were then questioning the proposition that societies were founded upon the sharing of common ultimate ends. Burma, Java and South Africa were manifestly not societies whose members shared such ends. But was the United States either? Many sociologists moved to the view that most societies were held together by the coercive power of state institutions. From such a standpoint Burma, Indonesia, South Africa, and the other African societies discussed, had to be understood less as societies than as states created by European imperialism which would be transformed when the dominant power was overcome. This favoured the use of a more general concept of pluralism, one which, for example, made it possible to argue that in the United States Afro-Americans shared the majority culture but were socially separate, resulting in a substantial degree of social pluralism but only minimal cultural pluralism. Pierre L. van den Berghe pushed this mode of analysis to its logical conclusion in his conception of pluralism as a set of properties characterizing heterogeneous societies. Since most states are heterogeneous, and since the approach he advocated entailed studying the entire society, any sharpness in the contrasts between Burma, Mississippi and Bahia was blunted.

Van den Berghe argued (first in 1958) that manifestations of racial prejudice had historically polarized around two ideal types of society which he called paternalistic and competitive. He compared these in respect of six independent variables (economy, division of labour, mobility, social stratification, numerical ratio, value conflict); nine dependent variables (race relations, roles and statuses, etiquette, forms of aggression, miscegenation, segregation, psychological syndrome, stereotypes of lower caste, intensity of prejudice); and two social control variables (form of government; legal system). To write of polarization implies that the poles are opposite ends of a continuum or scale on which a series of intermediate points can be located. Van den Berghe denied that this was his intention; the differences between his types were qualitative and not quantitative. Intermediate cases were inherently unstable and tended to move towards one of the ideal types, usually the competitive one. This argument the present author found unpersuasive. Situations of 'race contact' or forms of racial relations varied in too many ways. I thought it better to follow Park in conceiving of a series of orders of race relations which could develop out of initial contact; I called them institutionalized contact, acculturation, domination, paternalism, integration and pluralism (1967: 68–75). I also pointed to characteristic modes of change: 'acculturation leads fairly easily to integration'; domination often gave way to pluralism, whereas paternalism was more likely to be replaced by an integrated order. What I had done was to survey that academic literature which was conventionally labelled as dealing with racial relations, like sorting a set of filing cards into piles based upon the possession of common characteristics. In this way I had produced six categories and given them names, but the six did not differ from one another in any systematic way. Had I been using analytical instead of empirical categories I might have identified dimensions of difference and located empirical cases at different points on them, or have produced a bigger framework in which there might have been a number of empty cells as well as cells in which the best known cases could have been placed. Neither my scheme nor van den Berghe's was well designed for the analysis of relations in industrial cities or the structures governing face-to-face relations about which Hughes had written. My scheme, again like van den Berghe's, could help show how circumstances on the macro-sociological level might influence behaviour on the micro-sociological level, but it neglected the ways in which behaviour on the micro level could change the macro structures. Neither of us had any adequate explanation of change from one kind of order or type to another. As my critics pointed out, Afro-Americans had been thoroughly acculturated in the United States but the nature of their integration remained problematic.

Micro and macro

How to integrate the micro and macro approaches has been a long-standing problem. It was addressed by Hubert M. Blalock in *Toward a Theory of Minority Group Relations* (1967). He started at the micro level, seeing the individual as a person who utilized scarce means in order to attain goals within a patterned social system. As he acknowledged (1967: 49) this was an 'assumption that individuals will act more or less rationally so as to maximize their chances of attaining all important goals. They are expected to select the most efficient means . . . ' The first proposition he advanced was

> In general, the larger the number of feasible alternative means for achieving a given goal, the less likely it is that this goal will be incompatible with a second goal, in the sense that the achievement of the former will reduce the probability of attaining the latter, or vice versa.

Individuals sought to maximize their status, and to this end they avoided being identified with people of low status. There were many alternative means of increasing status and so it was compatible with many other goals. From this starting point, Blalock went on to formulate propositions about economic and status factors as determinants of discrimination. He recognized that in majority–minority relations the dominant group commanded greater resources, and discussed slavery as a type case, concluding that it was usually easier to control slaves by force if (i) they are not members of indigenous groups; (ii) they have been transported from long distances; and (iii) they have diverse cultural backgrounds. Blalock next examined four empirical situations to see what general propositions could be derived from their analysis. They were: (1) competition between white settlers and native peoples; (2) middleman minorities in peasant-feudal societies; (3) the Negro and organized labour in the United States; (4) the Negro and professional sports.

   Blalock contended that the exclusion of minority members from an occupation turned upon the costs and benefits to particular parties of such exclusion, the awareness of what was entailed, and the power of groups to make others accept their view of the facts or the priorities. He presented his conclusions in the form of general propositions making no mention of particular groups. Thus propositions 42 and 52 stated:

> The easier it is to evaluate accurately an individual's performance level, the lower is the degree of minority discrimination by employers.
> The lower the degree of purely social interaction on the job (especially interaction involving both sexes) the lower is the degree of discrimination.

The first of these is a more systematic way of saying that people are less inclined to discriminate when the costs to them of their doing so are evident. The second says that people already employed are less likely to resist the entry to their workplace of people belonging to other groups if their relations with them will be of only an impersonal kind. Blalock then added further propositions (to a total of 97) about, for example, the effect that variations in the relative size of a minority were likely to have upon the motivation of minority members to discriminate. His construction of a set of analytical concepts offers a good example of the nominalist method.

As Blalock's discussion showed, the task of integrating the micro and macro approaches is forbidding. Many, perhaps most, sociologists considered that there was urgent research to be conducted that did not require them to specify all the possible micro-sociological determinants of the data they utilized. One such line of enquiry which prospered in the United States in the 1970s was the study of status attainment, that is, of the factors associated with social mobility. The techniques developed for this purpose have been employed in the study of some other societies. For example, at the start of the 'troubles' in Northern Ireland in 1968 the number of Catholics occupying high status occupations was not proportionate to their numbers in the population. Was this due to discrimination? To approach this question it is necessary to allow for the influence of the family in assisting a child's education, shaping that child's socio-economic expectations and perhaps helping him or her to obtain employment. Since Catholics on average have lower status occupations the sociologist would expect Catholic children to do less well even in the absence of discrimination. In the 1968 data, Catholics had, on average, received 6 months less education and earned almost £3 per week less. The interrelation between family background, occupation, education, district of origin, sex, etc., can be measured by multivariate analysis. This shows that,

> most of the status differences disappeared once education and family background were held constant, while income differences remained significant . . . Catholic children born into elite families suffered substantial differences in education and status, while those born to average families were only slightly disadvantaged, if at all. By contrast, although Catholics generally have less education, those who nonetheless obtain advanced education then get higher status jobs than comparable Protestants. (Kelley and McAllister, 1984: 183–4)

Factors other than discrimination could account for some of the differences. Catholics may not have the same work motivation as Protestants. Higher status Catholics may be employed within their own community which, for various reasons, pays lower wages. The tendency for each community to 'look after its own' in what are regarded as internal matters is a kind of reciprocal discrimination that promotes disadvantages and should be distinguished from the kind of discrimination that is practised in areas controlled by the state, which ought to be above the two communities.

The analysis of status attainment is a technique which could be built out into a theory which would account for the differential influence of education upon the status attained by individuals from different kinds of families and with different levels of educational qualifications. Education would be measured by years of schooling, variations in the quality of the education provided being incorporated in the measure by calculations reflecting expenditure on school buildings and teacher salaries. This theory could treat racial status as a comparable factor, not because this presupposes differential ability but because membership of racial categories, like education, gives rise to various kinds of privilege and disprivilege. When detailed data have been collected it may be possible to separate influences that are often confounded, like racial status and the effects of being an immigrant. Where immigration is voluntary, incomers may be expected to catch up with the incomes of native workers after about 15 years (Chiswick, 1979). This is because migration is a selective process; the ambitious are more likely to migrate and to decide to settle. If they move to a country with a higher living standard they may be pleased to take up positions which are scorned by native workers and this may help them attain higher status eventually.

The status attainment approach informs a comprehensive study by Stanley Lieberson entitled *A Piece of the Pie* (1980). This addresses the question why the immigrants who entered the United States after 1880 from South, Central and Eastern Europe fared so much better than Afro-Americans. He assesses the influence of differences in conditions of settlement, health, participation in the political process, residential segregation, occupations, etc. He has to explain why it was that the position of blacks in the North in the twentieth century started to deteriorate as their numbers increased. Was it because the black migrants coming up from the South were less skilled and observed lower standards in their personal lives? Was it because white hostility increased? Lieberson advances a third explanation, stressing what he calls the latent structure of race relations:

> if an automobile changes speed as we vary the pressure on the gas pedal, we do not assume that the engine changes in character with more or less gas. Rather we assume that the potential range of speeds was always there and is simply altered by the amount of gas received. In similar fashion, it is fruitful to assume that the reason for race relations changing with shifts in composition is not due to radical alteration in the disposition of whites,

but rather that changes in composition affect the dispositions that existed all along.(1980: 375)

In other words, there was an increase in white hostility but not because of a simple shift in attitudes. Whites were hostile to anything or anyone who interfered with their progress towards their goals. When blacks became a greater threat, the task of fighting off black competition moved higher up the whites' scale of priorities. Lieberson also criticises what he calls 'the great non sequitur': the view that the failure of blacks to advance as fast as whites reflected ethnic deficiencies. His evidence shows that they were at a greater disadvantage in many ways: the life expectancy at birth in 1880 of blacks in three United States cities on the Eastern seaboard was 22 years for males and a little over 26 for females. Life expectancy at birth in the countries from which the European immigrants came was usually much higher; for example in Italy it was 34 years for males and nearly 35 years for females. Low average expectancies will reflect high infant mortality, but the differential rates suggest how much more difficult it would have been for black families to build up capital and help their children. Other differences had similar consequences. Blacks were barred from membership in craft unions; residential segregation made them pay more for their housing, and so on.

Such a conclusion leaves many questions unanswered. Why have relations in the United States followed a course different from the courses followed in other American countries to which white immigrants have gone? Why has the colour line remained so distinct when the divisions between white ethnic groups have eroded? Is racial status simply one 'factor' that can be measured against others when assessing attainment?

Rational choice

The status attainment approach has great merits. It permits the relative advantage and disadvantage of different groups to be compared more accurately than by any comparable method, especially since it allows for some of the ways in which individuals' circumstances change over time. This is a great improvement upon snapshot measures of conditions at particular moments. Use of this approach is dependent upon the availability of statistics, collected usually for administrative purposes. Since statistics are compiled in different ways in different countries, it is difficult to compare like with like across national boundaries. If theories are to furnish useful explanations they have to restrict their focus, so it is foolish to criticize them for failing to provide answers to questions they have not attempted to tackle. Nevertheless, as a prospective theory of racial relations, the status attainment approach seems unduly limited (even apart from the problems of data comparability) because it makes so little allowance for interaction between individuals (which is the central concern of symbolic interactionism) and does not link up with the analysis of motivation (one of the strengths of Blalock's venture). These deficiencies are ameliorated, I claim, in the Rational Choice Theory of Racial and Ethnic Relations (Banton, 1983a: 104–9).

Some have been misled by the name into assuming that this is a theory of rational choices; they ask about the criteria of rationality and about the implications of irrational choices. They have misunderstood the argument. The name is used to indicate that this theory is a member of a family of theories which start from a view of social action as the allocation of scarce means to competing ends. This kind of theory has been developed most systematically in economics but it is now increasingly deployed in geography, political science, social anthropology and social psychology as well as in sociology. It has sometimes been called exchange theory.

The version which is most useful in the study of racial and ethnic relations rests upon a series of presuppositions, the first of which states that (a) individuals act so as to obtain maximum net advantage. This assumption, sometimes called that of optimization, is generally acknowledged as a presupposition of all forms of rational choice theory. The second is that (b) actions at one moment of time influence and restrict the alternatives between which individuals will have to choose at subsequent moments. Such an assumption is necessary to many applications of rational choice theory though it is usually left implicit. By making it explicit it is possible to clear up two misunderstandings, one concerning the constraints upon choice, and the other about rationality. Presupposition (b) implies that actions have to be seen as the outcome of choice in situations in which some individuals command more resources than others. One person's lack of resources constitutes a constraint upon his or her range of options. Although they are two sides of the same coin, the relative disadvantage of one person is perceived more sharply than the corresponding advantage of the other, so the simplest way of drawing attention to the relation of choice to resources is to say that choice and constraint are two dimensions of action; they can neither be separated nor weighed against each other. Presupposition (b) might also be extended to make explicit the expectation that unless a society is affected by some disaster changes will result in a greater rationalization of social relations, reducing inconsistencies and resolving conflicts in the social pattern. This comes about as individuals seek to attain the goals held up to them as desirable in the course of their socialization. In industrial societies many consumers go to some length to discover what is the 'best buy'. After making a purchase they may conclude that they have failed to allocate means to ends in the optimum manner; if so, they seek to learn from that experience so that the next time they can make a better buy. It is their procedure that is rational. Just because a purchase turns out to have been a 'bad buy' does not mean that it was the result of an irrational choice. Consumers are impelled in this way to rationalize their purchasing. The rationality that is in question is not a property of some actions rather than others, but a criterion for studying the pattern of behaviour over time. Such an approach breaks away from Max Weber's attempted distinction between rational and non-rational action and links instead with his discussion of the process of rationalization (Banton, 1985b). As Weber argued, in every kind of society, capitalist, socialist, Islamic or Hindu, there are pressures making for the reduction of inconsistencies. People do share common ultimate ends (even if these are neither static nor the foundation of the social order); over the course of time they seem, often unconsciously, to rationalize their lives in terms of these values, whatever they may be.

The alternatives between which individuals have to choose may be more complicated than those facing the ordinary consumer. A more realistic analogy may be that of competition between a big company able to place a massive order, and a very small one that can be forced into bankruptcy. The former has greater resources and can get better terms when purchasing from a manufacturer, it can induce the manufacturer to stop supplying goods to its competitor, or, by temporarily reducing selling prices, force the small firm to cease trading. Like the big company, members of a dominant racial group may be able to select between many alternatives, while limiting those available to the minority; members of that group may feel they must take what is on offer because the only alternative is a rebellion that has no chance of changing the social order. The explanation of how a particular society came to be as it is constitutes a task for the historians, but sociologists can discern processes that are common to many societies, and, by analyzing them, may contribute to the historian's account of why members of different groups confront quite different alternatives.

The application of rational choice theory to social relations requires a reliance upon some further presuppositions, in particular two which may be formulated as principles: (c) the principle of prescriptive altruism has been advanced by Meyer Fortes (1983: 23) as a rule requiring recognition of binding mutual inter-dependence and a willingness to forego selfish gratification. The capacity for prescriptive altruism is generated in the relationship of mother and child and is developed in the process of social-ization. Humans can develop their potential only if they are brought up in social groups. They learn that they have obligations to those who are defined as fellow group members. They become psychologically depen-dent upon their identification with particular groups and upon the receipt of approval from people who represent them. Thus assumptions about group identity are part of the traditions transmitted from one generation to another as a consequence of the decisions covered in presupposition (b).

The analysis of inter-group relations then depends upon (d) the principle of group alignment. To attain their ends individuals may be obliged either to join with others in collective action or to follow a strategy that assumes others will engage in such action. Social groups result from and are main-tained by the goal-seeking actions of individuals, but each individual has many goals with different priorities. Short-term goals may be ordered as part of a strategy for attaining long-term goals. If the cost of attaining one goal increases, an individual may change to pursue another one and align himself or herself with a group that will be of more assistance for this purpose. Sometimes, too, individuals change their goals (as when someone decides to stop smoking!). A group is therefore to be understood as a col-lection of individuals aligned in a distinctive manner with respect to others. Individuals may be psychologically disposed to identify themselves with a particular group because of their socialization, but, as Dollard explained, groups are not maintained by inertia and they are continually forming and dissolving. They come into being in situations defined in particular ways and their continuation over time has to be accounted for by social pro-cesses. Immigrant parents may try to bring up their children to identify with the culture of the homeland. If they fail, as they so often do, this may be because the inducements the parents offer are less powerful than those offered by the children's peer group and by other features of life in the country of settlement.

Alignment can derive either from the psychological processes of identifi-cation or from the more sociological process of commitment. Some indi-viduals wish to keep their options open. They wait to see how they are approached before deciding how they will align themselves. Others indicate in advance that they are committed in some way (as by the Jewish skull-cap, the Sikh turban, the 'Afro' hair style, the Rasta 'locks' or tam in its red, black, green and golden colours). An individual who publicly com-mits himself to a group or a course of action takes a decision which has the effect of reducing future options. It is very important to group mobiliz-ation.

Seen from this viewpoint, racial and ethnic relations have at least five important characteristics which give rise to five corresponding and over-lapping theories. In the first place racial and ethnic groups are defined by their boundaries. To determine whether an individual does or does not belong to a group it is necessary to discover whether that person stands on one or the other side of a boundary. Of course, individuals belong to many groups, and group boundaries overlap too, but there are occasions when membership of a particular group is in question and that can be decided only by knowledge of where the boundaries are drawn. For example, if in North America, oil is found on land belonging to an Amerindian tribal group, many people may claim membership of the group and some rule must be used to decide who can share in any resulting benefits. In the second place – and this refers to more everyday circumstances – groups are identified by signs, such as those of phenotype (outward appearance), language and religion. In the third place, groups are also constituted by the way non-members regard others as members of groups with recognized places in the social system. In the fourth place, groups exist in historical time, their character being influenced by the relative privilege enjoyed by their ancestors or predecessors. In the fifth place, groups are maintained by the differential values of their members. It will be apparent that the second, third, fourth and fifth characteristics contribute to the definition and maintenance of the boundaries mentioned as the first. The five kinds of theory corresponding to these characteristics will be outlined in turn. Only the fifth has so far been elaborated in any detail or used in a way that approximates to the testing of hypotheses. The other four need to be developed further, but they must be outlined to give an indication of the potential of rational choice theory in this field.

The theory of *boundaries* states that

1. Individuals utilize physical and cultural differences in order to create groups and categories by the processes of inclusion and exclusion. Ethnic groups result from inclusive and racial categories from exclusive processes.

This asserts that the distinctions called racial and ethnic are the results of social processes utilizing physical appearance and that the processes continue over time. When relating to someone of different race an individual is unlikely to act in the same way as he or she would act when relating to a person of the same race. The individual would notice that the other person was of a particular complexion, and perhaps had a particular kind of hair or facial structure and would take these as signs that the other person was conventionally assigned to a different racial category from his or her own. This knowledge would then lead the individual to behave differently. Several things are to be noted about this view. Firstly, it is not 'race' but phenotypical features which serve as signs indicating assignment to a social category. Race is a second order abstraction. Secondly, this process is not limited to the sign value attributed to phenotypical variation. It applies equally to the assignment of people because they appear to be of a particular gender or (perhaps because of their costume) of a particular religion, or (perhaps because of their accent) of a particular linguistic group. Thirdly, the process operates in the same way in a society in which blacks rule whites as one in which whites rule blacks. The significance attributed to membership of a racial, gender or religious category varies from one set of circumstances to another and from one individual to another, for some people, knowing that others would discriminate, are inclined to act in the opposite way in order to display their disapproval of conventional values.

In his long list of propositions and sub-propositions Blalock distinguished minorities in terms of their visibility, size, power, etc., and avoided definitions based upon the folk concepts of the people whose behaviour he sought to explain. Yet in the application of his theory he regarded the nature of minority group membership as unproblematic. My version of rational choice theory goes beyond this position to take account of the factors which, in differing ways, make people feel themselves members of minorities. It utilizes two analytical concepts, those of exclusion and inclusion. These are processes at work in all situations of group creation and maintenance, and take different forms in different circumstances; it just so happens that in recent times and in the countries most frequently studied, ideas about race have mostly been used to exclude people from privilege while ideas about shared ethnicity have been used to create bonds of belonging together. This therefore makes possible a pair of definitions which do not depart uncomfortably from the folk concepts but permit greater precision of statement. In circumstances of group contact a common sequence has been for members of the more powerful group to display a high group consciousness, with a strong inclusive boundary round their group. They categorize others as non-members, often paying little attention to differences between groups within the excluded category. Since they treat all excluded people similarly, these may come together in a new alignment and develop a sense of belonging together, and thus an inclusive boundary, where they had none in the past. Thus what was a racial category may become an ethnic group as well. Afro-Americans provide a notable example of this.

2. When groups interact, processes of change affect their boundaries in ways determined by the form and intensity of competition; and, in par-

ticular, when people compete as individuals this tends to dissolve the boundaries that define the groups, whereas when they compete as groups this reinforces those boundaries.

A boundary is the product of alignment which in turn results from the action of individuals seeking their goals. Once individuals start to trade goods and services with members of another group they will create ties across the group boundary that will weaken it. A different set of circumstances arises when, say, members of the dominant group hire the labour of members of the subordinate group at a standard rate so that an employer who is willing to pay higher wages is prevented from doing so and members of the subordinate group cannot look around for an employer willing to pay them better. This is a situation of group competition in which hostility between groups is generated and the patterns of alignment reinforce the boundaries. In such circumstances the price of the goods or services traded is influenced by the power of the dominant group to set terms favourable to its members. That power is dependent upon a structure within the group that enables its leaders to keep potential deviants in check.

In this simple form the theory of boundaries is a theory of trade between two partners. Matters become much more complicated when inter-group relations involve three or more parties.

The theory of *signs* states that the nature of relations between groups based upon race, ethnicity, language, religion, etc. varies because of the characteristic that is the basis for group formation. Simple illustrations can be found by examining what is considered deviant behaviour. A religious group may be intolerant of theological idiosyncrasies (reading them as signs that a member's commitment to the group is questionable), but be uninterested in its members' political opinions, whereas a political group will see things the other way round. A racial, ethnic or linguistic group will have a conception of deviance only in so far as it is also a political group. From a sociological standpoint the two chief characteristics of groups based upon race are that membership is involuntary and that it is transmitted in association with kinship. It is involuntary in that other people assign individuals to racial categories independently of their wishes so that someone who does not wish to be identified with such a group may nevertheless have no alternative. Membership is also transmitted in families, so that individuals are usually assigned, and assign themselves, to the same categories and groups as their parents and kinsfolk. Thus the signs used for constructing racial groups have more far-reaching consequences than those which are the basis for most other kinds of groups, though in

Northern Ireland assignment to religious categories is almost as effective even if the signs are less evident. The signs used to allocate people to racial categories are highly visible and are often defined as relevant in a wide range of social situations, so that racial solidarity is easily evoked and the resulting social patterns may be reinforced by ideologies of difference.

Physical features signifying a degree of African origin have different sign values in Benin, Bahia and Baltimore. Within Baltimore more attention may be paid to variations in skin colour at a wedding reception than in a cinema queue. As has already been explained, a coffee-coloured complexion is, in Bahia, one factor among others in assessing someone's claim to status; in Baltimore it may have a comparable significance among Afro-American people but serve as a sign of category membership in an inter-racial context. Just how important category membership is, varies between public and private settings. To use the one word 'race' in connection with two such different social patterns is misleading. Genetic differences between the populations thought of as races by members of the general public can be described only statistically. Physical variation is continuous. It is human societies which rather arbitrarily draw distinctions and use them to create or reinforce social discontinuities.

The theory of *categories* has to account for the discontinuities in the assessment of status, explaining why, in the Deep South, complexion is the basis for categorical distinctions in inter-racial relations and why these distinctions are of more or less importance in different contexts. For example, it might be presumed that, since white domination rested upon control of the political system, the white rank order of discrimination would have placed the maintenance of black disfranchisement as its number one priority. Why should the bar against inter-marriage have occupied this place? Was it because it was a means of organizing white solidarity so that the whites could then enforce black disfranchisement? In what ways are the maintenance of categorical relations dependent upon the means of enforcement?

In a two-category system the maintenance of categories is facilitated by the general assumption that any gain by one side can be only at the expense of the other. The solidarity of one group evokes the solidarity of the other so that conflicts easily escalate. Northern Ireland provides an example of a polarized, two-category system based on assignment to religious (or, more properly, confessional) categories, but there are more relationships there in which religion is socially irrelevant than there were relationships in the Deep South of the 1930s in which racial status was irrelevant. In Northern Ireland marriage across the religious divide may be an occasion for regret or disapproval on the part of kinsfolk but it does not evoke the emotional response of the corresponding situation in the Deep South and South Africa; in both of these regions intimate contact has been considered polluting and inter-racial marriage has been proscribed by law. In most multi-category systems – like the so-called plural societies – the categories are based upon occupational monopolies. While the weaker groups may enter into coalitions to advance their political interests it may not be possible to maintain them for long.

The theory of *group power* is concerned with the terms on which members of groups exchange goods and services, and with the way power affects the implicit bargaining about their price. If the parties cannot agree upon a price, one of them may either withdraw from exchange or utilize political resources to change market conditions. After a period of conflict, exchange may start again on new terms. In the Weberian tradition power is defined as a potential, an ability to influence others or to get them to do what they would not otherwise do. Blalock (1967: 110) rejects this kind of definition. He notes that in the study of physics power is defined as work/ time, so that if two agents perform the same amount of work in different lengths of time, the one which does it quicker exercises more power. Perhaps influenced by the parallel, Blalock defines power as the actual overcoming of resistance in a standard period of time, while admitting that it may be difficult to tell when it has actually been exercised. The definitions of both Weber and Blalock conceive of power as the securing of submission or compliance, but sociologists have to study power as exercised within social relationships and therefore as involved in transactions over time. When the superior party exercises power he or she does so in order to obtain a service, and if the inferior party is reluctant to perform this service he or she may attempt to change the relationship so as to reduce the disadvantage. This may well succeed, for in the long run even the most brutal forms of slavery and subjection have been brought to an end. To study the exercise of power in respect of one action only is to overlook important features of its social character.

According to Anthony Heath (1976: 25–6) the great advantage of the rational choice theory of power is that it can be measured by the price it enables a man to secure for his services.

> To use the theory we have to know about the alternatives open to men and their valuation of them, and we can then make predictions about the consequential rate of exchange. *But we do not actually need to measure power itself directly.* Since power seems to be just about the most difficult

thing to measure in social science this must be counted a notable success for rational choice theory.

Power derives from such things as money, property, physical strength, knowledge, and the expectations others have about the sanctions that could be brought into play. These can all be considered as resources, indeed Blalock (1967: 113) defines resources as 'the actual sources of power, or those properties of the individual or group that provide the power potential or ability to exercise power'. Resources can lie unutilized; they contribute to power only when they are mobilized, so Blalock regards power as a multiplicative function of resources and the degree to which they are mobilized in the service of those exercising the power. While an individual can mobilize power in seeking his or her goals, a more important circumstance arises when one or more individuals mobilize their *collective* resources to improve their collective position in relation to another group. The effect of group power at one point in time then influences the alternatives open in future periods of time.

Thus the power of the whites in the Deep South was displayed in their ability to fix the wages and conditions of service governing the employment of blacks. Differentials in the employment and remuneration of blacks measured that power. Since blacks as a category were disadvantaged this constituted categorical discrimination. However, there were tensions within the white category. Some had a greater interest than others in the defence of the established order, because it protected them from black competition. Some believed that whatever might be their short-term interest, their long-term individual interest, or the long-term collective interest of their group, pointed towards the elimination of racial inequality. Yet even people who had an individual interest in promoting fair competition would not act to advance that interest if they believed that their neighbours would do it for them. Their position would have been like that of the 'free rider' who calculates that if a trade union representing people in his occupation were to win a pay rise he would benefit from it, but that the possibility of their winning a bigger rise were he to join is so small that it would not outweigh the costs to him of having to pay for his membership. So he takes a free ride at the expense of those who do support the union. The structure of white society in the Deep South, and the strength of its justifying ideology, were such that it was difficult for individuals to break ranks. The whites had mobilized to defend their privileges. Blalock (1967: 126) defined degree of mobilization as the proportion of total resources actually utilized or expended to achieve a given objective. Thus in the electoral field mobilization could be measured as the proportion of eligible voters who had registered and had cast their votes. Since in the Deep South the whites allowed only a token few blacks to register as voters they prevented blacks from mobilizing their electoral potential.

A group's resources include natural resources (like oil fields or a strategic location), physical capital (like systems of roads, railways and harbours constructed by earlier generations) and human capital (notably the education, skills and motivation of the people). In World War Two much of Germany's physical capital was destroyed. One school of theorists would argue that the human capital of the nation enabled both the Federal and the Democratic Republics to equal or surpass the national income of countries that in 1945 were more favoured in respect of natural resources and physical capital. These theorists would also maintain that human capital can be transferred, as when migrants with technical skills or high work motivation have gone to new countries and overtaken native groups in their average earnings. With technological progress human capital tends to grow (e.g. through knowledge of how to build ever more efficient machines) but some kinds of knowledge become obsolete. Motivations can be damaged by political instability and the fear that a man may not be able to reap where he has sown. Economic 'aid' to a poor country, if badly planned or administered, can leave that country more dependent than before. The process of deskilling associated with mass-production reduces the value of what were previously valuable talents.

In this way the theory of human capital can be used to explain the relative mobility of ethnic or racial groups, just as the theory of status attainment sets out to explain the mobility of individuals. Thomas Sowell (1983: 248) attests:

> Numerous confiscations of the wealth of Jews in Europe or of the Chinese in south east Asia have been followed by their rising again to prosperity and wealth. In the United States, penniless refugees from Cuba, Korea, or Vietnam have begun in the most menial occupations and within one generation produced a business-owning middle class.

He contends that the effect of enslavement was to destroy much of the human capital that Africans brought to the New World. Irresponsibility and evasion of work were pervasive under slavery and continued after it. Blacks moved out of the South into the Northern cities, in the late nineteenth century, under very unpropitious circumstances. Their prior experience was less valuable than that of European immigrants coming from urban backgrounds. So 'Blacks are unique only in how far they have come and the degree of opposition they have encountered' (Sowell, 1983:

132). This theory states that cultural characteristics determine people's responses to incentives. If the circumstances are such that they are satisfied by the rewards they receive, then the original attitudes are reinforced. People develop attention to detail, punctuality, perseverance, willingness to obey orders and a readiness to work as members of a team. These are constituents of human capital in an industrial society, and by drawing attention to them the theory can furnish a plausible explanation of why things happened as they did. Most of what pass as sociological theories can do this. The objection is that without an independent measure of human capital no one can tell how important it is or whether it is genuinely an independent variable.

The theory of *discrimination* is by far the most developed of the five kinds of theory mentioned earlier. Starting from a study by Sidney Webb of 'The Alleged Differences in the Wages Paid to Men and to Women for Similar Work' which was published in 1891, economists have elaborated a series of possible explanations which apply equally to discrimination based on race and on gender. A recent review recounts their history and compares seven of them. They differ in at least three ways. Two are based on differing assumptions about motivation; three on differing assumptions about market conditions; while two utilize different models (Lundahl and Wadensjö, 1984: 8–80). The first one deals with discrimination as the result of social custom. The discriminator treats less favourably all persons socially assigned to a particular category in the belief that this is required of him by other members of his group. Since it is the unfavourable treatment of those assigned to a category it may be called categorical discrimination. The second explanation is concerned with discrimination as the product of decisions made in conditions of uncertainty. The discriminator treats less favourably all persons socially assigned to a particular category in the belief that those in this category are less likely to possess the qualities he is seeking. This is called statistical discrimination. The third explanation seeks to account for discrimination resulting from monopsony (a situation in which there are many sellers but only one buyer); the fourth and fifth are products of what are called the dual labour market theory and the radical labour market theory and deal with other forms of imperfect competition. The sixth explanation, pioneered by Gary Becker, analyses discrimination in terms of a model of international trade (between a white society rich in capital and a black society rich in labour); while the seventh views discrimination as a result of inequalities in bargaining power.

The intensity and form of competition in a market influence the amount of discrimination that is possible and can reduce or increase any motivation to discriminate. In a competitive market the incidence of discrimination should decline. A white employer may be reluctant to hire black workers, believing them to be less qualified. If this belief is widespread, black workers will be unable to demand the same wages as white workers. If the belief is incorrect, a non-discriminating employer should be able to hire black workers and manufacture a product more cheaply; in this way he should either drive his competitors out of the market or force them also to hire blacks. In due course the black–white differential will be eliminated. If the first white employer does not hire blacks because he believes his white workers would object, his firm too can be threatened by a non-discriminating competitor. Similarly in a private housing market a white vendor may not wish to sell his house to a black purchaser, and may say this is because his white neighbours would not wish this. Yet if a black purchaser offers a higher price there must be a point at which the sale will be concluded (even if – and this is hypothetical – it has to be high enough to provide compensation to the neighbours). In a situation in which there is great hostility to black incomers it can be expected that a high 'colour tax' will be demanded to start with, and that this will subsequently decline if the whites discover that the results are not as alarming as they feared.

Buyers and sellers do not know how a market will react to future changes. They are short of information about future states, and it costs time and money to get information which will help them make the predictions on which their policies will have to depend. They will be averse from risky decisions when the consequences of mistakes are costly. This general principle leads, in the labour market, to what has been named 'the Statistical Theory of Racism and Sexism' (Phelps, 1972). It starts from an attempt to explain what is called search behaviour. This can be the search of one employer for an employee able and willing to perform a certain kind of work in return for a given reward, but it can equally be the search of a would-be worker for a job, a landlord for a tenant, a would-be house purchaser for a house, a woman for a husband or a sports team manager for a player. It assumes that the search carries a cost (because the searcher's time is scarce) and that there is a risk of a further cost if the person or situation selected turns out not to meet the specifications. When deciding whether a particular case falls within the acceptable limits a searcher will interpret the signs displayed. If he is an employer he may judge an applicant by interview, references, trial, or some combination of these. How much he invests in researching an applicant's qualifications will depend upon his estimate of the benefits derivable from increased expenditure on selection relative to the costs entailed by taking the first suitable person; this will include a calculation of how long the applicant, if appointed, will stay in the job and the difficulty of dismissing someone who proves unsatisfactory. The employer will interpret the available evidence in the light of beliefs deriving from previous experience and the impression gained from other sources. The employer may, for example, believe Norwegians to be honest, Nigerians disputatious and Namibians prone to sickness; such beliefs may be with or without empirical support. People generalize from the information available to them, often despite its being insufficient, and this can set up a self-fulfilling prophecy. If an employer concluded that red-haired people were excitable, he could decide against employing them for jobs requiring coolness; if they got cross about being discriminated against, this could then be taken as proof of their excitability.

Beliefs about the differential probability of members of different groups proving good employees lie behind the phenomena of occupational queueing as discussed by Lieberson (1980: 346–51, 377–9). An employer with, say, a largely Italian workforce might have a preference for Italian workers; if he could not get Italians he might prefer white Catholics, then white Protestants, and only if he could not get them would he employ blacks. It would be easier for the employer to maintain these beliefs if he never had any experience of workers from the groups at the end of the queue. If he did, and that experience was satisfactory, his preferences might change. This is a reason for rejecting Lieberson's analogy with an automobile engine. The engine in the latent structure of race relations has as one of its components a set of dispositions based upon beliefs about the probable skills or attributes of minority group members. That component can change and when it does the effect can be very important. It was for this reason that Gunnar Myrdal (1944: 68) attached so much importance to what he called the 'principle of cumulation'. This must be a major consideration in any comparison of the economic advance of Asian-Americans and Afro-Americans. As Lieberson writes, the initial response to Chinese and Japanese workers in the United States was every bit as violent as that towards blacks who sought to compete with whites. White resistance to Asian competition was so strong that it led to the cessation of Asian immigration, so that the numbers of Japanese and Chinese remained small relative to blacks. Because they were no longer perceived as a serious threat they were then able to establish themselves in some niches in the expanding West Coast economy and their subsequent advance has been very rapid. White prejudice has declined because they were successful and there is no longer so strong a disposition to discriminate against them. Social acceptability is often a reward for success rather than a precondition.

Search behaviour can give rise to statistical discrimination in which people assigned to a particular category are the victims of discrimination deriving from the discriminator's beliefs about the category as a whole. The discriminator may believe that there is a more than even chance that Nigerians will prove disputatious but consider that it is not worthwhile arranging some special selection procedure to identify the ones that are not. This form of discrimination is therefore rational behaviour judged by the conventional criteria of business reality even if it is not rational from the standpoint of a society troubled by hostility or inequality between groups. Some of the elements of the rational choice theory are brought together in the analysis of public goods (Banton, 1968: 26–8). In economic theory public goods are things like clean air, protection from foreign enemies, and a system of highways. If the air is clean for one person it is clean for all others. If one person is protected from foreign attack by the national army, so are all others. If a road is there for one driver, it is equally available to others. No taxpayer has a private right to the air he wants to breathe, to the services of the artillery, or to the roadway outside his house. Thus public goods are characterized by jointness of supply: once the good is produced for one person, it can be made available to others at little or no extra cost. They are also characterized by the way that they are external to ordinary market transactions. They may make trading possible, and increase national wealth, but those who produce them cannot charge users as they might charge them for private services. (Of course, there are schemes for charging road-users proportionate to use, as with differential licence fees for heavy vehicles, but these are as yet of a limited character.) The concept of a public good is helpful for defining the objectives of public policy in the realm of racial relations. Racial discrimination can be seen as a public bad corresponding to atmospheric pollution. In neither case are the negative consequences evenly distributed, but the overall effect of both is to reduce the welfare of the society as a whole. The equivalent of clean air is then racial harmony, though this is not a very good name since grossly unfair relations may for a time appear harmonious. Just as it is difficult to agree a positive definition of freedom, as a freedom *to* things, and more satisfactory to define freedom in terms of freedom *from* various kinds of oppression, so it is better to define racial harmony as an absence of discrimination and other features which embitter social relations or may come to do so.

Mobilization

There are remarkable variations in the extent to which groups use their resources to build up their collective power. In nineteenth-century Europe a sequence of groups developed nationalist movements and succeeded in creating their own nation states, yet Ernest Gellner (1983: 43) concluded from his study that there had been only one effective nationalism for every ten cases in which, had things been in some way different, comparable developments could have occurred. In the mid twentieth century one of the most notable social changes was the way Afro-Americans were able to increase their collective identification and exert greater influence upon the national stage. Why are some groups, in some circumstances, able to mobilize like this when so many never do?

For a long time it has been assumed that when individuals stand to gain from collective action they will organize as a collectivity, but there are variables which intervene between sharing interests and acting upon this basis. The rational choice theory, as this has been elaborated by Michael Hechter, Debra Friedman and Malka Appelbaum (1982), predicts that an individual will join in a collective action only when he expects the benefits of his participation to exceed the costs. The collective action is one designed to secure a public good, so that non-participants will also benefit from any success. This application of the theory culminates in an equation designed to specify the basic factors determining the individual's net benefit from participation in the action under consideration. They are (i) the amount of the public good he expects to obtain if the collective action succeeds; plus (ii) the amount of private reward; these together are then multiplied by (iii) his estimate of the probability of success; to this is added (iv) the amount of private reward expected for participation regardless of the probable outcome; then subtractions are made to allow for (v) the amount of private punishment if the action fails; and (vi) the cost of injury; these last two are then multiplied by (vii) their likelihood; to this is added (viii) the amount of private punishment the individual expects to receive if he does not join the collective action. This equation predicts when collective action is likely to take place; it also has implications about the likely forms of such action, predicting, for example, that forms which entail fewer personal costs for individuals will occur with greater relative frequency. It further implies that the position of an ethnic group in the stratification system has no direct bearing either on a member's decision to participate or on the group's propensity to engage in collective action.

The single most important variable influencing the values given to the component elements of the equation is group organization. Hechter and his associates explain that the organization supplies private goods to its members; it can prevent free-riding; and it controls the information available to members so that it can more easily persuade them that collective action can succeed. Sometimes organizations are set up to secure public goods for members of an ethnic group. Sometimes organizations which already exist for the purpose of supplying private goods to members (like churches and social clubs) can be redirected to seek political or economic benefits for the groups as a whole (i.e. public goods). Ethnic mobilization may then be a by-product of activity originally oriented towards some other goal.

This notion of a capacity for collective action as a by-product is important. It also points to a major limitation upon the utility of rational choice theory, namely, the extent to which present possibilities are always constrained by the products and by-products of past activities. Any theory has to start somewhere, so that some social scientists think it only reasonable that they should start at some point in time and take for granted the effect of previous history in producing groups that have developed distinctive cultures, created social institutions and acquired particular positions in structures of power. If it turns out that they have not started far enough back in time they can always move back their point of departure. The rational choice theory does not account for the values that people place upon their likes and dislikes though it can account for the patterns of behaviour produced by aggregates of individuals and why those patterns change in particular ways. It assumes, for example, that physical features have a given social significance, but critics ask how it was that the features in question came to be used in this way in the first place? This question can be dismissed on the same grounds as people dismiss the question whether the chicken came before the egg. But on the empirical level the problem does not always go away so easily. Several of the factors in the Hechter equation depend very much upon the individual's assessment of how others may react and of the kind of relationship in which the parties are involved. They may be more anxious to prevent their rivals obtaining a benefit than to obtain one for themselves. Some of these problems may be elucidated by using a very elementary application of the theory of games. Relations between groups are then seen to result from implicit processes of bargaining for collective benefit.

Inter-caste relations in Hindu India provide illustrations of what is called a zero-sum game. Members of one caste group may maintain that because of past misfortune they have been forced into a lower position in the caste hierarchy than they once occupied. They mobilize to try to have this alleged injustice rectified. Success would mean moving up the scale and forcing some other groups to move down one rank each, so that the first group's gain would be others loss; if the gains and losses are added up they cancel out and the sum is zero. A hierarchical system of ranking necessarily generates tension about the justice of relative positions and threatens social tranquility, but in the Indian system its divisive implications have been counterbalanced by the division of labour which gives each caste group a monopoly upon some trade. Since each group needs the others' economic services they do not normally push very far their disagreements about rank. One instance has been described however in which a dissatisfied group refused any longer to provide services for the Brahmins and therefore could not call upon them to officiate at marriages. They carried their resistance to the point at which an increasing number were not marrying (Harper, 1968). In such circumstances one group may be worse off and no other group may derive any benefit; this is a negative-sum game. It can be contrasted with the sort of change in which members of all castes are allowed to follow any occupation they wish; the result is likely to be an increase in the total wealth of the society, so that if everyone's gains and losses are added up the result is a positive sum. Inter-group competition is most fierce when the parties believe they are involved in zero-sum relations; a gain by one group is seen by another as necessarily a loss on their part. If the government of Malaysia, for example, makes a concession to the Chinese population it may be pressed to give some corresponding benefit to the Malays. Zero-sum tension can be most effectively resolved when energies are redirected into positive-sum competition. This in turn may depend upon acceptance of the view that the elimination of racial discrimination will be a public good.

Where group relations are on a zero-sum basis, each individual's consciousness of his or her group identity will be constantly reinforced. As Nathan Glazer and Daniel P. Moynihan (1965: 19–20) noted, some writers have conceived of ethnicity as a primordial attribute; they assume that everyone has an ethnic identity which may be fundamental to their very being. Other writers have been dubbed circumstantialists because they regard the character and intensity of ethnic consciousness as the product of circumstances. The opposition is partly the philosophical one of realism and nominalism already discussed, and partly a reflection of different experiences. For Jews, Sikhs, Afrikaners and people in Northern Ireland, ethnic boundaries often coincide with religious boundaries and the significance of group membership to many kinds of contact is constantly reinforced. In such circumstances, group membership may be of fundamental importance in the psychological development of individuals. They then see their ethnicity as something primordial. People may then place a higher value upon any benefits that collective action may bring to their groups. Collective action may be more easily organized because past activities have bequeathed an institutional framework.

The calculation of possible benefit may depend upon whether someone takes a short- or long-term view. An elderly person might believe that a change in the social order could be only beneficial in the long-term but fear that it would be painful and dangerous in the short-term. Readiness to take the long-term view might depend upon that person's age, occupation, number of children and group identification. When it is very difficult for anyone to calculate the likely risks, costs and benefits, much may depend upon the ability of political activists to persuade their fellows that the net benefits would be greater and the chances of success high. It is for this reason that Hechter's specification about the control of information supplied to group members is important. Activists are likely to be altruists in that their only private benefits will be the satisfaction they get from serving the cause to which they devote themselves. Once they start to gain support, then other group members may revise their estimation of the chances of success and support for the movement may gather strength like a snowball being rolled down a hill. The organization it creates will be able to act as a bargaining agency in negotiating with the institutions of the majority society.

In comparing different versions of rational choice theory it is useful to distinguish between act utilitarianism and rule utilitarianism. In philosophical discussion this is a distinction between two sets of criteria for judging the goodness or badness of actions, but in sociology it can be used to differentiate two kinds of assumption in the interpretation of behaviour. Act utilitarianism is the assumption that actions are intended to maximize net advantages. Rule utilitarianism envisages a two step process. It sees rules as so formulated as to maximize net advantages for those bound by them. Individual members of groups are expected to observe group rules, but they may calculate their individual costs and benefits of observance and comply with them only to the extent that maximizes their individual net advantages. Act utilitarianism usually lies behind theories which seek to account for the behaviour of individuals. The version of rational choice theory I have advanced claims only to account for aggregate behaviour. A manufacturer may be confident that if he spends a given sum on advertising, his sales will increase by a particular proportion. He may know to which subgroup in the population the advertizing should be directed, but he will not be able to predict which individual customers will make purchases. The expectation that a given number will increase their purchasing derives from a knowledge of how people have behaved on previous similar occasions and of their own pattern of preferences. There is no direct connection here with rule utilitarianism, but a version of the theory which limits itself to aggregate behaviour and allows for the influence of rules in generating costs and benefits is more realistic.

The rational choice theory of racial and ethnic relations resolves the

'micro-macro problem' by starting from individual behaviour and introducing into the analysis components which recognize the constraints to
which individual actors are subject and the way in which individuals are
organized in collectivities. One of its great merits is that it does not treat
groups as if they had a life of their own but shows how they are constituted
from individual behaviour and are subject to continual change as individuals respond to changes in their circumstances. Seen in historical
perspective, it synthesizes components of the ecological theory, structural-
functionalism, symbolic interactionism, and status attainment to constitute a comprehensive theory.

The consequences of the nation-state

In the earlier discussion of group boundaries it was claimed that once individuals start to trade goods and services with members of another group
they will create ties across the group boundary that will weaken it. A brief
but classic analysis of this process was advanced by Max Gluckman (1955:
140–52) in his account of the developments in Zululand after the
imposition of direct control by the British in 1887. The Zulu themselves
were divided and this facilitated the growth of alignments that crossed the
colour line. With the Zulu King in exile, some members of the royalist
section asked a British Native Commissioner to adjudicate in a dispute
between them. Royalist chiefs who, to start with, had refused government
stipends, decided to accept them. Some chiefs thought it advantageous to
align themselves with the new government while the Commissioners tried
to make use of them in their administration. In tax collecting, control of
hunting, pass-laws, and like matters, a steadily increasing minimum of
allegiance to the Commissioner was enforced. Thus 'desire for peace, for
White technical assistance, and for White money and goods, introduced
conflicts in Zulu allegiance, and thus led some Zulu – eventually almost all
Zulu – into cooperation with Whites'. Nor were the Whites without their
divisions. 'Missionaries who wanted to evangelize, educate, and improve
Zulu approached them with interests very different from Boer farmers:
churches of Zulu and Whites worshipping together arose. Traders and
[labour] recruiters had other interests.' In pursuit of various, and often
conflicting ends in the new social system, bonds were created between sections on opposite sides of the colour line which enabled that system to
work and to expand as a way of integrating economic and social activity.
Within it there was a deep cleavage, but in the late nineteenth century there
were many situations in which the black–white conflict was not obtrusive.

Under a different regime cross-cutting ties of class and religion could have strengthened until they balanced the opposition between black and white.

The circumstance which most prevents the growth of such ties is the existence of monopoly. In the South African case it has been the white monopoly of so much of the country's natural resources and so many of the best positions in the social and economic order. In plural societies like Burma and Malaysia the position was complicated by the entry of an immigrant minority attuned to a market economy and the unresponsiveness of the native peoples to the new incentives. Indian and Chinese middlemen seized control of the agricultural marketing. Peasant producers rapidly became indebted to them. Though there were cross-cutting ties between the small farmer and the middleman, and though they had certain common interests, these did not counterbalance the tensions in the relationship, and ethnic alignments sharpened until they threatened the political order. In the conditions of the plural society the growth of cross-ethnic alignments is a slow process but its reality is demonstrated by a recent study in Malacca Town, in a region of malaysia where inter-ethnic relations have a long history and where relations are more harmonious than in many other parts of the country.

Dr Sanusi Osman (1981) asked a sample of respondents belonging to the Malay, Chinese, Indian and Portuguese groups to comment upon five situations in which their ethnic identifications might run counter to other identifications, like those of class, religion and politics. The first was one in which the daughter of a Malay padi planter asked her father's permission to marry a Chinese boy who was working in the same factory. Respondents in all groups favoured inter-marriage, the rates varying between 81 and 89 per cent; many Malays insisted that permission should be conditional upon the bridegroom's agreeing to become a Muslim. The second question concerned the award of a scholarship; all groups, by percentages varying between 75 and 84, declared that the scholarship should be given to a young Portuguese who was the son of a fisherman because he deserved assistance more than the other young men whose parents were wealthier. Thirdly, people were asked about government action in evicting a group of Malays who had unlawfully built a squatter settlement on government land. On this issue there was more support for the squatters among Malays (40 per cent) than the non-Malays, but the responses reflected socio-economic as well as ethnic identification. Fourthly came a situation in which a Chinese employer threatened to dismiss 150 textile workers who had gone on strike. Again, Chinese respondents were no more likely to side with the Chinese employer than were the Malays or the other groups. Respondents with higher income, irrespective of ethnicity, were less likely to support the workers and more likely to blame both sides. Finally, when asked to choose between Malay and Chinese men, one of each with a high status and one of each with a low status background, as possible prime ministers, all groups preferred the low status Malay who was a trade union leader. Ethnic alignment was evident, and, among the Malays a class alignment within that framework, but middle- and high-income Chinese were more inclined than were low income Chinese, to prefer the trade unionist, apparently believing that someone with this background was more likely to be able to provide effective leadership. These results show that while ethnic alignment may be dominant at the most generalized level of national politics it can be less important in many other contexts, and that group boundaries are affected by the growth of common sentiment and the recognition of national interests.

The earlier discussion of Furnival's concept of the plural society served as a reminder of the tendency for colonial governments to permit and at times reinforce ethnic occupational monopolies, giving extra credence to the belief that they acted on the maxim 'divide and rule'. This inference has been questioned (Horowitz, 1985: 66–8, 75–6, 149–60). But Furnival's study also provided many examples of colonial governments' taking steps to bring benefits to native populations (such as health and educational services) well in advance of any demand for these services. Greater wealth permitted an expansion in governmental activity, an increase in the power of the state, and the growth in size of the public sector within the national economy. A private economic sector can exist only within a political unit that provides for the enforcement of contracts, and the working of this sector is greatly facilitated when government regulation permits the establishment of banks and systems of credit. Given such institutions, however, the private sector is self-regulating in that labour is rewarded according to the marginal value of its productivity, and so on. The public sector is different, in that within this sector resources are allocated by more subjective criteria. Governments decide what customs duties and taxes they will impose, and upon whom; they decide where the roads, schools and hospitals will be built, who will get the contracts, who will be employed in the civil service, and what their salaries will be. Control of the state's powers has always been a glittering prize and the value of that prize has not diminished with industrialization. These powers are not subject to the discipline of the private sector; public sector rewards may bear no relation to marginal productivity. Alvin Rabushka observes that in multi-racial societies the introduction of electoral politics causes candidates for office to appeal to racial constituencies; the need to form winning coalitions, whether by ballots or by rifles, converts communities of individuals into competing groups.

In the developed states of Europe and North America such conflicts can be contained, but in parts of the world where ethnic groups have not developed common interests, or a consciousness of common interests, group competition can be dangerous. The imperial power could limit racial discord by acting neutrally between groups or by enforcing a free enterprise economy upon them. What happened was that the shared consciousness which developed among people subjected to alien rule was an anti-imperialist consciousness which permitted common action in the pre-independence era but dissolved when the imperial power withdrew. The numerically largest group took control of the state power and used it to reward its own supporters. One of the ways in which it has done this is to remunerate them through the public sector where the costs of discrimination in employment are less evident. Members of the minorities are therefore inclined to enter the private sector where they have a better chance of being allowed to compete as individuals. Sometimes, as in East Africa, government power has been used to expel minorities.

The conclusion drawn by Rabushka (1974: 98) is that 'those who desire racial harmony should support the development and expansion of a free market economy in which government's role is restricted to providing the institutional framework within which market exchange can take place, and to defend that market system from those who seek to destroy it'. The formulation (rightly, in my view) assigns extensive and active functions to governments, even if Rabushka chooses not to acknowledge this when he says that the closer any society approximates perfect competition then the more likely is it that government intervention will cause racial tension. It was said long ago that all men would be monopolists if they could. Even in countries committed to the ideal of a free market economy like the United States many markets are heavily influenced by monopoly power and governmental enforcement of anti-trust legislation is essential. In other parts of the world there is little chance of free market economies being established without government regulation, for if the governments of underdeveloped countries were to allow powerful overseas companies to control their production section the result would be predictable. For lack of any countervailing power to balance that of the overseas company, the prices given for products would reflect conditions in the low-wage economy and not the prices those goods could command in the high-wage economy. Dissatisfaction in the former country would lead to a change of regime and the adopting of another trading policy (Furnival referred to one consequence of such an imbalance when he wrote that British rule opened up Burma to the world and not the world to Burma; the Burmese government has since adopted strong measures in order to restrain the influence of outside economic interests). Governmental intervention in economic activity can be productive of racial tension but it can equally be essential to the promotion of racial harmony. Only if a truly competitive market existed at the time in question (which would indeed be remarkable) might it be reasonable to prescribe non-intervention by the government.

Imperial rule can claim to have contributed in a very positive manner to the development of relations between persons of different ethnic and racial groups. In Africa one of its legacies is the existence of several large multi-ethnic states like those of Kenya, Nigeria, Zaire and Zimbabwe. All of them have managed to contain the tensions between their constituent ethnic groups and, in the cases of Nigeria and Zaire, to frustrate attempted secessions. The political framework developed by the British for the government of the Indian sub-continent was not sufficiently strong to withstand the pressures that led to its partition in 1947, or to the subsequent secession of Bangladesh from Pakistan. But, given their internal diversity, the very size of these states testifies to the merits of a political history which developed forms of government that transcended ethnic alignments. The nation-state with its doctrine of 'one man, one vote' suffers from inherent disadvantages in the promotion of inter-group harmony by comparison with imperial or theocratic rule in which ultimate authority is independent of the contending parties. When popular majorities prevail it is easy for an ethnic group with 55 per cent of the vote to insist upon policies unacceptable to another group with 45 per cent of that vote, so that the latter group then attempts to secede. The desire for national independence has been given a moral priority in the era of decolonization. It has been one of the values which individuals have sought to maximize; the costs to minorities of such preferences have rarely entered into the calculations of net benefit implicitly made by members of the majorities. Politicians could advance their own interests by appealing to purely ethnic constituencies and the long-term benefits of institutions transcending ethnic boundaries have been neglected. In an international order dominated by the political power that springs from technological advance, there are great advantages in creating large states or groupings of states. Of course, it is easier for the outsider to perceive these advantages. What happened in several parts of the world was that with the approach of independence, or shortly afterwards, different ethnic groups struggled either for control of the apparatus of the new nation-state or to improve their share of the power. In countries like Burundi, Rwanda and Zanzibar

(Kuper, 1977) this led to terrible massacres. Elsewhere the processes of ethnic polarization led to the expulsion of a minority or genocidal attack (Burma, Uganda, Indonesia), or contributed to partition (Cyprus). Malaysia has, with great difficulty, managed to restrain these processes but in Sri Lanka the position remains critical.

The concept of class as a set of individuals standing in a common relationship to a labour market is sometimes cast in a macro-sociological framework. This chapter has discussed its micro-sociological foundations, recognizing that individuals almost everywhere form coalitions in their struggles to curtail market competition, often by using the powers of the state to serve their sectional ends. The same processes, with minor variations, can explain the formation, on the one hand, of racial and ethnic groups, and, on the other, of social classes as conflict groups persisting over time. From the analysis of these processes models of social transitions can be derived (e.g. North, 1983) which help illuminate the histories of societies and regions. Some of these models deal with the processes of 'modernization'; others seek to generalize features of the contacts which have occurred between European imperial powers and small-scale technologically simple societies (e.g. Rex, 1986: 38–58). These models and rational choice theory both oversimplify reality but in different ways. The latter simplifies by isolating particular elements in behaviour. The former simplifies by generalizing about collectivities (planters, landlords, peasants, estates, castes, classes) not as aggregates, but as if all members of these categories had the same interests and experiences, and acted in unison. This procedure is that of methodological collectivism, though sometimes in a relatively weak form. Whether such simplifications are justified depends upon their utility in explaining the known evidence about societies and in directing the search for new evidence. Therefore, in the present stage of their development, these models are best assessed by their contribution to the study of particular historical sequences. They have not yet achieved any synthesis with a political appeal comparable to the Marxist model of historical change as the outcome of class struggle. Certain distinctive features of that model are considered in the next chapter.

5

RACE AS CLASS

The typologists sought to account for the special features of human races, and of the relations between them, by subsuming these within a general theory of the permanence of types. Social scientists have sought to account for the social aspects of racial differentiation by bringing these within the ambit of their own theories of group formation and group relations. To do so they have extended general theories by adding extra propositions designed to allow for the ways in which racial groups differ from other kinds of groups. However, among the social science theories there is a deep gulf between those discussed here in terms of status and class. It is an opposition between orthodox sociology and Marxism which is manifested in the conflict between weak and strong definitions of class. The sources of conflict can be traced back to two epistemologies, the one associated with the name of Kant and the other with that of Hegel, though the difference is also expressed as an opposition between positivism and realism and parallels the opposition between nominalism and realism discussed earlier. The simplest way of illustrating this difference is that teachers in the former tradition have asked their students 'what is your problem?' while those in the latter enquire 'what is the problem?'.

Epistemological assumptions

At present it is very difficult to describe the difference between the two epistemologies because there is no neutral ground. Any formulation must be framed from the standpoint of one or other of the two contending parties. A contemporary exponent of the Kantian approach, Sir Karl Popper, contrasts what he calls philosophical pluralism and philosophical monism. (The appropriateness of these names is disputable, and it should be noted that Kant did not subscribe to pluralism in the usual philosophical sense.) According to philosophical pluralism in Popper's terminology there are three worlds (i) the physical world of matter; (ii) the mental world of subjective states; and (iii) the world of objective knowledge which results from humans' attempts to understand what is around them. This knowledge 'is the product of men just as honey is the product of bees' (Popper, 1972: 154). In this tradition, a definition has to be suited to its purpose, depending upon the theory to be tested and developed. What appears to a research worker as a problem is decided by his training and his interest in following up a line of thought. He uses the theories of his subject to organize and refine his observations. Solving one problem he discovers more and from this activity of problem-solving an intellectual tradition emerges.

Those within the Hegelian tradition subscribe to what, by contrast, Popper calls philosophical monism. The observer is within the world, but there are laws of its development which he can grasp. The world of knowledge is not separate, and what men think they know is determined by their position in societies at particular states of their development. A person who has grasped the principles according to which the world is developing should use that knowledge to hasten its development, serving, in Marx's phrase, 'as a midwife to history'. Definitions must correspond to the nature of things defined and these can be understood only if they are located in the processes of change. A Marxist would be sceptical of the suggestion that it is possible to select a problem and then compare the power of orthodox and Marxist theories to resolve it. The Marxist insists that the task is not to interpret the world but to change it; therefore the social scientist should identify the politically significant problem and concentrate upon that.

The Kantian stance dominated social science in the United States during the first half of the twentieth century to such an extent that it was taken for granted. Twenty years passed before the seriousness of the challenge issued in Oliver C. Cox's *Caste, Class and Race* was appreciated by more than a small minority. The social movements of the 1960s brought an upsurge of interest in Marxism as an approach which promised to unite history and social science. As an exemplar of Marxism, Cox's work has grave defects (see Miles, 1980) but it is of prime historical significance for any discussion of how racial theories have developed.

What distinguished Cox's philosophy of social science can best be seen in his statements about how the phenomena of racial relations are to be defined. Early in that section of the book devoted to race he set out to eliminate certain concepts that he believed to be commonly confused with that of race relations. One of the concepts to be eliminated was that of racism, because studies of its origin substituted 'the history of a system of rationalization for that of a material social fact' (1948: 321). He did not state this explicitly, but it can be deduced that in his view material social facts could be understood only as features of historical constellations. He concluded that 'probably the crucial fallacy in Park's thinking is his belief that the beginnings of modern race prejudice may be traced back to the immemorial periods of human associations' (1948: 474). According to Cox, Park failed to appreciate the differences between the social formations of classical antiquity and of modern capitalism. Something quite new took place when Europeans appropriated territory in the New World and created a system of social relations based upon the principles of capitalism. For this system to develop, labour was required. The system could grow more rapidly if that labour, or a large section of it, could be bought and sold just like any other commodity and the labourers treated as chattels rather than as people. A supply of labour was found in Africa which could be marketed in this way since Africans were physically distinctive and could therefore be made subject to special laws. If white workers could be persuaded that black workers were different, then they might not perceive that the true interest of all workers lay in their taking common action against their exploiters. The 'material social fact' was therefore a complex system of relations which would develop in a historically predictable manner.

In 1948 Cox understood 'racism' to 'refer to a philosophy of racial antipathy' though more writers at that time seemed to define it as a doctrine, dogma or ideology according to which race determines culture (i.e. as a component of an explanation). I discussed its use as a concept in that sense in an address published in 1970. Cox commented privately on my address: 'if racism is not societally based – an emanation of a given society – it is not anchored in time and space. We become concerned with an historical study of intellectual usage . . . racism . . . can be dead only if changes in the society itself demonstrate it.' This suggests that, if not in 1948, then at a later date Cox was willing to regard 'racism' rather than 'race prejudice' as an appropriate name for 'the socio-attitudinal facilitation of a particular type of labour exploitation' (1948: 393). It is not a distortion of Cox's line of thought if, in accordance with a meaning that the name has acquired in the last twenty years, it is said that in Cox's view, racism was a new phenomenon that was part and parcel of the growth of capitalism. It had become the *explanandum* (that which is to be explained) instead of being part of an *explanans* (that which explains).

At one point Cox wrote that:

> we may think of race relations as that behaviour which develops among people who are aware of each other's actual or imputed physical differences. Moreover, by race relations we do not mean all social contacts

between persons of different 'races', but only those contacts the social characteristics of which are determined by a consciousness of 'racial' difference. Two people of different 'race' could have a relation that was not racial. (1948: 320)

This reads like the kind of definition found in orthodox sociology and suggests that Cox had not completely liberated himself from the position he was attacking. As can be seen from other parts of his book things were to be defined not by the parties' consciousness but by their functions in the social order; 'race relations . . . are labor-capital-profits relationships; therefore, race relations are proletarian-bourgeois relations and hence political-class relations' (1948: 336). In such circumstances it is to be expected that people will become conscious of actual or imputed physical differences, but the object of a study is a complex of relations existing on different levels (productive forces, relations of production and ideological forms) located in a historical sequence.

For Park, the phenomena of race relations had many facets, and presented many problems to the social scientist. Racial differentiation occurred in an ecological context as different human groups competed for resources. It could also be studied in terms of prejudice, an expression of the consciousness of a group seeking to defend a privileged position; in terms of social distance, as members of such a group regulated the kinds of relations they would enter into with varying sorts of non-members; in terms of personality, for example, the effect of occupying a socially marginal position; and so on. There were as many problems as there were useful ways of looking at the evidence. For Cox, there was one inclusive problem, the historical fact of racial differentiation; the sociologist's conceptual frame-work had to be adjusted to grasp the object of study and to reveal the principles which explained its changing character. The opposition between these two views is at root epistemological. For the intellectual tradition in which Park stood, knowledge grows from the ordering of evidence within the concepts defined by a theory; for Cox, knowledge was revealed in history to those who could study it unhindered by the biases of class interest.

Discussion of these issues has been hindered by the diversity of ways in which, especially since the late 1960s, the word 'racism' has been employed. For a scholar working within the strictly Hegelian tradition of Marxism, according to which underlying historical forces generate the social forms, what matters is that blacks, browns, reds, whites and yellows have been differentiated so that they occupy different positions within social orders although there is no biological justification for racial inequality. The influences upon the consciousness of individuals that stimulated them to differentiate themselves are worth investigating provided it is remembered that they lead to no final answer. The real determinants are to be found on a lower level, and they are structured by opposing class interests. Beliefs about race do not have the objective reality of class; they encourage a distorted view of social affairs; by acting as brakes upon the class struggle they delay the challenge from the working class. From this standpoint it is the fact of racial differentiation which matters and which should be the criterion for a definition of racism. To take a contemporary example, which may illustrate this point even if for some readers it may seem to neglect the magnitude and pervasiveness of racism, some of the British immigration laws are labelled racist because they exclude a greater proportion of non-white would-be entrants than white entrants; if they excluded equal proportions they would not be so labelled. What matters is not the intention of the people who passed the laws but their consequences. If, after a time, the laws no longer excluded a greater proportion of non-whites they would no longer be racist. This, of course, is not the only current sense in which the word 'racism' is used, but it illustrates how, for those who start from a particular reading of history, it is the fact of racial differentiation which should be the focus of interest and should guide the manner in which the building blocks of history are defined. Since scholars in the two traditions have different intellectual objectives they are bound to work with different definitions of concepts such as 'racism'.

According to Cox, the class struggle was the motive power behind the history of our era. 'Racial antagonism is part of this class struggle, *because* it developed within the capitalist system as one of its fundamental traits. It may be demonstrated that racial antagonism, as we know it today, never existed in the world before about 1492; moreover, racial feeling developed concomitantly with the development of our modern social system.' This reflects the strong concept of class as the key to history; racial division affects the class struggle, but, since class is the more important in the long-run, racial alignments have to be seen as influences upon class formation rather than the other way round. Cox did not wish to be read as stating that the white race was the only one capable of race prejudice. 'It is probable that without capitalism, a chance occurrence among whites, the world might never have experienced race prejudice.' A peculiar feature of his book is the way Chapter Sixteen, concerning the history of racial antagonism, suddenly yields place to a chapter describing seven situations of race relations. As the author is chiefly concerned with the qualities of social systems, the reader expects a typology that shows how structures of race relations are associated with particular social systems and phases of their development, but Cox advanced his seven situations simply as the major forms in which racial conflicts presented themselves in the modern world. A systematic typology would have stated the criteria of classification and would probably have ended up with a set of boxes, some of which might well have been empty.

Having defined race relations as 'that behaviour which develops among people who are aware of each other's actual or imputed physical differences', Cox had quite a lot to say about the kinds of awareness that characterized the various situations. The most important of these were the ruling-class and bipartite situations and it is under these headings that Cox compared the societies he knew best: Trinidad and the US South. The first three situations were of a different kind: stranger, original contact, and slavery. Stranger and original contact situations could develop later into either ruling class or bipartite situations. Slavery resembled the latter but had a different legal basis. The last two situations were also equivocal. Cox counted Brazil as representing an amalgamation whereas it seems on his criteria to belong in the ruling-class category. It is when describing the amalgamative situation that he chiefly discussed nationalism as 'an exploitative, socio-psychological instrument of actual or potential ruling classes'. The seventh category, the nationalistic situation, was described only briefly and inadequately; to deploy the theory that he stated elsewhere Cox would have needed to describe the material forces in Haiti in 1792 or India in 1857 which were the basis for the uprisings he mentioned. The nationalism of the underdogs appeared as the sort of process by which peoples lifted themselves up, but any suggestion that beliefs could be prime movers was in Cox's view mysticism and he pushed it out of sight. Relations necessary to the social system had pride of place. 'Haiti might be taken as the classic illustration of an exploited racial group which has achieved nationhood. Negro Americans will probably never become nationalistic; the numerical balance of the races will not allow the development of nationalistic antagonism on the part of the coloured people' (1948: 403). In this scheme the white ruling class was given a power to rule the minds as well as the bodies of the black citizens to an extent which was never possible even under slavery.

It may also be justified to examine Cox's typology from a different perspective and to ask whether there was not here another chain of reasoning of which the author was not himself fully aware and therefore did not develop as he might have done? Elsewhere Cox criticized Myrdal for assuming that beliefs about the nature of race were 'primary social forces'. Myrdal failed to acknowledge that the propagators of the ruling ideas in the United States knew that these beliefs were without objective justification but deliberately spread them because they served a purpose (1948: 531). This is a clear statement of the thesis that race is a political idea. If a sociologist adopts this viewpoint and defines race relations in terms of an awareness of 'actual or imputed physical differences', he should attempt to identify the kinds of political and economic structures which generate a racial consciousness. Cox did indeed present the bipartite situation as one in which 'definite racial attitudes are developed' but he did not analyze his seven situations in terms of the cultivation of racial beliefs or indeed in terms of exploitative relations. Some of his situations provided illustrations of neither of these and in this respect his typology was inconsistent with his own theories.

In his concluding chapter Cox handed down his judgement that the race problem of the United States 'is primarily the short-run manifestation of oppositions between an abiding urge among Negroes to assimilate and a more or less unmodifiable decision among racially articulate, nationalistic whites that they should not . . . the solidarity of American Negroes is neither nationalistic nor nativistic'. The racial policy of the country was formulated by Southern ruling-class whites and the Negro's political position was one of great weakness. For him to come to full manhood and citizenship the liberation of the Southern poor white would also be necessary. 'A great leader of Negroes will almost certainly be a white man, but he will also be the leader of the white masses of this nation.' Cox seems to have thought that he would need to be someone like Franklin D. Roosevelt (1948: 545, 581–2). Time has not dealt kindly with this diagnosis and it is necessary to ask whether there was anything in Cox's sociology that led him astray. It looks as if he overestimated the integration of the capitalist system and underestimated the independence of beliefs in social processes. In this connection his discussion of religious movements was symptomatic. He wrote, 'In all significant social revolutions, organized religion will necessarily be involved . . . the Church is normally rightist' (1948: 171). There was no recognition of religious belief as an inspiration in slave insurrections or in movements for status change. Religious belief has often been associated with the nationalism of unprivileged groups and it played a crucial part in the process by which black Americans attained a new consciousness of themselves. Oliver Cox's assumptions prevented him from seeing the significance in his own observation: 'One is amazed at the strength of the simple faith of the older, unlettered, rural Negroes. Powerless in the hands of their white exploiters, they go beyond them directly to their omnipotent God, almost happy in the assurance that retribution will come' (1948: 566). Here was something that was not determined by the needs of the social system, and it was out of this kind of psychological strength that a new movement emerged.

It may assist the further argument if I make one matter clear at this point. I accept, and I believe that every scholar standing in the Kantian tradition should accept, that it is perfectly feasible to write an account of the development of racial relations as a world phenomenon, especially over the past four centuries, regarding them as a consequence of the growth of European capitalism. In so doing it is reasonable to employ a philosophy of history which assumes ownership of the means of production in a context of technological innovation to be the predominant factor influencing class formation, and, thereby, the course of events. What is at issue is whether this view of history represents a personal preference on the part of the writer or is something corresponding to an objective reality. Is it a philosophy of history or a science of history? Does it operate with a model of society or does it state the laws according to which societies change? If someone takes the second of these two positions how does he or she prove the truth of these claims? It is for this reason that the epistemological issue is inescapable (on this, see Banton, 1986). To put the issue in this way is to make difficulties for those who rely on a Hegelian epistemology because to them their way of looking at things seems so superior to any alternative that they consider that what requires explanation is other peoples' failure to appreciate what should be obvious to them. (There are obvious parallels with the position of those who see history as record of God's relations with humanity.) The Hegelians are on stronger ground when they criticize the weaknesses in Kantian philosophy, in particular (from their standpoint) for its failure to allow for the way in which any scholar is himself part of a historical process. Yet if there is no reason to believe in an underlying level of historical determination, no one should be blamed for neglecting it. The main difference today between the orthodox sociologists and the Marxists lies in the questions they think should be asked rather than in the answers they give. The Marxists, because of their use of Hegelian epistemology, believe that it is possible to answer in a social scientific manner questions about the development of whole social systems. Moreover, since they believe that future developments can be anticipated and inform present-day politics, they contend that there is a moral obligation to direct research towards such issues. That is why a student should ask 'What is *the* problem?' The sociologists believe that, while it may be useful to ask such questions, they cannot be answered in a social scientific manner. Answers depend upon subjective assessments of what is significant. The student should start with a theory and choose a problem which will help him or her to improve the explanatory power of that theory. That is why they ask 'What is *your* problem?'

The scholars who are accounted Marxists differ significantly among themselves and the Marxist analysis of racial relations is still being developed. Those who take the position that Marxism offers a theory of history as the product of class struggle belong in what has been described as the Hegelian tradition. Those who believe that Marxism offers a model of society either belong in the Kantian tradition or are engaged in trying to bridge the gulf between the two. Though that gulf is very deep, bridges can be thrown across it in several places.

Despite their divergences, Marxists can agree with sociologists about what constitute satisfactory answers to certain kinds of questions. Marxists have tackled questions neglected by orthodox sociologists, and many of their contributions can be accepted and welcomed by sociologists who do not share their historical and political perspectives. For example, there need be no dispute about the importance of understanding the position of a group in relation to the processes of production, to the structure of power, and to the utilization of resources controlled by the state. There is therefore an area of overlap in the analysis of particular societies. The possibilities of theoretical overlap have been enhanced by the recent publication of Marxist studies which assume that societies are composed of individuals with resources of varying kinds who attempt to choose rationally between courses of action. This new approach has been called rational choice Marxism (Carling, 1987). So far, most Marxist writing relevant to racial relations has begun from the examination of particular societies. Therefore it is not yet possible to set out a class-based theory in a form parallel to the status-based theory of the previous chapter. The class-based writing has also taken forms which greatly increase the problems of selecting authors or studies for discussion. Acknowledging these difficulties, it may still be helpful to consider how one particular author, Edna Bonacich, has added to the understanding of racial relations in South Africa and the United States. This is not to claim that her approach is representative of neo-Marxist writing; only that it is of particular interest.

South Africa

In discussions of racial relations, South Africa and Brazil appear as opposite poles. In Brazil individuals can be classified according to skin colour and other physical features but there are no social categories corresponding to North American and European folk concepts. The visitor to Brazil who assumes that there is a distinctively racial element in relations between people of different appearance will not understand what is going on. In South Africa, by contrast, there are clear social categories recognized by everyone who lives within the country because group differences have been used by successive governments to create a hierarchy of privilege. The visitor who thinks of relations between these categories as expressions of physical differences will misunderstand the society every bit as much as his counterpart in Brazil. Physical features are used as signs that people are assigned to particular categories. South Africa, Brazil, North America and West European Countries have different social systems divided into different groups and categories. Relations between blacks and whites in South Africa have many dimensions that are not to be found in black–white relations in the other countries.

Edna Bonacich (1972, 1979, 1981a) concluded that none of the prevailing interpretations of black–white relations in South Africa was satisfactory. Those which have been classed as liberal failed to deal adequately with the connections between position in the labour market and position in the political structure. Those which have been classed as Marxist failed to explain the behaviour of the white workers. She argued against both these interpretations that ethnic antagonism is produced by the kind of competition that arises in split labour markets. The better jobs are reserved for a labour aristocracy whose members seize on the physical differences between them and their competitors to develop an ideology justifying their privileges. There is thus a pattern of conflict between three classes: a business class whose members want as cheap and docile a labour force as possible; a higher-paid working class and a lower-paid one. The interests of the higher-paid workers are threatened by the third class, because the very weakness of that class ensures that it can easily be controlled by the business class. From the difference in the *initial* price of labour a complex class struggle develops which exacerbates the relations between different groups of workers.

The key problem in contemporary South Africa, according to Bonacich (1981a: 239) is: why is South Africa apparently trying to prevent the full absorption of the African population into the capitalist sector? Any political analysis must depend upon a solution to this puzzle. To find an answer it is necessary to go back to the increased demand for labour generated when first the mining and then the manufacturing industries started to compete with the farming sector. The demand for craftsmen and other skilled workers could be met only from the immigrant white labour force and this gave them a corresponding leverage in demanding a share of the profits from exploiting the country's valuable natural resources. There was also a demand for unskilled labour which could be met either by whites or blacks. The native Africans were not much attracted to wage labour so the business class had to recruit Africans from outside South Africa's boundaries. Indentured workers were also recruited from India and China. It was in farming that black workers first succeeded in competing successfully with whites. Their progress offended white farmers and politicians. The Natives Land Act of 1913 was introduced apparently to exert greater control over black labour and to block this opening (see Banton, 1983a: 220–1, summarizing research by Francis Wilson). During World War One black workers became better established in the gold mining industry; fairly soon they could be used to fill jobs that had previously been reserved to whites. As profitability declined this became more attractive to the employers and occasioned the Rand strike of 1922.

Capital, writes Bonacich, is attracted to cheap labour of any colour, and, if permitted, would have made more use of blacks, displacing high-priced white labour. White workers therefore had a choice. They could follow an inclusionist policy, trying to bring Africans into the working-class movement, helping them to raise the price of their labour, and thus ending the split in the labour market. Or they could follow a protectionist policy, attempting to prevent any undercutting of their own position by limiting capital's access to cheap labour and creating a kind of caste system. The policy options were mutually exclusive. If either were to succeed it had to eliminate the other. The inclusionist alternative was unattractive because the African 'reserve army of labour' seemed so huge; there was so much potentially cheap black labour within the country that frontier control, important as it might be, could not suffice; the South African business class was particularly powerful because the employers controlled the mining compounds and could easily act against attempts to unite white and black labour; Afrikaner workers, with their rural history and frontier ideology, were ill-disposed towards inclusionist strategies; finally, after the suppression of the Rand strike political power was utilized to create a state apparatus ready to suppress the earliest moves in such a direction. It was therefore mistaken to infer that the antagonism of white workers towards blacks resulted from their having been either duped or bribed by capital. The first of these false explanations suggested that capitalists had developed an ideology of racism to deflect white workers' hostility away from their real enemy; the second saw white labour, especially its leadership, as having been bought off. Bonacich rejected the second because she read the evidence of displacement as indicating that capital would sooner dispense with costly white labour than pay the price of bribery. (For further evidence and supporting argument on both of these points, see Lipton, 1985: 183–226.) Bonacich also argued that the black struggle for liberation had been shaped by the white class struggle; the reactionary stance of white labour had pushed the conflict towards a racial rather than a class confrontation. This then added to the forces delaying the incorporation of the African population in the capitalist sector.

This attempt to explain why the African population was not being so absorbed has been sharply criticized by Michael Burrawoy (1981). Where other writers have perceived the split labour market as one factor underlying the present social order, Bonacich, he says, has represented it as the factor which above all else determines racial antagonism: 'she inverts the logic of enquiry by constructively appropriating history to illuminate a theory rather than appropriately constructing a theory to illuminate history'. Thus the matter at issue is not just whether Bonacich has answered the question but whether she had asked the question that Burrawoy believes to be crucial. He doubted whether a theory of racial antagonism was possible. He argued that to understand the differential access of races to resources required a theory of the more general allocation of resources, which in turn presupposed a theory of capitalism. To understand why the African population was not being absorbed into the capitalist sector it was necessary, according to Burrawoy, to look at the parts played by the state apparatus, at the difference between individual and class interest, at the specificity of South African development, at the events of different historical periods, and so on.

In Bonacich's rejoinder (1981b) she observed that Burrawoy's way of posing the problem was remarkably like sociological functionalism. When the state supported a colour bar it was said to be acting in the interests of the capitalist class by reproducing a system of exploitation. When the state attacked the colour bar it was said to be acting in the interests of a capitalist class which required 'a more flexible approach to apartheid'. Whatever action it took concerning trade unionism was similarly 'explained'. The underlying assumption was therefore ideological. Bonacich protested, 'It is the racial aspect of the South African social structure that I was trying to explain, not every aspect of the social structure.' In that event she should have defined her problem more closely. She has not advanced a very satisfactory explanation of why South Africa is apparently trying to prevent the full absorption of the African population into the capitalist sector, what she has done is to explain the constraints bearing upon the strategies of the white workers, and, in a more limited way, upon those of the major white employers, plus the significance of these constraints for ethnic antagonism (in itself a significant achievement!). Though they might be criticized in detail there is nothing of a general kind about these explanations which should make them unacceptable to a sociologist who starts from the perspective of race as status; indeed the question of whether black and white labour is substitutable has long been a central issue for those who study discrimination in labour markets in the terms of neo-classical economics.

United States

The split labour market theory helps explain some important features of black–white relations in United States history. Bonacich (1976) singled out the abolition of slavery (dated from 1863 but a subject of controversy over many years) as a key question. Some whites who were against slavery nevertheless opposed the granting of any rights to free blacks. Others seemed to favour slavery, yet fiercely resisted proposals to extend it to new territories as the United States frontier moved westwards. Since the whites in both North and South agreed that blacks were inferior, why should they have fought one another so bitterly from 1861 to 1865?

Black workers and white workers were substitutable forms of labour. They could, when permitted, perform the same work. To use black slaves, an employer first needed the capital to purchase them, but thereafter his costs were much lower than if he hired free white labour. Originally it had been possible to purchase white labour also, by buying up the indentures of immigrant workers who had been given a passage because they had entered into such a contract. Buying indentures gave the purchaser a right to a man's labour for only a specified number of years and it was never politically possible to establish any form of servile labour by whites. Blacks were different because they were more easily segregated and controlled, so that in some states at some periods an employer owned his slaves as he owned his farm animals. Black workers could therefore be made to work longer hours than whites, making their labour cheaper to the employer. The capitalists brought in black slaves to develop Southern agriculture and a split labour market was created as the white owners of small farms were pushed out of the fertile lands most suited for cotton plantations. Thus slavery created a powerful capitalist class based on cheap labour and it weakened the bargaining position of free workers and small farmers (who were nearly all white).

Bonacich maintained that there was a continuous process whereby white workers were displaced by black. Slaves were used in textile and tobacco manufacturing, in the iron industry, in sugar refining and rice mills, on the docks, canals, and railroads, and in mining, construction, and lumbering. Some slaves became skilled workers who, when not needed on the plantations, were hired out by their owners. Faced with this kind of competition, many white workers left the South. Others tried to reserve certain jobs for whites only, adopting what Bonacich called the caste solution. Their ability to do so was increased by the extension of the franchise in the 1830s which enabled white workers and small farmers to exercise greater influence. This was also a period in which laws were passed to restrict the right of slave owners to give slaves their freedom. It has frequently been argued that such legislation expressed the slave owners' fears of slave insurrection since free blacks were seen as a disruptive influence. Bonacich suggested to the contrary that slave owners had no collective interest in preventing the manumission of individual slaves. Other slave societies with strong slave-owning classes permitted individual manumissions, while the Northern and Western regions of the United States, which had no slaves, produced as many laws directed against free blacks as the South. From this, she inferred that the pressure for the Southern legislation against manumission probably came from the white working class.

Outside the South, white workers feared any moves which threatened the introduction of cheap labour. They therefore approved the maintenance of slavery in the South while opposing its extension. Behind their support for slavery in the South lay the fear that abolition might mean the northward migration of former slaves to increase the competition for jobs in their regions; even though this would be free labour, it would be the labour of people willing to work for lower wages and therefore a considerable threat. White workers in the United States were thus faced with a problem comparable to that of white workers in South Africa. Were they to protect their short-run interests by trying to set up a kind of caste system which would reinforce the split in the labour market and acknowledge their right to the better paid jobs, or were they to adopt the radical inclusionist policy of trying to build a working-class movement that transcended racial differences? Bonacich's essay deals with the period 1830–63 when this problem had to be addressed by the first trade unions, which were craft unions representing skilled trades. Other evidence which she does not review (see Banton, 1983a: 378–9) shows that where black craftsmen were already established, the union had to include them. Craft unions formed in later periods were discriminatory from the outset. As in South Africa, the white class struggle influenced the form taken by the black liberation movement.

The split labour market theory is therefore able to throw new light onto inter- and intra-racial tensions in this period. Its exposition is less persuasive when arguing that 'Abolition of slavery occurred, in part, because there were major classes of whites whose interests were at odds with the perpetuation of the "peculiar institution".' Spokesmen for those interests rarely spoke in such terms and Bonacich's own scheme does not provide very much support for the interpretation. Conflicts between North and South had been reduced by negotiation in the past; whether they could have been negotiated in 1861 no one can know. Any assumption that the Civil War was inevitable is purely a supposition and takes it out of the realm of causal explanation to which social scientists' theories are directed.

Passing over several intervening decades, Bonacich took up the story again to contend that a split labour market analysis helps explain the higher level of unemployment among Afro-Americans in the industrial era. According to the census of 1930 the level of black unemployment was lower than that of whites, but afterwards it started to rise until by 1954 the black rate was twice the white rate. That disparity had persisted. Operating with her three-class model, Bonacich maintained that employer paternalism led black workers to feel that they had more to gain by allying with capital than with white labour. She quoted Marcus Garvey as saying, 'If the Negro takes my advice he will organize by himself and keep his scale of wage a little lower than the whites . . . By doing so he will keep the good will of the white employer.' Since white workers would never help blacks to get jobs, it was a good tactic for them to take jobs offered to them because the white workers had gone on strike. By the 1930s the white workers' strategies for preventing competition from black workers were in disarray. Then the New Deal changed the picture; the National Industrial Recovery Act introduced protections for trade union activity and empowered the President to prescribe minimum rates of pay. This made it difficult for blacks to be used as cheap labour, though it was only in this way that they had any chance of improving their share of the job market. Bonacich nevertheless maintained that once white fears about cheap labour had been allayed, white unions could become more active in recruiting black support, so that one of the short-term consequences of the 1933 Act was that black and white labour were able to come together in a 'radical coalition'. Protective legislation had shifted the balance of power against the employers and threatened some of these with bankruptcy. The capitalist class could respond in one or more of three ways. Firstly, by relocating part of the industrial process overseas to make use of cheaper foreign labour. Secondly, by relocating in parts of the country – such as the South – where labour was unorganized and relatively cheap. Thirdly, by investing in machinery to reduce their labour force. They followed all three courses; blacks suffered from their consequences more than whites did, because the black workers were less educated, had less seniority in the lay-off queue, were less easily able to migrate or commute when factories were moved out of the highly-taxed central cities, and were less able to protect their interests when decisions about jobs were taken. Capitalists, in this view, do not benefit from black unemployment; they are ready to utilize cheap black labour when they can, but government regulations, job requirements, location, and other factors, including white prejudice, reduce these opportunities.

An alternative explanation of higher black unemployment (Lewis, 1985: 62–6) is that especially since the 1950s wage levels for unskilled labour have been rising faster than productivity, so that the demand for this kind of labour has not kept up with the increase in its supply due to mechanization (especially in agriculture), increased female employment and illegal immigration from Mexico. A higher proportion of black workers were unskilled so that their unemployment rates increased more than those of white workers.

Great Britain

Relations between white capitalists, white workers, and immigrant workers from the New Commonwealth who settled in Britain after 1948, can be usefully analyzed in terms of the split labour market theory, but the pattern is less clear-cut than in the United States, and so very much less distinct than in South Africa that it raises the question whether it is not mis- leading to describe the British labour market as racially split. The differ- ences are better comprehended if they are seen as arising from a queueing process in which there is a hierarchy of job preferences. This alternative view is the more appropriate because to begin with the racial minority was so small.

From 1948 (when the immigration from Jamaica started), for about ten years, there was no opposition from white workers to the employment of blacks. There were two main reasons for this. The blacks (mostly from the West Indies) were British subjects from British colonies. White people in Britain believed that their country benefited economically from owner- ship of colonies and accepted that, if this relationship was to continue, they had obligations towards any colonials who were resident, perhaps temporarily or in small numbers, in what was called the 'mother country' (Banton, 1983c). Secondly, the period 1948–58 was one in which the demand for labour exceeded the supply. White workers abandoned the less attractive, less well-paid jobs and moved to others. First black workers and then Asian workers were recruited to fill the vacancies that resulted. They contributed less than one per cent of the labour force, and were scarcely any threat. A caste-like pattern was established with the immigrant workers taking the jobs white workers did not want. The availability of a reserve army of labour reduced the pressures on employers to invest in automated production and provided them with concealed subsidy in that they did not have to provide the extra housing or meet the additional social services costs which fell upon the municipal authorities in the areas of settlement.

Writers in the Marxist tradition have debated the relationship of New Commonwealth workers to the indigenous working class. Robert Miles (1983: 152–3) has distinguished three positions. Firstly, that the immigrant workers form part of a unitary working class – despite all the evidence of a special discrimination against them. Secondly, that they constitute an underclass which cannot be assimilated into the working class – a view which, he says, sees no explanatory significance in their being immigrants with attributes associated with their countries of origin. Thirdly, that they constitute a distinct stratum within the working class – an argument that fails to relate the characteristics of such a stratum to other divisions within the working class. Miles argues that migrant workers should be seen as constituting a racialized fraction within the working class; his argument, it will be noted, concerns the first generation of immigrants only. Like other writers in this tradition, Miles has been concerned to uncover the ways in which the powers of the state have been used to define the position of migrant workers. (Indications of how he stands in relation to these other writers may be derived from Miles, 1984.) Miles notes parallels with migrant labour in Germany, France and Switzerland, but adds that 'it was not until 1971 that British capital had made available to it the political/legal framework for a migrant labour system determined by contract' and that since then British capital has been faced with a surplus rather than a shortage of labour so that it had no reason to make much use of that framework. If the framework has not been utilized, the processes leading to its creation contribute little to any explanation of the social position of New Commonwealth workers.

This approach, when applied to relations in Britain, is less rewarding than is the application of the split labour market theory to South Africa and the United States. Why then should there be controversy about the immigrant workers' class position? Miles (1982: 167) writes: 'There is a world of difference between observing that certain industries in Britain were facing a labour shortage in the 1950s and arguing that the process of capital accumulation and the uneven development of the capitalist mode of production created the need for labour migration and the means by which that need could be met.' The world of difference relates, surely, to the desire to fit a whole set of observations into a synoptic interpretation of the course of history. Those who draw inspiration from Marx must believe that the main source of political change within the present phase of capitalism lies within the proletariat. Therefore it is important to discover in what relationship the New Commonwealth minorities stand with respect to the progressive forces in the white proletariat. Marxists work with a conception of history that resembles a level of explanation similar in some ways to those discussed in the section of Chapter 3 that deals with reductionist explanations. They may accept the explanations of social relations discussed in connection with the view of race as status, while maintaining that these are but partial theories which should be synthesized in a comprehensive theory of social change and subordinated to this. To revert to Miles' statement, there need be no dispute about the effects of excess demand for labour in Britain in the 1950s. The issues are whether the capitalist mode of production develops in a predictable way creating both a new demand and a new supply of labour, and whether propositions about such historical sequences have a similar status to propositions about the effects of labour shortages in particular industries at particular times, or are instead, as I believe, expressions of a philosophy of history.

A simple comparison may help to make quite clear the nature of the argument. A Danish anthropologist once went out on a polar bear hunt with an Eskimo. The hunt was unsuccessful, and the Eskimo explained, 'No bears have come because there is no ice. There is no ice because there has been too much blowing weather. There has been too much blowing weather because we humans have offended the spirits.' The Dane might have agreed with the first two propositions, but, in place of the third, said that there had been too much blowing weather because a deep depression had been moving up the coastline. He would probably have been satisfied with that kind of explanation and not felt obliged to explain why the depression had been moving up instead of down the coastline, or why it had come this week instead of last week. The claim that it was sent by the spirits is an attempt to answer these extra questions. It is a claim that does not have the same empirical basis as the propositions which account for the absence of bears in terms of weather conditions. Similarly Marxists and non-Marxists can agree about many of the correlates of labour demand in the 1950s. The relations between this demand and the regulation of immigration on the one hand, and the expected returns to investment in automation, on the other, can be empirically determined. To fit observations about the labour shortage into an interpretation of the development of capitalism, however, is comparable with the claim that bad weather was sent by the spirits. The interpretation may be correct, but it belongs in a different kind of discourse, one of a more subjective character (although Marxists claim a special objectivity for their interpretations).

Conclusion

The tensions between groups in South Africa, the United States and Great Britain are shaped by differences of power. One group has been in a controlling position in respect to others; its members have enjoyed higher social rank and have used their position to ensure that their children succeed them in their privileged status. An analysis which started instead from the relations between Hausa, Ibo and Yoruba in Nigeria, Sinhalese and Tamils in Sri Lanka, and Malays, Chinese and Indians in Malaysia, would point to different conclusions about the nature of racial or ethnic conflict. Such an analysis has been carried through by Donald L. Horowitz. He draws a distinction between ranked and unranked social systems, maintaining that it is useful to see them as contrasting kinds of system even if in the real world no social system conforms completely to either model. In ranked systems, like that of South Africa, the boundaries of ranked ethnic groups tend to coincide with the lines of class; conflict between these groups points in the direction of revolution. Unranked systems, like that of Nigeria, consist of groups which try to act like mini-states; their conflicts are more likely to result in the partition of the state or the attempt of groups to secede from it. This simple picture has then to be qualified. Horowitz (1985: 36) observes that in a given country some groups may be ranked in relation to each other but not in relation to further groups. In South Africa, Afrikaners are ranked in relation to Zulus, but not necessarily in relation to English-speaking whites; nor are Zulus ranked in relation to Xhosas. In a generally unranked federal political system like that of Nigeria, one group may be more than proportionately represented in the elite, or may control a state government and rank above the members of minorities from other ethnic groups. The reality is therefore one of two dimensions to ethnic interaction; one that stems from differences of rank and power; another that arises from expectations associated with cultural differences. The first is evident in conflicts over material resources; the second in conflicts motivated by group pride.

Class analysis presumes that the dimension of rank is more important than that of group sentiment. Status analysis does not deny the dimension of rank (after all, the very word status is used to denote both differences on a scale of prestige and differences of rights attaching to positions independent of rank). Whether the one dimension or the other is the more important therefore depends upon the question the research worker is seeking to answer. Not all class analysts are Marxists, but most of them – and certainly all who are Marxists – would, as has been explained earlier in this chapter, reject the presumption that the research worker is free to choose the question that is to be studied. They would contend that differences in group sentiment are ultimately the product of differences in rank and that the research worker's choice of question is socially conditioned. They claim that they can provide a more comprehensive explanation of present-day relations by showing that these are predictable consequences of historical processes. There is here an obvious parallel with the theory of evolution as a body of reasoning that offers a comparable synthesis of experimental research as validating a process by which the very subject matter of research is transformed.

Discussing the scientific status of Darwinism (by which he meant the theory of evolution by natural selection, comprehending all the five theories distinguished by Mayr, and in the form which Julian Huxley called 'The New Synthesis') Popper (1974: 168) stated: 'I have come to the conclusion that Darwinism is not a testable scientific theory, but a metaphysical research programme – a possible framework for testable scientific theories.' In similar fashion, it can be said that Marxism offers a metaphysical political programme which includes a set of guidelines for research and a framework for the interpretation of findings.

The parallel with evolution is the closer because evolution is not necessarily a process of increasing differentiation. When Darwin studied sexuality among barnacles, he could be concerned with the way two sexes appeared where previously there had been one. In some circumstances, though, hermaphroditism could be a better solution of the problem of maximum fertility when there were few sites on which they could reproduce. Equally, some species die out either in spite of the way they have been evolving or because of the way in which they have been evolving. Evolution is not necessarily progressive in the way that humans judge progress. The Darwinian theory predicts that if organisms are classified according to their resemblances and differences, the resulting classes can then be related to one another as parts of a branching tree. If different characteristics demanded different trees, this could demonstrate that something was wrong with the theory. The same line of descent had to be deducible from all the organs and structure of a particular species. Since differences between classes can now be quantified in respect of many enzymes and proteins, this greatly increases the explanatory power of the theory, enabling parts of it to be tested (so in this respect Popper was wrong), but it does not permit any more than very limited predictions about the future evolution of any species or subspecies.

Marxists see history as a progressive development in some respects comparable to organic evolution. They do not claim to predict the future of particular societies, but believe that they can identify the components of change so that their understanding of its character has improved in a manner comparable to the results of testing in other areas of social science. They presume that by viewing racial groups in class terms something more can be learned than when they are seen purely in status terms. This is a matter of belief. Marxists cannot prove their interpretation of change in a way that convinces those who stand in the Kantian tradition. What is surely not a matter of belief, however, is that the challenge offered by Marxism has been beneficial to the study of racial relations. It has obliged orthodox sociology to confront new questions and Marxists have had to improve their arguments in response to counter-attacks, so that on empirical issues the gulf between the two positions may be unimportant.

The Kantian perspective is often interpreted as counselling restraint. A research worker is advised to address only those questions which, in the current state of knowledge, he or she may be able to answer. In all probability no theory will seem altogether satisfactory. The only course is to select the least unsatisfactory and seek to improve it. Yet some social science theories are so rudimentary that the research worker who neglects more imaginative possibilities in order to follow the formula may come to regret it. Even the theories of physical science are problematic from some standpoints. In his autobiography Popper (1976: 149) explained that when he wrote a postscript to *The Logic of Scientific Discovery* he stressed that he had 'rejected all attempts at the justification of theories, and that I had replaced justification by criticism'. On another occasion (1972: 265) he added:

> A scientific result cannot be justified. It can only be criticized, and tested. And no more can be said in its favour than it seems, after all this criticism and testing, better, more interesting, more powerful, more promising, and a better approximation to truth, than its competitors.

One of the problems with the positivist approach is its tendency to rely on what Gellner (1985: 58) has called a granular metaphysic, conceiving of the world as consisting of discrete grains which can be separated from each other for purposes of analysis. 'Things in themselves' cannot be fully comprehended, yet every research worker must be able to locate them in some metaphysical view of the world. Criticism can lead people to modify their metaphysical views but these are usually several steps removed from any process of trying to confront theories with empirical observations.

The limitations of the positivist approach are often manifested in discussions of social policy. When arguing about what should be done to ameliorate racial discrimination people have to make assumptions about the nature of social groups. Are black people so different from white people that any policy should assume that they will continue to be different? If so, what is the nature of the difference? If not, what factors are responsible for the present differences? Such questions rest upon assumptions as to what creates the black category. The Marxist believes that in the long-run the fundamental identities are those of class, so that the short-run problem is to understand the process of class formation and the ways in which racial identities constitute impediments. Those who see racial groups as fashioned by circumstance must draw upon their personal philosophies of history and of human nature whenever they envisage likely future developments and the chances that these might be influenced by social policies. Unlike Hegelianism, positivism cannot provide the tools required to legitimate its philosophical position (Gellner, 1985: 67).

Racial theories, as these have been formulated in Europe and North America over the last two centuries, have been embedded in the political and social life of the societies to which their authors and readers have belonged, but they have stimulated a growth in knowledge which is independent of those societies. As yet no one has attempted to identify the external influences which might have contributed to the recent rise in interest in class analysis, or, indeed the externalist approach to the history of science. If external factors are often important they must be at work in the present as well as in the past, but the manner in which they work changes. As subjects develop, in the way that genetics has created its own internationally recognized experimental techniques, so the external influences bear upon the selection of problems rather than upon the procedures by which they are tackled. Looking back upon studies of the relations between people distinguished by race (or what was thought to be race) it is possible to discern an internal history created by scholars struggling for the autonomy of their own disciplines. Perhaps the central question which people have asked is: why are they not like us? To begin with, those who asked the question may have identified the particular 'they' as a group of whom they had only limited or inaccurate knowledge. The question became more interesting once it was possible to treat the 'they-group' as one among many others, and to accept that the questioners themselves belonged to another such group whose peculiarities had to be explained by the same principles.

The first comprehensive answer was one which conceptualized race as lineage. It said that 'they' were not like 'us' because 'they' belonged to a genealogical group which had acquired special characteristics either because of divine intervention or because of its distinctive environmental experience. The weakness of this answer was that it could not satisfactorily explain how environment affected the transmission of inherited characters.

A second answer was that peoples were different because they represented different racial types. The differences had existed either since the creation or for as long a period as there was reliable evidence. This argument smuggled in a significant change in the meaning of the word race. Previously race was not a label for a classification like species, but a name for a line of descent. Since, however, the differences to be classified derived from descent, the implications of shift in meaning were not properly appreciated. The weakness of this answer was that it failed to account for evolution.

The third answer replied that other peoples were different because they were separate subspecies. Because of genetic variability, mutation, genetic drift, and natural selection, regular differences could appear and subspecies could in time become separate species. To say that a set of individuals constituted a subspecies was therefore like a snapshot classification at a particular moment in time. It did not reflect the significance of their shared history or the relations between them. To refer to racial groups as populations was an improvement because it represented them as more than the results of snapshot classification. However, this was still an answer to only half the question. The conceptualizations of race as lineage and race as type attempted to explain why people were both physically different and culturally different. Race as population offered a satisfactory explanation of physical differentiation but it could interpret cultural differentiation only by analogy, on the assumption that the ecological processes governing unconscious behaviour could explain as much about humans as they could about animals.

The ecological theory enabled the sociologist to reply that they were not like us because of the positions we occupied and the nature of the relations between us and them, but ecological factors alone could not account for the differences in wealth, power and social position of racial groups which formed parts of the same society. So it is now said that racial minorities differ because they are of unequal social status; this is the outcome of an interaction between their own preferences and skills, and the ways they are regarded by others. The physical difference serves as a social sign, indicating to people whether another person is a fellow group member or an outsider. The significance of such an assignment varies, of course, from one place, one time, one social setting, to another. Those who see race in terms of class claim that it is possible to explain those variations of place, time, and setting, but the explanations they offer take the form of historical interpretation and point to political prescription rather than to procedures by which they can be tested. In recent years the class perspective has been the basis for a constructive critique of the status perspective and a reminder of the way that theorists, far from being neutral figures, are influenced by their own social commitments. If support for the class perspective were to disappear some replacement would still be desirable to criticize sociological orthodoxy and to draw attention to its limitations.

This book has set out to show that past mistakes about the influence of race in human affairs can be better understood by tracing them to theories which attempted in the circumstances of their own time to account for observed differences. Some of those differences persist and will continue to trouble future generations. Any policies to reduce racial inequality must be based on some understanding of the nature of the problems, and that understanding must be of a theoretical character. The critical study of how present theories have been developed out of past ones can help research workers identify ways of moving forwards.

Bibliography

Bannister, Robert C. (1979) *Social Darwinism: Science and Myth in Anglo-American Social Thought*. Philadelphia: Temple University Press.

Banton, Michael (1959) *White and Coloured: The behaviour of British people towards coloured immigrants*. London: Cape.

(1967) *Race Relations*. London: Tavistock.

(1977) *The Idea of Race*. London: Tavistock.

(1983a) *Racial and Ethnic Competition*. Cambridge: Cambridge University Press.

(1983b) Categorical and statistical discrimination, *Ethnic and Racial Studies*, 3: 269–83.

(1983c) The influence of Colonial status upon black–white relations in England, 1948–58, *Sociology*, 17: 546–59.

(1985a) *Promoting Racial Harmony*. Cambridge: Cambridge University Press.

(1985b) Mixed motives and the processes of rationalization, *Ethnic and Racial Studies*, 8: 534–47.

(1986) Epistemological assumptions in the study of racial differentiation, pp. 42–63 in Rex, John and Mason, David, editors, *Theories of Race and Ethnic Relations*. Cambridge: Cambridge University Press.

Barker, Anthony J. (1978) *The African Link: British Attitudes to the Negro in the Era of the Atlantic Slave Trade, 1550–1807*. London: Frank Cass.

Beddoe, John (1885) *The Races of Britain*. Bristol: Arrowsmith.

(1912) *The Anthropological History of Europe* (revised edition, originally 1891). Paisley: Gardner.

Bendyshe, T. (1865) The history of anthropology, *Memoirs read before the Anthropological Society of London*, 1: 335–458.

Biddiss, Michael D. (1970) *Father of Racist Ideology: The Social and Political Thought of Count Gobineau*. London: Weidenfeld & Nicolson.

(1976) The politics of anatomy: Dr Robert Knox and Victorian Racism, *Proc. Roy. Soc. Med.*, 69: 245–50.

Blalock, Hubert M. (1967) *Toward a Theory of Minority Group Relations*. New York: Wiley.

Blome, Hermann (1943) *Der Rassengedanke in der deutschen Romantik und seine Grundlagen im 18 Jahrhundert*. Munchen & Berlin: Lehmann.

Blumenbach, J. F. (1865) *The Anthropological Treatises of Johann Friedrich Blumenbach*. London: Anthropological Society of London.

Blumer, Herbert (1958) United States of America, *International Social Science*

Bulletin, 10: 403–47, reprinted at pp. 87–133 in UNESCO, *Research on Racial Relations*, 1966, Paris: UNESCO.

Blumer, Herbert and Troy, Duster (1980) Theories of Race and Social Action, pp. 211–38 in UNESCO, *Sociological Theories: Race and Colonialism*, Paris: UNESCO.

Boas, Franz (1940) *Race, Language and Culture*. New York: Free Press.

Boissel, Jean (1971) Un Théoricien des races, précurseur de Gobineau: Victor Courtet de l'Isle, *Etudes Gobiniennes*: 203–14.

(1972) *Victor Courtet 1813–1867. Premier théoricien de la hierarchie des races*. Paris: Presses Universitaires de France.

Bonacich, Edna (1972) A theory of ethnic antagonism: the split labor market, *American Sociological Review*, 37: 547–59.

(1976) Advanced capitalism and black/white race relations in the United States: a split labor market interpretation, *American Sociological Review*, 41: 34–51.

(1979) The past, present and future of split labor market theory, *Research in Race and Ethnic Relations*, 1: 17–64.

(1981a) Capitalism and race relations in South Africa: A split labor market analysis, *Political Power and Social Theory*, 2: 239–77.

(1981b) Reply to Burrawoy, pp. 337–43 in *ibid*.

Boyd, William C. (1950) *Genetics and the Races of Man*. Boston: Little, Brown.

Broca, Paul (1864) *On the Phenomenon of Hybridity in the Genus Homo*. London: Longman Green for Anthropological Society (originally 1859–60).

(1874) *Memoires d'Anthropologie*, 5 vols. Paris: Reinwald.

Buenzod, Janine (1967) *La formation de la pensée de Gobineau et 'l'Essai sur l'inégalité des races humaines'*. Paris: Nizet.

Burrawoy, Michael (1981) The capitalist state in South Africa: Marxist and sociological perspectives on race and class, *Political Power and Social Theory*, 2: 279–335.

Cairns, H. A. C. (1965) *Prelude to Imperialism: British Reactions to Central African Society, 1840–90*. London: Routledge.

Carling, Alan (1987) Rational choice Marxism, *New Left Review*, forthcoming.

Carus, Carl Gustav (1849) *Denkschrift zum hundertjährigen Geburtsfeste Goethes: Ueber ungleiche Befähigung der verschiedenen Menscheitstämme für höhre geistige Entwickelung*. Leipzig: Brockhaus.

Chadwick, H. Munro (1945) *The Nationalities of Europe and the Growth of National Ideologies*. Cambridge: Cambridge University Press

Chakravati, Nalini Ranjan (1971) *The Indian Minority in Burma: The Rise and Decline of an Immigrant Community*. London: Oxford University Press.

Chambers, Robert (1844) *Vestiges of the Natural History of Creation*. London: Churchill, reprinted Leicester University Press, 1979.

Chiswick, Barry R. (1979) The economic progress of immigrants: some apparently universal patterns, , pp. 357–99 in Fellner, William, editor, *Contemporary Economic Problems*. Washington, D.C.: American Enterprise Institute.

Coleman, William (1964) *Georges Cuvier, Zoologist: a study in the history of evolution theory*. Cambridge, Mass.: Harvard University Press.

Cox, Oliver C. (1948) *Caste, Class and Race: a study in social dynamics*. New York: Monthly Review Press.

Crook, John Hurrell (1980) *The Evolution of Human Consciousness*. Oxford: Clarendon Press.

Curtin, Philip D. (1964) *The Image of Africa, British ideas and Action, 1780–1850*. Madison: University of Wisconsin Press, and London: Macmillan.

Darwin, Charles Robert (1871) *The Descent of Man*. London: Murray.

Davis, Allison, Gardner, Burleigh B. and Gardner, Mary (1941) *Deep South: A social anthropological study of caste and class*. Chicago: University of Chicago Press.

Desmoulins, A. (1826) *Histoire Naturelle des Races Humaines*. Paris.

Dollard, John (1937) *Caste and Class in a Southern Town*. New York: Doubleday Anchor.

 (1938) Hostility and fear in social life, *Social Forces*, 17: 15–26.

Down, John Langdon (1866) Observations on an ethnic classification of idiots, *Clinical Lectures and Reports of the London Hospital*, 3: 259–62.

 (1887) *On Some of the Mental Affections of Childhood and Youth*. London: Churchill.

Echevaria, Durand (1957) *Mirage in the West: A History of the French Image of American Society*. Princeton: Princeton University Press.

Edwards, W. F. (1829) *Des caractères physiologiques des races humaines, considérés dans leur rapports avec l'histoire: lettre à M. Amédée Thierry*. Paris: Compère Jeune.

Erickson, Paul (1981) The Anthropology of Charles Caldwell, M.D., *Isis*, 72: 252–6.

Fenton, C. Stephen (1980) Race, class and politics in the work of Emile Durkheim, pp. 211–38 in UNESCO, *Sociological Theories: Race and Colonialism*. Paris: UNESCO.

Finot, Jean (1906) *Race Prejudice*. London: Constable.

Fortes, Meyer (1983) *Rules and the Emergence of Society*. London: Royal Anthropological Institute Occasional Paper 39.

Frazier, E. Franklin (1957) *Race and Culture Contacts in the Modern World*. Boston: Beacon Press.

Freeman, Derek (1974) The evolutionary theories of Charles Darwin and Herbert Spencer, *Current Anthropology*, 15: 211–37.

Fredrickson, George M. (1971) *The Black Image in the White Mind: the Debate on Afro-American Character and Destiny. 1817–1914*. New York: Harper & Row.

Froude, James Anthony (1886) *Oceana, or England and her Colonies*. New edition 1894. London: Longmans, Green, and Co.

Fryer, Peter (1984) *Staying Power: The history of black people in Britain*. London: Pluto Press.

Furnivall, J. S. (1948) *Colonial Policy and Practice: a comparative study of Burma and Netherlands India*. Cambridge: Cambridge University Press.

Gellner, Ernest (1983) *Nations and Nationalism*. Oxford: Blackwell.

 (1985) *Relativism and the Social Sciences*. Cambridge: Cambridge University Press.

Ghiselin, Michael T. (1969) *The Triumph of the Darwinian Method*. Berkeley and Los Angeles: University of California Press.

Gluckman, Max (1955) *Custom and Conflict in Africa*. Oxford: Blackwell.

Gobineau, Le Comte de (1853–5) *Essai sur l'inégalité des Race humaines*. Paris: Firmin-Didot. Page references are to the edition of 1967 (Paris: Belfond).

Gobineau, Arthur de (1915) *The Inequality of Human Races*. London: Heinemann [translation of Vol. 1 of Gobineau (1853–1855)].

Gould, Stephen Jay (1977) *Ontogeny and Phylogeny*. Cambridge, Mass.: Harvard University Press.

(1981) *The Mismeasure of Man*. Harmondsworth: Penguin.

Greene, John C. (1959) *The Death of Adam: Evolution and its Impact on Western Thought*. New York: Mentor Books.

Gumplowicz, Ludwig (1875) *Rasse und Staat: eine untersuchung uber das gesetz der staatenbildung*. Vienna: verlag der Manzschen Buchhandlung.

(1881) *Rechsstaat und Socialismus*. Innsbruck: verlag der Wagner'schen universitaets-buchhandlung.

(1883) *Der Rasenkampf: sociologische untersuchungen*. Innsbruck: verlag der Wagner'schen universitaets-buchhandlung.

Halliday, R. J. (1971) Social Darwinism: a definition, *Victorian Studies*, 14: 389–405.

Harper, Edward B. (1968) Social consequences of an 'unsuccessful' low caste movement, pp. 36–65 in Silverberg, James, editor, *Social Mobility in the Caste System in India*. Comparative studies in society and history, supplement 3. The Hague: Mouton.

Heath, Anthony (1976) *Rational Choice and Social Exchange: A critique of exchange theory*. Cambridge: Cambridge University Press.

Hechter, Michael, Friedman, Debra and Appelbaum, Malka (1982) A theory of ethnic collective action, *International Migration Review*, 16: 412–34.

Hofstadter, Richard (1955) *Social Darwinism in American Thought* (revised edition). Boston: Beacon Press.

Horowitz, Donald L. (1985) *Ethnic Groups in Conflict*. Berkeley: University of California Press.

Horsman, Reginald (1981) *Race and Manifest Destiny: The origins of American Racial Anglo-Saxonism*. Cambridge, Mass.: Harvard University Press.

Hughes, Everett C. (1946) The knitting of racial groups in industry, *American Sociological Review*, 11: 512–19, reprinted at pp. 175–88 in Hughes, Everett C. and Hughes, Helen McGill (1952) *Where Peoples Meet: racial and ethnic frontiers*. Glencoe, Ill.: The Free Press.

(1973) *Personal Communication*, 14 November.

Hunt, James (1865) On the Negro's place in nature. *Memoirs read before the Anthropological Society of London 1*, 1863–4: 1–64.

(1870) On the acclimatisation of Europeans in the United States of America, *Anthropological Review*, 8: 109–37.

Huxley, Julian S. and Haddon, A. C. (1935) *We Europeans: A Survey of Racial Problems*. London: Jonathan Cape.

Jordan, Winthrop D. (1968) *White over Black: American attitudes towards the Negro, 1550–1812*. Chapel Hill: University of North Carolina Press. Abridged Edition (1974): *The White Man's Burden: historical origins of racism in the United States*. New York: Oxford University Press.

Keith, Sir Arthur (1931) *The Place of Prejudice in Modern Civilization*. London: Williams and Norgate.

Kelley, Jonathan, and McAllister, Ian (1984) The genesis of conflict: religion and status attainment in Ulster, 1968, *Sociology*, 18: 171–87.

Killian, Lewis M. (1970) Herbert Blumer's contribution to race relations, pp. 179–90 in Shibutani, Tamotsu, editor, *Human Nature and Collective Behaviour: Papers in Honour of Herbert Blumer*. New Brunswick, N.J.: Transaction Books.

Kiple, Kenneth F. and King, Virginia H. (1981) *Another Dimension to the Black Diaspora: diet, disease and death*. Cambridge: Cambridge University Press.

Klemm, Gustav (1846–52). *Allegemeine Cultur-Geschichte der Menschheit*. 10 vols. Leipzig: Teubner.

(1851) *Grundideen zu einer allgemeinen Cultur-Wissenschaft. Sitzungsberichte der philosophisch-historischen Classe der K. Akad. der Wissenschaft*. Wien.

Knox, Robert (1850) *The Races of Men: a fragment* (second edition 1862). London: Renshaw.

(1857) *Man: his structure and physiology; popularly explained and demonstrated*. London: Balliere.

(1863) Ethnological inquiries and observations, *Anthropological Review*, 1: 246–63.

Kroeber, Alfred (1917) The superorganic, *American Anthropologist*, 19: 163–213.

Kuhn, Thomas (1962) *The Structure of Scientific Revolutions*. Chicago: University of Chicago Press.

Kuper, Leo (1974) *Race, Class and Power: Ideology and Revolutionary Change in Plural Societies*. London: Duckworth.

(1977) *The Pity of it All: Polarization of racial and ethnic relations*. London: Duckworth.

Lapouge, Georges Vacher de (1899) *L'Aryen: son rôle social*. Paris: Albert Fontemoing.

(1887) L'Anthropologie et la science politique, *Revue d'Anthropologie*, 15 May, 15.

Lasker, Bruno (1929) *Race Attitudes in Children*. New York: Henry Holt.

Latham, Robert Gordon (1850) *The Natural History of the Varieties of Man*. London: Van Voorst.

Lee, Frank F. (1961) *Negro and White in Connecticut Town*. New York: Bookman Associates.

Lewis, W. Arthur (1985) *Racial Conflict and Economic Development*. Cambridge, Mass.: Harvard University Press.

Lieberson, Stanley (1980) *A Piece of the Pie: Blacks and White Immigrants Since 1880*. Berkeley: University of California Press.

Lind, Andrew W., editor (1955) *Race Relations in World Perspective*. Honolulu: University of Hawaii Press; reprinted 1973, Westport, CT: Greenwood Press.

(1966) Race relations in the islands of the Pacific, pp. 229–48 in *Research on Racial Relations*. Paris: UNESCO.

Lipton, Merle (1985) *Capitalism and Apartheid: South Africa, 1910–1986*. Aldershot: Gower.

Lorimer, Douglas A. (1978) *Colour, Class and Victorians: English Attitudes to the Negro in the Mid-nineteenth Century*. Leicester: Leicester University Press.

Lundahl, Mats, and Wadensjö, Eskil (1984) *Unequal Treatment: A study in the Neo-Classical Theory of Discrimination*. London: Croom Helm.

Lyman, Stanford M. (1972) *The Black American in Sociological Thought*. New York: Putnam's.

Mayr, Ernst (1982) *The Growth of Biological Thought: Diversity, Evolution, and Inheritance*. Cambridge, Mass.: Harvard University Press.

Miles, Robert (1980) Class, race and ethnicity: a critique of Cox's theory, *Ethnic and Racial Studies*, 3: 169–87.

(1982) *Racism and Migrant Labour*. London: Routledge.

(1984) Marxism versus the sociology of 'race relations'? *Ethnic and Racial Studies*, 7: 217–37.

Morton, Samuel George (1839) *Crania Americana: or, A Comparative View of the Skulls of Various Aboriginal nations of North and South America, to which is prefixed an Essay on the Varieties of the Human Species*. Philadelphia and London.

(1844) *Crania Aegyptica: or, Observations on Egyptian ethnography*. Philadelphia and London.

Murray, Gilbert (1900) The exploitation of inferior races in ancient and modern times, pp. 118–57 in *Liberalism and the Empire*, three essays by Francis W. Hirst, Gilbert Murray and J. L. Hammond. London: Johnson.

Myrdal, Alva and Gunnar (1941) *Kontakt med Amerika*. Stockholm: Bonniers.

Myrdal, Gunnar with the assistance of Sterner, Richard and Rose, Arnold (1944) *An American Dilemma: the Negro problem and modern democracy*. New York: Harper.

North, Douglas C. (1983) A theory of institutional change and the economic history of the Western World, pp. 190–215 in Hechter, Michael, editor, *The Microfoundations of Macrosociology*. Philadelphia: Temple University Press.

Nott, J. C. and Gliddon, G. R. (1854) *Types of Mankind: or Ethnological Researches*. Philadelphia: Lippincott and London: Trubner.

(1857) *Indigenous Races, or New Chapters of Ethnological Enquiry*. Philadelphia: Lippincott and London: Trubner.

Osman, Sanusi (1981) *The National Unity Policy and Ethnic Relations in Malaysia with special reference to Malacca Town*. Unpublished Ph.D. thesis, University of Bristol.

Park, Robert E. and Burgess, Ernest W. (1921) *Introduction to the Science of Sociology*. Chicago: University of Chicago Press.

Park, Robert E. (1950) *Race and Culture*. Glencoe, Ill.: The Free Press.

Patterson, Orlando (1975) Contest and choice in ethnic allegiance: a theoretical framework and Caribbean case study, pp. 305–49 in Glazer, Nathan and Moynihan, Daniel P., editors, *Ethnicity: Theory and Experience*. Cambridge, Mass.: Harvard University Press.

Pearson, Veronica (1973) Telegony: A Study of this Belief and its Continued Existence. Unpublished M.Sc. thesis. University of Bristol.

Perraton, H. D. (1967) British attitudes towards East and West Africa, 1880–1914. *Race*, 8: 223–46.

Phelps, Edmund S. (1972) The statistical theory of racism and sexism, *American Economic Review*, 62: 659–61.

Pierson, Donald (1942) *Negroes in Brazil: A Study of Race Contact at Bahia*. Chicago: University of Chicago Press; reprinted, 1967, Carbondale: Southern Illinois University Press.

Poliakov, Leon (1974) *The Aryan Myth: a history of racist and nationalist ideas in Europe*. London: Chatto, Heinemann, for Sussex University Press.

Popper, Sir Karl Raimund (1957) *The Poverty of Historicism*. London: Routledge & Kegan Paul.

(1972) *Objective Knowledge: An Evolutionary Approach*. Oxford: Clarendon Press.

(1974) *Unended Quest: An Intellectual Biography*. London: Fontana, 1976 edition.

Powdermaker, Hortense (1939) *After Freedom: A Cultural Study on the Deep South*. New York: Atheneum.

Prichard, James Cowles (1826) *Researches into the Physical History of Mankind* (second edition). London: Arch.

(1843) *The Natural History of Man*. London: Balliere.

Quatrefages, A. de (1879) *The Human Species*. 2nd edition. London: C. Kegan Paul.

Rabushka, Alvin (1974) *A Theory of Racial Harmony*. Studies in International Affairs 11. Columbia, SC: University of South Carolina Press.

Rex, John (1968) The Sociology of a Zone of Transition, pp. 211–31 in Pahl, R. E. (ed.), *Readings in Urban Sociology*. Oxford: Pergamon.

(1986) *Race and Ethnicity*. Milton Keynes: Open University Press

Sloan, Philip R. (1973) The Idea of Racial Degeneracy in Buffon's *Histoire Naturelle*, pp. 293–321 in Pagliaro, Harold E. (ed.), *Racism in the Eighteenth Century*. Studies in Eighteenth-Century Culture, 3. Cleveland: Press of Case Western Reserve University.

Smith, Bernard (1960) *European Vision and the South Pacific 1768–1850: a study in the history of art and ideas*. Oxford: Clarendon Press.

Smith, Charles Hamilton (1848) *The Natural History of the Human Species*. Edinburgh: W. H. Lizars.

Smith, Samuel Stanhope (1787) *An Essay on the Causes of the Variety of Complexion in the Human Species*. Second edition 1810. Cambridge, Mass.: Harvard University Press.

(1810) *An Essay on the Causes of the Variety of Complexion and Figure in the Human Species*. Revised edition, reprinted and edited by Winthrop D. Jordan. Cambridge, Mass.: Belknap Press of Harvard University Press, 1965.

Sorokin, Pitirim A. (1928) *Contemporary Sociological Theories*. New York: Harper.

Sowell, Thomas (1982) *The Economics and Politics of Race: An International Perspective*. New York: William Morrow.

Stanton, William (1960) *The Leopard's Spots: scientific attitudes towards race in America 1815–59*. Chicago: University of Chicago Press.

Stocking, George W. (1968) *Race, Culture and Evolution: Essays in the history of evolution*. New York: Free Press.

(1973) From Chronology to Ethnology: James Cowles Prichard and British Anthropology, 1800–1850, pp. ix–cx in J. C. Prichard, *Researches into the Physical History of Man*. Chicago: University of Chicago Press.

(1973) What's in a Name? The Origins of the Royal Anthropological Institute, *Man*, 6: 369–90.

Sumner, William Graham (1906) *Folkways: A Study of the Sociological Importance of Usages, Manners, Customs, Mores, and Morals*. New York: New American Library.

Thomas, William I. (1904) The Psychology of Race Prejudice, *American Journal of Sociology*, 9: 593–611.

Thuillier, Guy (1977) Un anarchiste positiviste: Georges Vacher de Lapouge, pp. 48–65 in Guiral, Pierre, and Temime, Émile, editors, *L'idée de race dans la pensée politique française contemporaine*. Paris: Editions du Centre Nationale de la Recherche Scientifique.

van den Berghe, Pierre L. (1967) *Race and Racism*. New York: Wiley. Revised edition 1978.

(1981) *The Ethnic Phenomenon*. New York: Elsevier.

Voegelin, Erich (1933a) *Die Rassenidee in der Geistesgeschichte von Ray bis Carus*. Berlin: Junker & Dunnhaupt.

(1933b) *Rasse und Staat*. Tübingen: Mohr.

Vogt, Carl (1863) *Lectures on Man: his place in creation and in the history of the earth* (edited by James Hunt). London: Longman, Green for Anthropological Society, 1864.

Washburn, S. L. (1963) The study of race, *American Anthropologist*, 65.

Watson, George (1973) *The English Ideology: Studies in the Language of Victorian Politics*. London: Allen Lane.

Weber, Max (1978) *Selections in Translation*, ed. W. G. Runciman. Cambridge: Cambridge University Press.

Williams, E. E. (1944) *Capitalism and Slavery*. Chapel Hill, N.C.: University of North Carolina Press; New York: Harper Torchbooks, 1965.

Williams, Robin M., Jr., in collaboration with John P. Dean and Edward M. Suchman (1964) *Strangers Next Door: Ethnic Relations in American Communities*. Englewood Cliffs, N.J.: Prentice-Hall.

Index